S0-BIJ-726

WORDS OF PROTEST, WORDS OF FREEDOM

An Anthology

WORDS OF PROTEST, WORDS OF FREEDOM

POETRY OF THE AMERICAN CIVIL RIGHTS MOVEMENT AND ERA

EDITED BY Jeffrey Lamar Coleman

DUKE UNIVERSITY PRESS DURHAM AND LONDON 2012

See page 349 (which is considered an extension of this page) for additional copyright information.

Printed in the United States of America on acid-free paper ∞

Designed by Heather Hensley

Typeset in Arno Pro by Tseng Information Systems, Inc.

Library of Congress Cataloging-in-Publication Data appear on the last printed page of this book.

Duke University Press gratefully acknowledges the support of the Mary Duke Biddle Foundation, which provided funds toward the publication of this book.

CONTENTS

"A gun / Struck, as we slept, a caring public man"

13

"Mighty mountains loom before me and I won't stop now"

14

PREFACE

I became interested in the relationship between poetry and the civil rights movement as a graduate student at Arizona State University in the early 1990s. I had recently left Madison Avenue and my job at Young and Rubicam, the country's largest advertising agency, as a copywriter to pursue a Master's of Fine Arts degree in creative writing. I enrolled in an English course that focused on the language of the civil rights movement, taught by Dr. Keith D. Miller, who had recently completed *Voice of Deliverance: The Language of Martin Luther King, Jr., and Its Sources.* In an attempt to synthesize the required course materials with my interest in poetry, I decided to write an essay about poems and poets of the civil rights movement. Logically enough I decided to visit Hayden Library, the main library on campus, to locate and borrow the *Anthology of Civil Rights Movement Poetry* as part of my research for the essay. The Internet and its multiple search engines were not yet available. The library's database informed me that there was no such text. I typed in "poetry of the American civil rights movement." Again my search came up empty. I then typed "poetry, civil rights." Still there were no desired matches. I repeated my search from a few different angles, but to no avail. Surely this must be some kind of mistake, I thought.

I had learned from personal research and from Dr. Miller's course that the movement had received a great deal of scholarly attention. I knew that there were numerous books that contained poems written during and about the period. In addition, many of those poems had been selected for inclusion in relevant anthologies by black and white editors, including *The Black Poets, American Negro Poetry, The Negro Caravan, Campfires of the Resistance, The Poetry of Black America, Beyond the Blues, Black Fire,* and *Understanding the New Black Poetry.* I was also aware that one could find several historical accounts, most notably *Eyes on the Prize,* of the more memorable events of the movement, including the Emmett Till murder of 1955, the Little Rock crisis of 1957 and 1958, the bombing of the Sixteenth Street Baptist Church in Birmingham in 1963, the murders of James Chaney, Andrew Goodman, and Michael Schwerner in Mississippi in 1964, the murder of Malcolm X in 1965, the birth of the Black Panther Party in 1966, and the assassination of Martin Luther King Jr. in 1968. However, as my search in Hayden Library indicated, a history of the movement from the perspective of poets and their poems had not been published. A poetic companion to *Eyes on the Prize,* or a collection of poetry stemming from and contextualized within the movement itself, did not exist. In fact it eventually occurred to me that unlike the Vietnam War the civil rights movement, the most transformative social movement of twentieth-century America, did not exist in any meaningful or substantive manner in the literary world. For reasons unknown, the movement had not produced a collective poetic voice or record, a single stanza-filled volume intended to cut across lines of race, class, and gender for the purpose of documenting the goals and challenges of the movement.

I should note that my budding interest in this subject did not occur in a vacuum. My time in Arizona was marked by the ongoing controversy over a paid holiday for Dr. King. A few years prior to my arrival in Arizona, Evan Mecham, the newly elected governor, rescinded the state holiday honoring King. This move set off protests against the state. While the NAACP, Stevie Wonder, and tourism boycotts gave visibility to the issue surrounding the holiday, it was the National Football League that made the greatest impact. The NFL decided to withhold the Super Bowl from Arizona until the paid state holiday was reinstated.

Mecham, who was no stranger to linguistic foibles, once informed *Arizona Trend* magazine, "I've got Black friends. I employ Black people. I don't employ them because they're Black. I employ them because they are the best people who applied for the *cotton-picking* job." Although he was impeached before I set foot in the state, the turmoil surrounding his short tenure in office was still very much present. For example, letters to the editors of both the campus newspaper and the local paper, the *Arizona Republic*, reflected what seemed to be a commonly held sentiment: not only could the taxpayers of the state of Arizona not *afford* such a holiday, but many of them felt that King was not *deserving* of a holiday. This sentiment came about amid recent allegations that King had plagiarized parts of his dissertation and that he had at times been unfaithful as a husband. These two charges seemed to be proof enough for those who made up the vocal minority that the late civil rights leader was unworthy of being honored with a paid holiday. Of course, there were always those who would respond to an editorial or a letter to the editor with one of their own, claiming to be ashamed of being white, and therefore guilty by association of being anti-King, antiblack, or just downright racist. This was all very interesting to observe, but I reached a point where I felt that such attacks on King, the civil rights movement, and even mildly liberal ideas were also attacks on King's vision of an integrated society. Arizona State University, with approximately forty-two thousand students, was one of the largest in the country. At the time I enrolled African Americans constituted about 2 percent of the student body. There were days when I did not see many, if any, of them. What I began to hear and feel was not so much that the state could not afford the holiday, but that it wanted nothing to do with King or his social vision. The residual impact of Mecham's rescission, combined with Miller's class on the language and history of the movement, undoubtedly gave rise to my interest in the poetry of the 1950s, 1960s, and early 1970s.

Searching for and finding pertinent poems from the movement years soon became a hobby I indulged as often as possible. This approach led to the discovery of a few poems initially and then to an American studies dissertation on the civil rights movement poetry of Amiri Baraka, Gwendolyn Brooks, Michael S. Harper, and Alice Walker at the University of New Mexico in the late 1990s. Curiosity and the excitement of discovery propelled me to keep searching, until I had found hundreds of poems that could easily be classified as poems from and about the movement, enough poems to start thinking about placing them in a single volume. Many, many years later *Words of Protest, Words of Freedom: Poetry of the American Civil Rights Movement and Era* has become that single, but by no means exhaustive, volume. I apologize to writers I have unintentionally overlooked and excluded. My sincerest hope at the moment is that I have been able to do justice not only to the period, but also to the writers I have included.

ACKNOWLEDGMENTS

This book would not have been possible without the insight and generous assistance of Ken Wissoker and Leigh Barnwell, my editors at Duke University Press. Ken's support of the anthology was evident from the very early stages of contact, and he was instrumental in shepherding the book through the various stages of the publication process. Likewise, Leigh's feedback and unwavering encouragement were essential to the completion of the book, especially with respect to the permissions process.

I thank the cover artist, as well as the book's designer, Heather Hensley.

I would also like to thank four St. Mary's College of Maryland alums who provided invaluable research assistance as undergraduates. Toby Bates, Simone Fields, Lindsay Pack, and Brandon Scott made countless trips to the library to gather books for me and conducted biographical and bibliographical searches. I am forever in their debt.

Most importantly, I would like to thank my wife, Ynez, and our children, Nadia and Javier, for their love and support over the years. This book would not exist without their patience and understanding.

Introduction JOURNEY TOWARD FREEDOM

The election of Barack Obama in 2008 was the result of social activism that occurred several decades earlier, during the height of the civil rights movement. Obama's surprising ascension can be linked to the dream of Dr. Martin Luther King Jr. and other activists who envisioned a society in which race would not be seen as a hindrance or impediment to achieving the American dream or to enjoying the proverbial rights of life, liberty, and the pursuit of happiness. Like most visionaries, King, who always came across as a poet in his speeches, toiled and suffered in the present in order to alleviate or eliminate the suffering of others in the future. This fact is evident in his life of diligent, patient activism, and in the words he left behind. The night before his assassination, for example, he claimed, "I might not get there with you . . . but we, as a people, will get to the Promised Land." Many Americans view Obama's victory as a testament to King's prophecy. The barriers King and other civil rights workers encountered and struggled against day after day and march after countless march appeared to crumble and vanish, or at least seemed less formidable and restrictive on the evening of 4 November 2008. The historic election proved that the highest office in the land and the position of leader of the free world were no longer off-limits to Americans of African descent or to the offspring of interracial couples. President Obama's success seemed to signal a seismic cultural shift in our perception of people of color in America and of America in general. After all, not too long ago someone of Obama's background would have been viewed as an affront, to put it mildly, to those intent on keeping segregation alive for the sake of white racial purity and power. His victory was thus surreal for many old enough to recall King and the period of Jim Crow, but it was made real in large part by those of you between the ages of eighteen and twenty-nine who cast your vote for the junior senator from Illinois. You were Obama's most energetic and reliable constituency during the campaign and were as emphatic about him as earlier generations were for King and John F. Kennedy. I was fortunate enough to witness firsthand the genuine excitement Obama created in college students, a group typically considered too apathetic or cynical to care about politics or voting. He was able to strike a deep and resounding chord with the vast majority of my students. Regardless of the assignment in my Literature of the American Civil Rights Movement course, for example, students somehow found a way to steer the discussion toward Obama, and this was *before* the election. Yes, this generation, like students and youth during the movement years, coupled its hope for a better future with a profound desire for change and led Obama's candidacy into the Promised Land King spoke of on 3 April 1968.

Unlike during the King years, we now live in an undeniably multicultural America that attempts to honor the history and contributions of citizens from varied backgrounds. Some have even suggested that we now live in a "postracial" society, a society in which racial identity no longer matters or can be easily transcended. While such claims are unfortunately premature, they do shed light on the advancements America has made as a result of the civil rights movement. The movement, through both subtle and demonstrative methods, provided a blueprint for all citizens interested in helping America to become a more perfect mosaic. The movement called for action and for activists ("direct nonviolent action" was the term preferred by Dr. King) and in the process provided a strategy and vocabulary for social change. Ordinary citizens came to realize not only the potency of their individual voice, but also the power of collective and communal demands. The tone, style, and ideology of the message changed from the 1950s to the early 1970s (ranging from nonviolent civil rights to pro-self-defense black power), but the objectives were always centered on the liberation and advancement of the African American community. Quite often, as *Words of Protest, Words of Freedom* makes clear, poetry figured prominently in the articulation of and struggle for justice and equality in America.

Poetry, due to its ability to speak concisely and directly or metaphorically to any given situation, was the art form writers and everyday people chose to voice opposition to social and political conditions. The genre was viewed as accessible in the sense that one could turn to poetry in either the heat of the moment or much later, during moments of reflection and contemplation. Poetry could also be easily shared at meetings, readings, and demonstrations. As Broadside Press, founded by Dudley Randall in 1965, realized with its series of single poems, poetry could also be folded and carried in pockets, wallets, and purses to share with others, or placed on bulletin boards or refrigerators in the workplace or home. Poetry was, and still is to some degree, viewed as art of the people, for the people, and by the people. In this sense, poetry was viewed as a democratic art form that possessed the ability to empower the artist in an era when the refrain "Power to People!" could be heard at Black Panther Party rallies and in songs by the Chicago-based quartet the Chi-Lites, such as "(For God's Sake) Give More Power to the People," and by John Lennon ("Power to the People"). As with music, one could make powerful statements and rage against "the System" or "the Man" in multiple ways in a poem, especially in coffeehouses, which were precursors to today's popular spoken-word circuit. In fact many poets of the black arts movement from roughly 1965 to 1975 wrote with an oral performance in mind. Lines and stanzas that appeared ordinary on the page often took on an extraordinary life of their own when read aloud and performed before an audience. These poets viewed public readings as a vital communal experience, as a way of connecting to "the people" they often wrote about and intended to inspire and uplift, and as a way to remove the traditional separation between artist and community. Of course, not everyone wrote poetry with performance in mind. Many writers took an approach to the genre that was viewed as better suited for academic circles and sensibilities. These writers usually wrote with a reading audience in mind instead of a listening audience. They wanted their poems to succeed primarily on the printed page, where they could be read, reread, and contemplated. While the individual poets and groups of poets represented in *Words of Protest, Words of Freedom* were not always in agreement with respect to political objectives, poetics, or literary assessment, they were united by the civil rights movement's call for freedom and justice. Regardless of the approach, many viewed poetry as a viable, if not essential artistic element in the pursuit of civil and human rights in the United States. This pursuit of democracy, or journey toward freedom, as I often call it in the classroom, has an extensive history that stretches much further than the twenty-year period captured in this anthology. No ideal or myth is as valorized or closely identified with American life and history as that of freedom, and African Americans have a long and unique relationship with that ideal. The height of literary productivity with respect to the movement occurred between 1955 and 1975, but the history that informs much of the poetry and perspectives of the period extends at least to the previous century.

Demands for civil and human rights can be found in various forms in every decade stretching back to the seventeenth century, when captured Africans were brought to the U.S., but the seeds of the contemporary black freedom movement were planted after Emancipation, at the rise of the notoriously divisive Jim Crow era. Although former slaves were now technically free and had enjoyed protected rights for approximately a decade during the period of Reconstruction, Jim Crow laws and their attendant set of social etiquette of the late nineteenth century were designed to strip away those rights and keep blacks legally and socially subordinate. Gone, presumably, were the days of legalized shackles, chains, and corporeal abuse of slaves, especially in southern and border states, but those physical fixtures of enslavement were replaced by state-supported laws and social codes that legalized and reinforced the assumed superiority of whites and the inferiority of blacks. For those who had been enslaved and freed, the rise of Jim Crow was certainly an unwelcome reminder of the past. Jim Crow culture mandated social hierarchy based on racial classification; whites were considered the only first-class citizens of the land, and blacks were virtually powerless to challenge their designation as second- or lower-class citizens. The notion of social or racial equality was not to be entertained by blacks or sympathetic whites. Instead both groups were expected to behave in a manner that kept alive the mentality of the master-slave relationship of the recent past. This arrangement called for segregation in the most literal sense of the term, an arrangement that is probably impossible for today's generation to fathom. For example, the races were not to socialize in public or private, including houses of worship, neighborhoods, schools, the workplace, juries, and public transportation facilities. In addition, signs were posted in public areas indicating which water fountain and restroom a "colored" person was permitted or forbidden to use. Whether written or unwritten, spoken or unspoken, the laws and social codes of the Jim Crow era were clearly communicated, and at the heart of that communication was the insistence that blacks, even if free, had no rights that whites were required to acknowledge or respect.

Blacks of the late nineteenth century confronted systemic and entrenched resistance, a form of oppression less physically destructive than the institution of slavery, but no less crippling in matters of economic independence, social equality, and personal or legal redress. They realized that it would take concerted and committed effort to be considered *worthy* of the promises and fruits of American culture, especially of the most coveted American ideal of all: Liberty. They likely recalled or heard in the air around them the echo of George Horton's early nineteenth-century poem "On Liberty and Slavery":

How long have I in bondage lain,
    And languished to be free!
Alas! and must I still complain—
    Deprived of liberty.

Indeed they must have wondered if they would ever live an unencumbered life. Surely they saw the bounty of America before them and realized they were not yet privy to the riches of the land. They came to realize they would have to commit to a sustained struggle to enjoy even the most basic aspects of civil and human rights. They would have to withstand and combat the violence of racist extremists and terrorists like the Ku Klux Klan, weather the indignity of always having to succumb to whites in public, suffer the demoralizing effects of economic oppression, and persevere amid social and legal restrictions. They would often, in the words of the poet Paul Lawrence Dunbar in 1895, have to "wear the mask that grins and lies" and appear content in order to ensure personal and communal safety. However, they did not realize that their efforts, among the most laudable and heroic the country has ever produced, would not be enough to earn them during their lifetime true independence and all the rights and privileges that accompany full American citizenship. Furthermore they could not have realized that their efforts, not as individuals, but as a collective, as a race, would have to be sustained beyond the nineteenth century and into the second half of the twentieth century before Jim Crow would be dismantled.

When I discuss with students this difficult and protracted journey toward freedom, I often find it helpful to draw parallels between the nineteenth and twentieth century in order to provide a broad and hopefully fuller view of the freedom struggle. For example, I remind them that the Civil Rights Act of 1875, which outlawed discrimination in most public places during Reconstruction, was ruled unconstitutional by the U.S. Supreme Court in 1883. When the Civil Rights Act was struck down after only *eight years,* the Court essentially legalized discrimination and provided cover for those who wished to deny certain services to blacks. However, the short existence of the Civil Rights Act of 1875 was not the main tragedy that resulted from the Court's actions. The chief tragedy is that a comparable piece of legislation would not be implemented for nearly *ninety years,* not until the Civil Rights Act of 1964 was passed. This act and the Voting Rights Act of 1965 are among the most significant legal victories of the era. Combined the two acts made most forms of discrimination in America illegal, which was one of the main objectives of the civil rights movement. I also remind students that the *Plessy v. Ferguson* decision in 1896 that made "separate but equal" segregation the law of the land would stand firm for *fifty-eight years,* until the *Brown v. Board of Education* ruling in 1954. Simply put, blacks existed in and struggled against a climate of legalized discrimination, segregation, and violence for close to a century *after* the Emancipation Proclamation. This fact helps explain why the most frequently referenced theme in African American literature and culture from slavery through the civil rights movement to the present is freedom. After all, what would a slave imagine and desire most? What else could an indebted sharecropper imagine? And what else could Dr. King dream for blacks and America if not freedom?

The journey from the onset of the Jim Crow era to the sit-ins, boycotts, marches, and speeches commonly associated with the civil rights movement was tortuous, bloody, and often deadly, as *Words of Protest* makes clear, but it is a journey that helped define America's moral character. The movement challenged the country to decide whether all Americans are entitled to the promises of unalienable rights, or if some Americans can justifiably be denied those rights. The country, of course, eventually decided to side with justice, but that decision was not reached swiftly or voluntarily. Segregation, once firmly established, proved to be an obstinate institution to overcome, but liberation-minded organizations such as the National Association for the Advancement of Colored People (NAACP) and the National Urban League were founded in the early days of the freedom movement—1909 and 1910, respectively—to organize and assist the black community in obtaining voting rights, deterring lynching, and finding jobs. Similar groups emerged later in the century, including the Congress of Racial Equality (CORE) in 1942, the Southern Christian Leadership Conference (SCLC), which King founded in 1957, and the Student Nonviolent Coordinating Committee (SNCC) in 1960. These groups did not always agree philosophically, but they were united by the desire for the prize of freedom. Regardless of the limitations they faced, they held fast to the promise of America. Their determination reminds me of the poem by Langston Hughes titled "Freedom [2]," written in 1943. The poem hinges on the spirit of freedom that cannot be burned, imprisoned, or lynched, because in the end freedom "stands up and laughs" and says, "*You'll never kill me!*" The leaders and members of these organizations possessed the same spirit and resolve. They prodded, debated, and advocated for the black community regardless of the perils they encountered. Collectively they are responsible for the majority of social and legal advancements enjoyed by African Americans in the twentieth century. In addition to these organizations, prominent leaders such as Ida B. Wells, Booker T. Washington, W. E. B. Du Bois, and Marcus Garvey spearheaded liberation efforts early on, while individuals more familiar to today's generation—Rosa Parks, Martin Luther King Jr., and Malcolm X—are usually noted as civil and human rights leaders from the 1950s forward. These leaders, regardless of the time period, relied on the efforts of unheralded individuals from all walks of life who joined forces to protest black oppression at the local, state, and national level.

They often risked their livelihoods and lives to resist a status quo that sought to dehumanize them at every turn. They contributed in substantive ways inside established advocacy organizations, but their contributions could also be found in black churches and other local grassroots efforts that often caught momentum and evolved into larger regional or national protests. In short, ordinary people organized with other ordinary people across town, across states, across the country, and sometimes across the globe—without the conveniences of the Internet, social networks, or other modern technological advances—for the sake of establishing democracy in America. These followers or foot soldiers planned, promoted, and participated in boycotts, marches, and other forms of social protest. The efforts of leaders and nonleaders alike required patience, perseverance, and an almost inconceivable capacity for self-sacrifice, but they eventually forced America to, in the words of Dr. King, "rise up and live out the true meaning of its creed."

The poems in this anthology capture the "true meaning," history, and spirit of the civil rights movement from the mid-1950s to the mid-1970s, a period in which writers in America and elsewhere were most active in their attempts to address many of the movement's most crucial episodes and turning points. *Words of Protest, Words of Freedom* comprises two themes; the first is major events of the era, the second is the literary, social, and political climate of the civil rights era.

"What is a civil rights movement poem?" This is a question I am often asked when I discuss this volume with friends, family members, colleagues, and students. Briefly, this genre consists of poems that address the events, individuals, and social conditions of African Americans from the *Brown* decision through at least the mid-1970s. In fact the poems from that period could easily lead readers through the tumultuous timeline of the civil rights movement. They allow readers to (re)experience such events as bus boycotts, sit-ins at lunch counters, Freedom Rides, marches, and the evolution of America's racial climate. Overwhelmingly the poems fall into one of two categories: those that directly address crucial movement-related historical moments and those that are not necessarily event-specific, but—much like the Movement itself—concern racial oppression and discrimination or the movement-related social unease of the period as a whole. Poems in the first category are located in chapters 1–13, while poems from the second are located in chapter 14. It should also be noted at this juncture that each chapter of the anthology contains its own introduction. These brief introductions are intended to place the poems in historical context but are not intended to serve as comprehensive or exhaustive treatments of the subjects covered in each chapter. Likewise most poems are mentioned, if only briefly, in the sectional introductions for the purpose of illustrating how they contribute to the narrative of their respective chapter. Of course, not every significant moment of the movement is documented in chapters 1–13; unfortunately I could not find poems for certain era-related events or could not unearth poems in numbers sufficient to constitute chapters.

The poems in chapter 14 provide readers with a broader sense of the social and political climate of the period. The presence of violence and death that characterizes several of the first thirteen chapters is not as evident in chapter 14. The works contained here, unlike those in previous chapters, do not attend to specific events. Instead this chapter contains poems that speak to issues of personal and cultural identity and to a nonviolent rather than retaliatory ideology of resistance. Additionally poems in this section chronicle civil rights protests, marches, and demonstrations held in spite of imminent violence, and offer instruction and wisdom to fellow poets and activists. The poems also stress the need for blacks to counteract an array of detrimental issues in the community, especially fiscal inequities. There are also poems that evoke racial conditions and injustices implicitly or metaphorically, often in the process of addressing seemingly unrelated social problems.

Taken together, all fourteen chapters offer an exciting perspective of the United States during its civil rights years, a perspective not previously captured in a single volume of poems. One of the more extraordinary aspects of this particular genre is that it mirrors the movement in terms of its democratic composition of writers. African American poets were not alone in voicing opposition to their status as second-class citizens in America. Writers, regardless of race, and sometimes regardless of nation, contributed to its foundation. The genre was multiracial, multicultural, and multinational long before those terms gained currency in the country. Even more interesting is the fact that the writers gathered here, as is often the case with artistic periods, were for the most part unaware that they were contributing to a genre. They were not consciously writing verses for the sake of creating civil rights movement poetry. There was no call for submissions of movement-themed poems or poems representative of the period. In fact most writers were unaware that such a development was taking place, that a host of other conscientious writers were simultaneously documenting in poetry the most significant social movement of twentieth-century America. Yet one by one they composed lines and stanzas that complemented each other and formed an ongoing dialogue with each other. This eclectic collection of voices sharing common themes could appear to be an unlikely gathering if one considers that numerous poets hailed from different if not competing schools of poetry. For example, there are writers gathered here from the beat, black arts, Harlem Renaissance, and négritude movements, among others. While these movements are quite different in a number of ways, they are connected by their resistance to the social status quo, and part of that resistance involved the civil rights movement. The Beats, for example, who were mostly white, did not see the need to conform to the overwhelmingly conservative American culture of the 1950s and 1960s, including its sexual and literary practices. As a whole the Beats did not protest racial conditions in America on a regular basis, but members such as Anne Waldman and Allen Ginsberg broached the subject at times in their writing and during public demonstrations. On the other hand, the Harlem Renaissance and négritude movements, whose members shared African descent, were primarily concerned with issues of race in America and around the world. The artistic height of the Harlem Renaissance was in the 1920s and 1930s, while the négritude movement, which was influenced by the energy and philosophy of the Harlem Renaissance and consisted of French-speaking artists and thinkers, was formed in France in the 1930s in opposition to European cultural domination. Négritude members felt that cultural contributions from Africa and her offspring had been too long overshadowed by slavery and colonialism. Simply put, both movements desired to represent the African diaspora, especially in matters relating to race, including issues relevant to civil rights. Langston Hughes is the most prominent member of the Harlem Renaissance in this collection; Aimé Césaire, Nicolás Guillén, and Léopold Sédar Senghor represent the négritude movement. The black arts movement, formed in the mid-1960s, was the literary representative of the black power movement in America and sought to instill a sense of racial pride in the African American community during the 1960s and 1970s. In poems, novels, plays, and essays, members of the black arts community, including Amiri Baraka and Nikki Giovanni, stressed the significance of black culture and history in a predominantly white society. But regardless of literary affiliation, few writers in this volume wrote solely in a civil or human rights vein, and some writers are clearly represented more often than others (many are represented by a single poem), but when viewed collectively it becomes apparent that a distinctive yet diverse poetic movement was taking shape in the United States and abroad. With the benefit of hindsight and historical perspective we can now view that literary period through the lens of civil rights.

One purpose of this anthology is to honor and give voice to poets who were not "poets" in the sense that they devoted their lives to the art form or received accolades for their efforts. An extraordinary aspect of the civil rights movement with respect to poetry is that it inspired ordinary citizens, regardless of their affiliation with the movement, to put down in verse their thoughts and emotions about pivotal historical moments of the movement or about the cultural climate of the period as a whole. While many of these poets did not possess the genius of a Langston Hughes or a Gwendolyn Brooks, they did possess an ability to craft meaningful poems. This anthology desires to mirror the movement to the extent that well-known and lesser-known (or unknown) individuals worked side by side to sustain the movement. For example, scholars and the general public usually think of King in association with the movement, but hundreds of unheralded citizens sustained and propelled the movement by participating in sit-ins, marches, and other forms of social protest. These citizens participated because they saw the struggle for equality and democracy as a worthwhile and essential endeavor. The same is true of everyday citizens who decided to pick up a pen or pencil or sit before a typewriter to do *something* to help the cause or to deal with the emotional and psychological impact of the political and social conditions. Although many of the poems collected in this volume were written by the most influential poets of late twentieth-century America, including writers who would later win prestigious literary prizes, among them the American Book Award, National Book Award, Pulitzer Prize, and Nobel Prize for Literature, this anthology also seeks to honor individuals who never received the same level of recognition.

The writers in this collection, the esteemed and the unheralded, believed in the social advancement of African Americans. The civil rights movement's primary objective was to combat racial injustices stemming largely from segregation and to complete the journey toward freedom that began in the Jim Crow era. Social segregation produced segregation in the arts as well. The literary world suffered from this problem in equal if not greater parts than society at large during the 1950s, 1960s, and 1970s. However, numerous poets rejected divisions of this kind, and their attitudes about America were reflected in their art. They rejected the view that blacks deserved to be treated as second-class citizens and that whites, simply by birthright, were entitled to the various riches of American life. The historical period is the dominant rubric that unites the writers in this collection, but they are connected by other aspects of their craft as well. The typical elements of poetry are present, such as hyperbole, satire, irony, personification, and experimentation, but many readers will likely respond to or recall the presence of tragedy in these works. As mentioned earlier, elegies for those associated with the era are well represented here, starting with Emmett Till in 1955 and ending with Robert F. Kennedy in 1968. Closely tied to the presence of elegies in this anthology is unpleasant and disturbing imagery. This element appears in many of the elegies but occurs in other poems as well. For example, the imagery created or implied in chapter 2 about the Little Rock public school integration crisis is quite disturbing. The same can be said of the poetic descriptions of the riots, rebellions, and uprisings in chapter 8. Likewise the poems in chapter 10, "'In the panic of hooves, bull whips and gas': Selma to Montgomery Voting Rights March, 1965," contain extremely unsettling depictions. However, as one reads through this volume one will discover that in the midst of tragic stanzas there exists the unifying goal, the shared and common hope and dream that America will become America. This dream stretches from the first to the last poem in this anthology. It exists, usually unspoken or unacknowledged on a literal level, as the overriding concern of each poem. The works and their authors do not all agree on how to achieve democracy and equality in America, but the subject is present on page after page. In this sense, these poems—poems that recall and record the most transformative movement of twentieth-century America—are arguably among the most *American* poems of the century. They provide a glimpse of Americans at their worst and of Americans at their transcendent best as well.

I would like to add that *Words of Protest, Words of Freedom* is the culmination of nearly two decades of interest in the history and poetry of the period roughly between 1955 and 1975. Along the way my respect for the enormous sacrifices made by movement leaders and foot soldiers alike deepened exponentially. Those individuals risked their physical and psychological well-being for the sake of my generation and subsequent generations. Likewise my respect for the writers contained in this volume also deepened, for they left behind a literary history that directly complements existing accounts in other disciplines, a record of American literature that has for too long been overlooked or not adequately contextualized. In fact these writers left behind poems that in and of themselves could guide readers through many of the defining moments of the civil rights movement. They left behind a collective expression of socially conscious and aesthetically diverse creativity that when viewed as part of the continuum of contemporary American poetry is formidable enough to constitute its own genre. They left behind a twentieth-century legacy of the social and political line and stanza, a legacy that can now be categorized as *Poetry of the American Civil Rights Movement and Era.*

1

"Had *she* been worth the blood?"

THE LYNCHING OF EMMETT TILL, 1955

Emmett Till, a fourteen-year-old from Chicago, was visiting relatives in Money, Mississippi, during the summer of 1955 when he made the mistake of flirting with Carolyn Bryant, a married white woman. Roy Bryant, Carolyn's husband, and J. W. Milam, her brother-in-law, later abducted Till at gunpoint, tortured and shot him, and dumped his body into the Tallahatchie River. Although the men were charged with murder, both were acquitted by an all-white male jury in Sumner, Mississippi. The two men later profited from the murder by confessing their crimes for pay to *Look* magazine. Till's murder, which predates Rosa Parks's refusal to give up her bus seat to a white man in Montgomery, Alabama, was for many the event that led to their initiation into the freedom movement.

Elegies written for Emmett Till approach his murder and memory from a variety of perspectives, but they all share a sense of remorse and anger, albeit at times implicit or contained. Rhoda Gaye Ascher's "Remembrance," published in 1969 in *Freedomways,* is an excellent example. While the poem's tone is decidedly somber, the third stanza reveals the speaker's frustration, especially at the perceived indifference of the white community. Ascher's poem emphasizes the lack of respect many white Mississippians held for Negro life, even the life of a murdered teenage boy.

Similarly Gwendolyn Brooks conveys her disgust of the murder and subsequent trial in a seemingly restrained, indirect manner in "A Bronzeville Mother Loiters in Mississippi. Meanwhile, a Mississippi Mother Burns Bacon." Brooks accomplishes this feat by focusing on the interior and domestic life of Carolyn Bryant instead of the death of Emmett Till. Furthermore the violence that occurs in the poem is initiated by Roy Bryant, one of the men responsible for Till's death, but is directed at his wife and children instead of Till.

Nicolás Guillén, the celebrated Cuban poet who in 1961 was named the National Poet of his country, wrote "Elegy for Emmett Till" in 1956, the year following the murder. Guillén directs his frustrations directly at the state of Mississippi and its citizens.

The Mississippians Guillén admonishes are the subject of satirical denial in John Beecher's "The Better Sort of People." Beecher, a distant nephew of the author and abolitionist Harriet Beecher Stowe, chooses for his narrator an educated, cultured citizen of the Magnolia State who is "against the kind of thing / the ignorant rednecks do" and insists "it was unnecessary / to beat that little Negro boy to death" (lines 19–22). The speaker represents "the better sort of people" of white Mississippi who disapprove of Till's fate at the hands of the lesser sort of murderous white Mississippians.

However, for many, there was little or no distinction between the two classes of Mississippians explored in Beecher's poem. Langston Hughes, for example, makes clear in "Mississippi—1955" that the entire state was viewed as a land of sorrow, pain, blood, and above all else, "terror" (6). Likewise Eve Merriam's blues-influenced poem "Money, Mississippi" describes the town and its inhabitants in a succession of refrains as dirty, bloody, rotten, filthy, and evil (8, 16, 24, 32, 40). Aimé Césaire's "On the State of the Union" does not dichotomize white Mississippians. His poem makes no behavioral or socioeconomic distinctions, but Césaire does employ a similar brand of condemnation.

Remembrance

Broken on the hard sea the dead waves float
Downstream. The night cries are gone now. The Moon,
Returned from her hiding, lights the faceless rafts
Deserted by yesterday's children.

The water lives; its foams combine, tickling
The childish face of death no chains can hold
Like Grandpa's lather — now, the old days, son, were different —
Downstream, delta lips are red, no future here.

The other boy will fish tomorrow,
Snag his life on this young log; classify
It; green wood, kindling, nigger — and childlike
Go and tell his Pa it spoiled his fishing.

Take a rotting log from the circling river,
Wear it, piercing your heart, in remembrance.

Rhoda Gaye Ascher, 1969

:::::

The Better Sort of People

Our Negroes here are satisfied
They don't complain about a thing
except the weather maybe
whenever it's too cold to fish
for cat along the riverbank
But when they get away from here
up to Chicago or Detroit
and stay away awhile and then come back with notions
about the right to vote
or going to school with white folks
we sometimes have to get it through their heads

who runs this country
They're better off down here
or why don't they stay up yonder?
A lot of them keep coming back
but somehow they've been spoiled
and need the fear of God
thrown into them again
Mind you I'm against the kind of thing
the ignorant rednecks do
I think it was unnecessary
to beat that little Negro boy to death
and throw his body in the Tallahatchie
He was uppity
no doubt about it
and whistled at a white woman
He probably learned that in Chicago
so we ought to make allowances
A good horsewhipping should have been enough
to put him back into his place
and been sufficient warning to him that
if he ever got fresh again
he wouldn't live to see Chicago
Those rednecks that abducted him
I doubt if even they
really meant to kill him when they started
working on him
They just got too enthusiastic
Like I say the better sort of people
down here in Mississippi
we love our Negroes
We wouldn't harm them for the world
This violence you hear so much about
is all the fault of low-down rednecks
poor white trash

John Beecher

A Bronzeville Mother Loiters in Mississippi.

Meanwhile, a Mississippi Mother Burns Bacon.

From the first it had been like a
Ballad. It had the beat inevitable. It had the blood.
A wildness cut up, and tied in little bunches,
Like the four-line stanzas of the ballads she had never quite
Understood — the ballads they had set her to, in school.

Herself: the milk-white maid, the "maid mild"
Of the ballad. Pursued
By the Dark Villain. Rescued by the Fine Prince.
The Happiness-Ever-After.
That was worth anything.
It was good to be a "maid mild."
That made the breath go fast.

Her bacon burned. She
Hastened to hide it in the step-on can, and
Drew more strips from the meat case. The eggs and sour-milk biscuits
Did well. She set out a jar
Of her new quince preserve.

. . . But there was something about the matter of the Dark Villain.
He should have been older, perhaps.
The hacking down of a villain was more fun to think about
When his menace possessed undisputed breadth, undisputed height,
And a harsh kind of vice.
And best of all, when his history was cluttered
With the bones of many eaten knights and princesses.

The fun was disturbed, then all but nullified
When the Dark Villain was a blackish child
Of fourteen, with eyes still too young to be dirty,
And a mouth too young to have lost every reminder
Of its infant softness.

That boy must have been surprised! For
These were grown-ups. Grown-ups were supposed to be wise.
And the Fine Prince—and that other—so tall, so broad, so
Grown! Perhaps the boy had never guessed
That the trouble with grown-ups was that under the magnificent shell of adulthood, just under,
Waited the baby full of tantrums.

It occurred to her that there may have been something
Ridiculous in the picture of the Fine Prince
Rushing (rich with breadth and height and
Mature solidness whose lack, in the Dark Villain, was impressing her,
Confronting her more and more as this first day after the trial
And acquittal wore on) rushing
With his heavy companion to hack down (unhorsed)
That little foe.
So much had happened, she could not remember now what that foe had done
Against her, or if anything had been done.
The one thing in the world that she did know and knew
With terrifying clarity was that her composition
Had disintegrated. That, although the pattern prevailed,
The breaks were everywhere. That she could think
Of no thread capable of the necessary
Sew-work.

She made the babies sit in their places at the table.
Then, before calling Him, she hurried
To the mirror with her comb and lipstick. It was necessary
To be more beautiful than ever.
The beautiful wife.
For sometimes she fancied he looked at her as though
Measuring her. As if he considered, Had she been worth It?
Had *she* been worth the blood, the cramped cries, the little stuttering bravado,
The gradual dulling of those Negro eyes,
The sudden, overwhelming *little-boyness* in that barn?

Whatever she might feel or half-feel, the lipstick necessity was
something apart. He must
never conclude
That she had not been worth it.

He sat down, the Fine Prince, and
Began buttering a biscuit. He looked at his hands.
He twisted in his chair, he scratched his nose.
He glanced again, almost secretly, at his hands.
More papers were in from the North, he mumbled. More meddling
headlines.
With their pepper-words, "bestiality," and "barbarism," and
"Shocking."
The half-sneers he had mastered for the trial worked across
His sweet and pretty face.

What he'd like to do, he explained, was kill them all.
The time lost. The unwanted fame.
Still, it had been fun to show those intruders
A thing or two. To show that snappy-eyed mother,
That sassy, Northern, brown-black—

Nothing could stop Mississippi.
He knew that. Big Fella
Knew that.
And, what was so good, Mississippi knew that.
Nothing and nothing could stop Mississippi.
They could send in their petitions, and scar
Their newspapers with bleeding headlines. Their governors
Could appeal to Washington . . .

"What I want," the older baby said, "is 'lasses on my jam."
Whereupon the younger baby
Picked up the molasses pitcher and threw
The molasses in his brother's face. Instantly
The Fine Prince leaned across the table and slapped
The small and smiling criminal.
She did not speak. When the Hand

Came down and away, and she could look at her child,
At her baby-child,
She could think only of blood.
Surely her baby's cheek
Had disappeared, and in its place, surely,
Hung a heaviness, a lengthening red, a red that had no end.
She shook her head. It was not true, of course.
It was not true at all. The
Child's face was as always, the
Color of the paste in her paste-jar.

She left the table, to the tune of the children's lamentations, which were shriller
Than ever. She
Looked out of a window. She said not a word. That
Was one of the new Somethings—
The fear,
Tying her as with iron.

Suddenly she felt his hands upon her. He had followed her
To the window. The children were whimpering now.
Such bits of tots. And she, their mother,
Could not protect them. She looked at her shoulders, still
Gripped in the claim of his hands. She tried, but could not resist the idea
That a red ooze was seeping, spreading darkly, thickly, slowly,
Over her white shoulders, her own shoulders,
And over all of Earth and Mars.

He whispered something to her, did the Fine Prince, something
About love, something about love and night and intention.

She heard no hoof-beat of the horse and saw no flash of the shining steel.

He pulled her face around to meet
His, and there it was, close close,
For the first time in all those days and nights.
His mouth, wet and red,

So very, very, very red,
Closed over hers.

Then a sickness heaved within her. The courtroom Coca-Cola,
The courtroom beer and hate and sweat and drone,
Pushed like a wall against her. She wanted to bear it.
But his mouth would not go away and neither would the
Decapitated exclamation points in that Other Woman's eyes.

She did not scream.
She stood there.
But a hatred of him burst into glorious flower,
And its perfume enclasped them—big,
Bigger than all magnolias.

The last bleak news of the ballad.
The rest of the rugged music.
The last quatrain.

Gwendolyn Brooks, 1960

:::::

The Last Quatrain of the Ballad of Emmett Till

AFTER THE MURDER,
AFTER THE BURIAL

Emmett's mother is a pretty-faced thing;
    the tint of pulled taffy.
She sits in a red room,
    drinking black coffee.
She kisses her killed boy.
    And she is sorry.
Chaos in windy grays
    through a red prairie

Gwendolyn Brooks, 1960

On the State of the Union

I imagine this message in Congress on the State of the Union:
situation tragic,
left underground only 75 years of iron
50 years worth of sulphur and 20 of bauxite
in the heart what?
Nothing, zero,
mine without ore,
cavern in which nothing prowls,
of blood not a drop left.

EMMETT TILL
your eyes were a sea conch in which the heady battle
of your fifteen-year-old blood sparkled.
Even young they never had any age,
or rather more than all the skyscrapers
five centuries of torturers
of witch burners weighed on them,
five centuries of cheap gin of big cigars
of fat bellies filled with slices of rancid bibles
a five century mouth bitter with dowager sins,
they were five centuries old EMMETT TILL,
five centuries is the ageless age of Cain's stake.

EMMETT TILL I say:
in the heart zero,
of blood not a drop,
and as for yours may it hide my Sun, may it mix with my bread:
—"Hey Chicago Boy
is it still true that you're worth
as much as a white man?"
Spring, he believed in you. Even at the edge of night, at the edge of the MISSISSIPPI rolling its bars, its barriers, its barriers, its tomb-like avalanches between the high banks of racial hatred.
In spring rushing its murmurs into the portholes of eyes.
In spring hound-calling the bovine panic in the savannas of the blood.

In spring slipping the gloves from its fine hands in a burst of shells
  and siliquae,
loosener of fear clots, dissolver of the clots of hatred swollen with
  age and in the flow of blood—streams carrying the hazardous
  rubric of stalked beasts.
            But They
they were invulnerable, sluggish as they were,
and mounted, massively, on bizarre immemorial billygoats
            —"CHICAGO BOY" . . .
All gone with the bleating of the racial wind
He listens in the blue bush of veins
to the steady singing of the blood bird,
he anticipates above the banks of sleep
Sun, the rise of your furtive step,
a vehement fish, in the astonishing blue field.

Then night remembered its arm
a vampire's flabby flight suddenly hovering
and BIG MILLAM's Colt 45
wrote the verdict and the State of the Union in rust letters
on the living black wall:
20 years of zinc
15 years of copper
15 years of oil
            and the 180th year of these states
            but in the heart unfeeling clockwork
            what, nothing, zero,
            of blood not a drop
            in the white heart's tough antiseptic meat?

Aimé Césaire, 1960
Translated from the French by Clayton Eshleman and Annette Smith

Temperate Belt

Reflections on the Mother of Emmett Till

Mascara and sun blurred her cheeks when
those final words stammered from Mississippi
to the sallow veins in Spain; but
she could spin that top again; faster
than the tilt-a-whirl above his grave.

Sidewalk barker in yellow silk, she
shook that tiny skull until
pity bled from our eyes; stuffed
with cotton candy and paper dolls, we
rode the rides and caught the ring
of organ pipes in our glands.

The white-haired liberal
made us heave behind the tent; his
skins reaked with deadlines, with columns
of mutilations. He and we
by the hymns of paper boys
exchanged the night below her wooden stand.
From the backdrop
where everyone's weight is guessed
a diplomat emerged with the stars
brushed his shoes
on the parchment of his legs, drew
speeches from his sleeves.
This son of souvenirs,
drumming in the lobby,
scattered his wings and slipped away.

Still her music pulsed
day and night, charming fewer
and fewer; tents began to fold and
disappear one by one.
In this vacant lot of petitions

of papercups, we saw her
once or twice, lying in the tracks
of the tilt-a-whirl, full of quarters
among the weeds that sprung from his grave.

Durward Collins Jr., 1962

:::::

Emmett Till

I hear a whistling
Through the waters.
Little Emmett
Won't be still.
He keeps floating
Round the darkness,
Edging through
The silent chill.

Tell me, please,
That bedtime story
Of the fairy
River Boy
Who swims forever,
Deep in the treasures,
Necklaced in
A coral toy.

James A. Emanuel, 1963

Elegy for Emmett Till

In North America
the mariners' rose has its southern petal
stained with blood.

The Mississippi flows,
O ancient river, brother of the Black,
with open veins beneath its waters,
the Mississippi as it flows.
Its grand breast heaves
and from its deep guitar,
the Mississippi flows,
come sobs of bitter tears.

The Mississippi flows,
and the Mississippi as it flows
sees mute trees with
ripened moans for fruit;
the Mississippi flows,
and the Mississippi as it flows
knows crosses of burning fire,
the Mississippi as it flows,
and men of terror and screams,
the Mississippi as it flows,
and nocturnal bonfires
with white men dancing
in a cannibal light,
and nocturnal bonfires
with a black man always burning:
the obedient Black,
his torn bowels wrapped in smoke,
his guts choked with fumes,
his abused sex . . .
there in the alcoholic South,
there in the South of insult and lash,
the Mississippi as it flows.

And now, O Mississippi,
O ancient river, brother of the Black,
now a fragile youth,
a flower from your banks,
not yet a root of your trees,
a trunk in your forests.
a stone in your bed,
a cayman in your waters . . .
scarcely a child,
a dead child, murdered, alone,
black.

A boy with his top
his pals, his neighborhood,
a Sunday shirt,
a movie ticket,
his desk and his blackboard,
his bottle of ink,
his baseball glove,
a boxing program,
his picture of Lincoln,
a U.S. flag . . .
black.

Black, murdered, alone: this boy who tossed a rose of love
at a passing girl
who was white.

O ancient Mississippi,
O king, O heavy-cloaked river!
Here detain your train of ripples,
your azure, ocean-flowing coach:
see this slight body,
this adolescent angel
on whose shoulders
had not yet healed the scars
of where there once were wings.

Feel the absent contour of this brow,
smashed by stone and stone,
by lead and stone,
insult and stone.
Look upon this gaping breast
where once-warm blood is hard and caked.
Look, and in the night made bright
by a catastrophic moon,
the endless night of the Black
with its subterranean phosphorescence.
Look, and in the night made bright,
speak Mississippi: can you contemplate
with eyes of water gone blind,
with Titan arms indifferent,
this mourning, this crime,
this minimal death yet unavenged,
this cadaver colossal and pure?
Look, and in the night made bright,
you—so heavy with fists and birds
and dreams and metals—
look, and in the night made bright,
O ancient river, brother of the Black,
look, and in the night made bright,
look, and in the night made bright,
speak . . .
Mississippi!

Nicolás Guillén, 1956

Translated by Roberto Márquez and David Arthur McMurray

Mississippi—1955

(To the Memory of Emmett Till)

Oh, what sorrow!
Oh, what pity!
Oh, what pain
That tears and blood
Should mix like rain
And terror come again
To Mississippi.

Come again?
Where has terror been?
On vacation? Up North?
In some other section
Of the nation.
Lying low, unpublicized?
Masked—with only
Jaundiced eyes
Showing through the mask?

Oh, what sorrow,
Pity, pain,
That tears and blood
Should mix like rain
In Mississippi!
And terror, fetid hot,
Yet clammy cold,
Remain.

Langston Hughes, 1955

Money, Mississippi

(News Item: "Yesterday, in Money, Mississippi, the mutilated body of a 14-year-old Negro boy from Chicago was found in the river.")

From Chicago to Mississippi
Young Emmett Till went down,
Down to visit some kinfolk
In a Mississippi town.

> Now the name of that town is Money,
> The name of that town is Money,
> Name of that town is Money,
> Dirty Money town.

Emmett Till never came back
From that Mississippi town.
Two white men murdered Emmett Till
In that Mississippi town.

> And the name of that town is Money,
> The name of that town is Money,
> Name of that town is Money,
> Bloody Money town.

Two white men shot him down
In that Mississippi town,
Threw him into the river
And left him there to drown.

> Oh, the name of that town is Money,
> The name of that town is Money,
> Name of that town is Money,
> Rotten Money town.

Drag the river for Emmett Till
In that Mississippi town;
Drag the river for Justice,
Justice floating face down.

For the name of that town is Money,
The name of that town is Money,
Name of that town is Money,
Filthy Money town.

Where that young boy went to his death,
The murderers went free;
Where they let that young boy die,
They let the killers go free.

Where the name of that town is Money,
The name of that town is Money,
Name of that town is Money,
Evil Money town.

Raise up the body of Emmett Till
From that muddy river town;
Raise up the body of Justice
In that bloody Money town.

Bring home the body of Emmett Till
From that terrible Money town.
Bring home the body of Justice
With her blood-stained shining crown.

Eve Merriam, 1956

:::::

Salute

Murderers
of Emmett Till
I salute you
and the men
who set the

murderers
free I salute
you. Twice.

I salute
the brothers
of charity
who let Bessie
Smith bleed to
Death. She
had the wrong
blood type.
It wasn't white.

I salute
all self-anointed
men
who dole out freedoms to other
men.

I could go on. But won't. I
salute everything, all things
that infect me with this knot
twisted in your subconscious; knot
of automatic distrust, unraveled.
I salute everything, all things
Worthy of my confusion, my awe,
my fury, my cursing, which never
looks good in print . . . worthy of
my tears . . . ALL HONORABLE MEN!
I salute you.

You could go on . . . But won't.

Oliver Pitcher, 1962

2

"Godfearing citizens / with Bibles, taunts and stones"

THE LITTLE ROCK CRISIS, 1957–1958

The *Brown v. Board of Education of Topeka* decision made segregated public educational facilities illegal on 17 May 1954. However, many states refused to acknowledge the Supreme Court decision that overturned *Plessy v. Ferguson* of 1896 and continued to operate "separate but equal" schools. Racism, xenophobia, and traditionally divisive southern customs and politics caused many whites to oppose the ruling. One of the more contentious and publicized resistances to *Brown* occurred in Little Rock, Arkansas, in 1957. Governor Orval Faubus, a staunch segregationist, was so opposed to the prospect of black and white children attending school together that he summoned the National Guard to Little Rock's all-white Central High School on 4 September. The troops prevented nine black students from entering the school, a move that appeased the enraged mob of white adults stationed outside the school but infuriated integrationists and President Eisenhower. The crisis continued until Eisenhower deployed one thousand members of the 101st Airborne Division to the city nearly three weeks later. On 25 September the riot-trained troops escorted the Little Rock Nine, the nine African American children selected from approximately eighty candidates, through the doors of Central High, successfully integrating the Little Rock public school system. The students at the forefront of the struggle were Melba Patillo Beals, Elizabeth Eckford, Ernest Green, Gloria Ray Karlmark, Carlotta Walls Lanier, Thelma Mothershed-Wair, Terrence Roberts, Jefferson Thomas, and Minnejean Brown Trickey.

In response to the school integration crisis and the media attention surrounding Arkansas, Gwendolyn Brooks wrote "The *Chicago Defender* Sends a Man to Little Rock." She captures the aggressive actions of the adult mob surrounding Central High School and the overall tension that existed. Seemingly anything at the crowd's disposal was hurled at the Little Rock Nine.

Robert Hayden's "School Integration Riot" also brings to mind the scene at the school. Not only does Hayden capture the hypocrisy and pseudo-Christianity of many southern whites, but he also recalls the cruelty the Little Rock Nine endured.

Nicolás Guillén's poem "Little Rock," much like his "Elegy for Emmett Till," contains an abundance of condemnation for the social and political climate of the United States, especially the South.

The abuses Brooks, Hayden, Guillén, and others describe continued in varying forms until only five of the nine students remained in Little Rock. The other four left and took high school correspondence courses through the University of Arkansas. In September 1958, after Ernest Green became the first African American to graduate from Central High School, Governor Faubus ordered all the public high schools in Little Rock closed. The schools remained closed until 12 August 1959, nearly two months after a federal court ruled the governor's act unconstitutional.

The *Chicago Defender* Sends a Man to Little Rock

In Little Rock the people bear
Babes, and comb and part their hair
And watch the want ads, put repair
To roof and latch. While wheat toast burns
A woman waters multiferns.

Time upholds or overturns
The many, tight, and small concerns.

In Little Rock the people sing
Sunday hymns like anything,
Through Sunday pomp and polishing.

And after testament and tunes,
Some soften Sunday afternoons
With lemon tea and Lorna Doones.

I forecast
And I believe
Come Christmas Little Rock will cleave
To Christmas tree and trifle, weave,
From laugh and tinsel, texture fast.

In Little Rock is baseball; Barcarolle.
That hotness in July . . . the uniformed figures raw and implacable
And not intellectual,
Battling the hotness or clawing the suffering dust.
The Open Air Concert, on the special twilight green . . .
When Beethoven is brutal or whispers to lady-like air.
Blanket-sitters are seldom, as Johann troubles to lean
To tell them what to mean . . .

There is love, too, in Little Rock. Soft women softly
Opening themselves in kindness,
Or, pitying one's blindness,
Awaiting one's pleasure

In azure
Glory with anguished rose at the root . . .

To wash away old semi-discomfitures.
They re-teach purple and unsullen blue.
The wispy soils go. And uncertain
Half-havings have they clarified to sures.

In Little Rock they know
Not answering the telephone is a way of rejecting life,
That it is our business to be bothered, is our business
To cherish bores or boredom, be polite
To lies and love and many-faceted fuzziness.

I scratch my head, massage the hate-I-had.
I blink across my prim and penciled pad.
The saga I was sent for is not down.
Because there is a puzzle in this town.
The biggest News I do not dare
Telegraph to the Editor's chair:
"They are like people everywhere."

The angry Editor would reply
In hundred harryings of Why.

And true, they are hurling spittle, rock,
Garbage and fruit in Little Rock.
And I saw coiling storm-a-writhe
On bright madonnas. And a scythe
Of men harassing brownish girls.
(The bows and barrettes in the curls
And braids declined away from joy.)

I saw a bleeding brownish boy . . .

The lariat lynch-wish I deplored.

The loveliest lynchee was our Lord.

Gwendolyn Brooks, 1957

:::::

Little Rock

(for Enrique Amorim)

A blues cries tears of music
in the clear morning air.
White South draws its lash and strikes.
Little black children pass through pedagogical rifles
to their school of terror.
Once inside the classroom
Jim Crow will be their teacher,
sons of Lynch their playmates;
and there will be at every desk
of every child that's black
bloody ink and flaming pens.

This is the South, the never-ending curse of the South!

In that Faubus-world,
beneath the hard Faubus-sky of gangrene,
a black child is free:
        not to be in school among the whites,
to stay peacefully at home,
        not to walk out in the streets,
to be martyred by beatings,
        not to whistle at a white woman,
to be killed by spit and lead,
        and even to lower his head . . . *yes,*

bend his back . . . *yes,*
fall to his knees . . . *yes,*
in that free world . . . *yes,*
of which John Foster Stupid speaks from airport to
airport:
while that tiny white ball,
that pretty, tiny, white, presidential ball
(golf) rolls like the smallest of planets
over fine, stiff, clean, chaste, tender,
sweet, green grass . . . *yes*!

Now then, ladies,
gentlemen, girls,
old men, rich men, poor men,
Indians, Mulattoes, Negroes, Zambos,
think what it would be:
a world all South,
a world all blood and lash,
a world of white schools for whites,
a world of Rock and all Little,
a world all Yankee and all Faubus . . .

Consider that a moment.
Imagine for just one instant!

Nicolás Guillén, 1958
Translated by Roberto Márquez and David Arthur McMurray

:::::

School Integration Riot

I have no words, no words for this.
Obscene, inhumane, vile —
Oh, none of these, none of these will serve.
They limp, they falter

while Godfearing citizens
with Bibles, taunts and stones
advance upon a weeping child.

Outrageous, cruel—no;
these are whimpers lost
in clamourings of the mob.
No words, I have no words for this.
O Muse, befriend me now
that I may find release
from silence not to be endured.

Robert Hayden, ca. 1960

:::::

My Blackness Is the Beauty of This Land

My blackness is the beauty of this land,
my blackness,
tender and strong, wounded and wise,
my blackness:
I, drawling black grandmother, smile muscular and sweet,
unstraightened white hair soon to grow in earth,
work-thickened hand thoughtful and gentle on grandson's head,
my heart is bloody-razored by a million memories' thrall:

remembering the crook-necked cracker who spat
on my naked body,
remembering the splintering of my son's spirit
because he remembered to be proud
remembering the tragic eyes in my daughter's
dark face when she learned her color's meaning,

and my own dark rage a rusty knife with teeth to gnaw
my bowels,

my agony ripped loose by anguished shouts in Sunday's
    humble church,
my agony rainbowed to ecstasy when my feet oversoared
    Montgomery's slime,

ah, this hurt, this hate, this ecstasy before I die,
and all my love a strong cathedral!
My blackness is the beauty of this land!

Lay this against my whiteness, this land!
Lay me, young Brutus stamping hard on the cat's tail,
gutting the Indian, gouging the nigger,
booting Little Rock's Minnejean Brown in the buttocks and boast,
    my sharp white teeth derision-bared as I the conqueror crush!
Skyscraper—I, white hands burying God's human clouds beneath
    the dust!
Skyscraper—I, slim blond young Empire
    thrusting up my loveless bayonet to rape the sky,
then shrink all my long body with filth and in the gutter lie
as lie I will to perfume this armpit garbage,
While I here standing black beside
wrench tears from which the lies would suck the salt
to make me more American than America . . .
But yet my love and yet my hate shall civilize this land,
this land's salvation.

Lance Jeffers, 1970

3

“The FBI knows who lynched you”

THE MURDER OF MACK CHARLES PARKER, 1959

Nearly four years after Emmett Till’s abduction and murder, Mack Charles Parker was forcibly removed from a Poplarville, Mississippi, jail and lynched. Till’s death had intensified the civil rights movement and increased national and international awareness of America’s racial crisis, but actions taken against Parker reminded the state and country that racists remained active and vigilant. While Till and Parker were both seized and tortured in Mississippi, the similarities of their respective cases appear to start and end there, for Parker’s alleged crime and death never generated the media attention Till received, and the details surrounding his case are not nearly as widely known as Till’s. However, those little-known details and the mysteries that still surround them are among the most intriguing of the unsolved cases of the civil rights era.

Parker, a twenty-three-year-old African American from

Lumberton, Mississippi, was arrested on 24 February 1959 for allegedly raping and kidnapping June Walters, a married, pregnant white woman. Quite often in racially hostile regions such as Mississippi the slightest inference of abuse of a white female at the hands of a black male was enough to deem the alleged guilty in the court of popular opinion. Unfortunately Parker fell victim to this long-standing practice. According to FBI documents titled "*Summary of Investigation of the Abduction of Mack Charles Parker from the Pearl River County Jail, Poplarville, Mississippi, April 24–25, 1959*" released under the Freedom of Information Act, "a band of hooded or masked men, eight to ten in number," stormed the jail around midnight on 24 April, three days before Parker's scheduled trial, and drove off with the prisoner. Parker's body was retrieved from the Pearl River ten days later, on 4 May. An autopsy revealed that he had died from "a penetrating wound in the left auricle of the heart." Although many members of the mob confessed or were identified by the FBI, and despite the fact that both a county and a federal grand jury reviewed the case, no one was ever arrested or indicted for Parker's murder. His innocence or guilt was never determined.

Poems written in response to Parker's abduction from jail and subsequent murder place the tragedy in a broader historical context, usually in order to decry the ubiquitous nature of injustice in Mississippi. For example, Philip Abbot Luce's poem "Mack C. Parker" reads like a plain-spoken history of the case and serves as a scathing indictment of the FBI, the citizens of Poplarville, and the state of Mississippi. Whites who kill blacks, the poem contends, are never punished in Mississippi, especially for lynching. The poem also claims that Parker's death at the hands of the mob represents the state's 478th lynching.

Keith E. Baird's poem focuses on the impact of Parker's death on the black male psyche and the desire for affirmative self-definition. Inherent in the poem is the notion that Parker was wrongly accused, or at the least, a rush to judgment was made regarding his culpability in the rape of June Walters.

According to Pauli Murray's "For Mack C. Parker," such hasty decisions have often resulted in individuals being unnecessarily "cornered and trapped," "bludgeoned and crushed," and "hideously slain" (1–3). These lines echo and confirm Luce's description of Parker's murder as a "slaughter." Murray connects Parker's death to the decline of biblical brotherhood: “Each vainly rubbing the ’cursed spot / Which brands him Cain.” Murray, the first black woman to be ordained in the Episcopal Church, turns to *The Book of Common Prayer* for guidance in this poem and in the complementary poem, “Collect for Poplarville.” The speaker of “Collect” turns to faith and prayer for courage. The poem also calls for nonviolent Christian-based resistance instead of physical retaliation.

:::::

Poplarville II

Be nice, have patience, wait, have faith, you say;
To whom, and why, what for, in whom? I ask.
How long must last this yearning for the day
When they will see a Man and not the Mask?
’Tis they who forged that mask for us to wear,
That we might draw the water, hew the wood,
Give thanks for labours, and with hope in prayer
Should bear the chains and deem them for our good.
Mack Parker’s murderers walk abroad and mock
At Justice travestied to set them free,
And Africa and Asia note with shock
These tidings from the land of Liberty.
While Law delays, this cannot be gainsaid:
That I am BLACK, and Mack Charles Parker DEAD.

Keith E. Baird, 1962

Mack C. Parker

(In April of 1959, a young Negro worker, Charles Mack Parker, was dragged from his jail cell in Poplarville, Mississippi and lynched. To him this poem is dedicated.)

Your mother cried:
"He was innocent, I'm
sure he was innocent."
Yet you became Mississippi's
478th
        lynching
Your battered body
was found in the
Pearl River.
In 1955 it was
        Emmett Till.

Screaming—
        the steps of the
        jail covered with
        the blood from where
        your head pounded them—
you were dragged
away into the
night.

A woman in Poplarville
told me—
        "Everyone in town is sure that
        the murderers couldn't have
        been from Mississippi."

Because you
        "looked like"
the man that
        "raped"
a white woman
you were lynched.

You died but your known
killers are free.

White killers
        (of Negroes)
are never convicted
        in Mississippi

Two grand juries refused to
indict the slayers.
We, the American people,
do indict them.

The FBI knows who
        lynched you.
The people of Poplarville know who
        lynched you.
Both grand juries know
        the names of the eight men who
        lynched you.

Your death like that of
        Emmett Till
        George Lee
        Lamar Smith
Convicts the people of Mississippi.

Beaten
        Lynched
                Murdered
Yet you are still alive
in the hearts of all those
that struggle for freedom in
the United States.

You died and your killers
remain free.
Your slaughter can only show
the world that there is no
justice in Mississippi.

Phillip Abbott Luce, 1962

:::::

For Mack C. Parker

(Victim of lynching in Mississippi, 1959)

> In the hour of death,
> In the day of judgment,
> *Good Lord, deliver us!*
> — THE BOOK OF COMMON PRAYER

The cornered and trapped,
The bludgeoned and crushed,
The hideously slain,
Freed from the dreaded waiting,
The tortured body's pain,
On death's far shore cast mangled shrouds
To clothe the damned whose fear
Decreed a poisoned harvest,
Garnered a bitter grain.
For these who wear the cloak of shame
Must eat the bread of gall,
Each vainly rubbing the 'cursed spot
Which brands him Cain.

Pauli Murray, 1970

Collect for Poplarville

(Adapted from the Book of Common Prayer)

Lighten our darkness, we beseech thee, O Lord;
        Teach us no longer to dread
                hounds yelping in the distance,
                the footfall at the door,
                the rifle butt on the window pane.

And by thy great mercy defend us from all perils
        and dangers of this night;
                Give us fearlessness to face
                        the bomb thrown in the darkness,
                        the gloved hand on the pistol,
                        the savage intention.
                Give us courage to stand firm against
                        our tormentors without rancor—
                Teach us that most difficult of tasks—
                        to pray for them,
                        to follow, not burn, thy cross!

Pauli Murray, 1970

4

"Fearless before the waiting throng"

THE LIFE AND DEATH OF MEDGAR EVERS

One of the individuals responsible for bringing the Emmet Till and Mack Charles Parker cases to the public's attention and for seeking justice for both parties was Medgar Evers of the NAACP of Jackson, Mississippi (Evers-Williams and Marable 257). In fact the Parker case so infuriated the usually nonviolent-minded Evers that he remarked to his wife, Myrlie, "I'd like to get a gun and start shooting" (Tyson 556).

Evers, who became the NAACP's first field secretary in Mississippi in 1954, the year of the *Brown* decision, was one of the state's most visible and active civil rights leaders. In addition to his involvement with the Till and Parker cases, he was also instrumental in the campaign to register James Meredith as the first black student at the University of Mississippi at Oxford in 1962, introducing him along the way to Thurgood Marshall of the NAACP Legal Defense and Educational Fund. In the end

Meredith's admission also required the assistance of President Kennedy, who took the unusual step of federalizing Mississippi's National Guard to help protect Meredith from two thousand pro-segregation rioters on campus (Vollers 92–95). Evers eventually became a dominant force for the rights of blacks in one of the country's most hostile and racially divided states. In the process he gained a national reputation as well—one that never rivaled those enjoyed by Dr. King and Malcolm X—but one that earned him respect for his willingness to confront some of Mississippi's most entrenched racists. Around 12:30 A.M. on 12 June 1963, Medgar Evers was assassinated by Byron De La Beckwith Jr., a known white supremacist. Evers was left to die on his front doorstep after being shot in the back. Not surprisingly, Beckwith and others viewed Evers and the black community as threats to traditional white authority and conspired to have him eliminated. His murder was intended as a message to other activists involved in the movement and to the black community as a whole. Beckwith was tried twice in 1964, but both proceedings ended in mistrials. He was eventually convicted on 5 February 1994, almost thirty-one years after Evers's death.

The narrator of Aaron Kramer's "Blues for Medgar Evers" regrets not being by the activist's side when Evers was rushed to the hospital after being shot. Kramer's poem also incorporates and uses as a refrain "Turn me loose" (6, 18), the final phrase Evers uttered before dying at the University of Mississippi Hospital (Vollers 129).

David Ignatow's homage, "For Medgar Evers," suggests that Evers and his antagonists were connected by humanity but also by the acknowledgment of their mortality. Similarly the speaker of R. D. Coleman's "American" is forced to contemplate his own mortality as a black man in a segregated and violent America.

Gwendolyn Brooks's "Medgar Evers" makes clear that Evers lived during a time in which change and new ideas were often met with resistance. Nonetheless the poem ends on an optimistic note, focusing on the worldly, visionary qualities of the slain NAACP officer. Those same qualities are at the heart of Margaret Walker's "Micah." Not only is Evers a man who "cried out his Vision to his people" and "spoke out against Oppression" during his lifetime, but he is also depicted as someone who will leave a noble legacy and continue to impact society long after his death (3, 6).

Medgar Evers

For Charles Evers

The man whose height his fear improved he
arranged to fear no further. The raw
intoxicated time was time for better birth or a final death.

Old styles, old tempos, all the engagement of
the day—the sedate, the regulated fray—
the antique light, the Moral rose, old gusts,
tight whistlings from the past, the mothballs
in the Love at last our man forswore.

Medgar Evers annoyed confetti and assorted
brands of businessmen's eyes.

The shows came down: to maxims and surprise.
And palsy.

Roaring no rapt arise-ye to the dead, he
leaned across tomorrow. People said that
he was holding clean globes in his hands.

Gwendolyn Brooks, 1968

:::::

American

In memory of Medgar Evers

Without a mirror,
In longsleeves,
my hands behind me
and my pants breaking
on the laces of my shoes,
I am as black as the next man.

I am an American man
of tragic country, divided
          and poor,
America on the mantelpiece,
Crime with the evening meal,
O my American dust is eyeless
          in anger and pain.
And when I die,
Blood what will you be,
Who will shoot me,
What will my mirror say
Here or in Jackson?

He has died in his battle with death,
He has died in his fight for life,
How has he died, he has died worse than death
And lost his life in the bargain.

R. D. Coleman, 1964

:::::

For Medgar Evers

They're afraid of me
because I remind them of the ground.
The harder they step on me
the closer I am pressed to earth,
and hard, hard they step,
growing more frightened
and vicious.
                    Will I live?

They will lie in the earth
buried in me
and above them a tree will grow
for shade.

David Ignatow, 1968

:::::

Blues for Medgar Evers

I should have been there when darkness
came around your neck like a noose:
—not night, but that other darkness
choking, tight as a noose,
till even you couldn't stand it
and you whispered: "Turn me loose!"

I should have begged them to go faster,
but what would have been the use?
They drove till they couldn't drive faster,
but it wasn't any use.
Turning the corners of Jackson
is not the same as turning you loose.

We'd better watch out for triggers.
We'd better pray hard for a truce.
The hand that turned that trigger
turned more than a bullet loose.
My hand should have been on your forehead
when you whispered: "Turn me loose!"

Aaron Kramer, 1964

Micah

In Memory of Medgar Evers of Mississippi

Micah was a young man of the people
Who came up from the streets of Mississippi
And cried out his Vision to his people;
Who stood fearless before the waiting throng
Like an astronaut shooting into space.
Micah was a man who spoke against Oppression
Crying: Woe to you Workers of iniquity!
Crying: Woe to you doers of violence!
Crying: Woe to you breakers of the peace!
Crying: Woe to you, my enemy!
For when I fall I shall rise in deathless dedication.
When I stagger under the wound of your paid assassins
I shall be whole again in deathless triumph!
For your rich men are full of violence
And your mayors of your cities speak lies.
They are full of deceit.
We do not fear them.
They shall not enter the City of good-will.
We shall dwell under our own vine and fig tree in peace.
And they shall not be remembered in the Book of Life.
Micah was a man.

Margaret Walker, 1970

5

"Under the leaves of hymnals, the plaster and stone"

THE SIXTEENTH STREET BAPTIST CHURCH BOMBING, 15 SEPTEMBER 1963

On 15 September 1963 four young African American girls lost their lives when fifteen sticks of explosives destroyed the Sixteenth Street Baptist Church of Birmingham, Alabama. Primarily responsible was Robert Edward Chambliss, a Birmingham Klansman also known to his friends in the Eastview 13 Klavern as "Dynamite Bob." The four who died in the church were Addie Mae Collins, Carole Robertson, and Cynthia Wesley, all fourteen, and Denise McNair, eleven. Approximately twenty others were injured (Hampton and Fayer 171–72). Two African American boys, Virgil Ware, thirteen, and Johnny Robinson, sixteen, were shot and killed in separate incidents the same day (Harris 130). The bombing, an attempt to terrorize, intimidate, and prevent the black community from fully cooperating in school integration, went unpunished for more than a decade, even though an eyewitness claimed to have seen Chambliss and three other men plant the bomb. Chambliss was convicted in 1977 and died in prison in 1985; Thomas Blanton and Bobby Frank Cherry were sentenced to life in prison in 2001 and 2002, respectively, more than thirty years after the explosion. Cherry died in prison in 2004 at the age of seventy-four. Herman Cash, the fourth suspected bomber, died in 1994. He was never charged with a crime.

The historic March on Washington, which took place on 28 August, a few weeks before the bombing, was largely responsible for a newfound sense of optimism. However, the terrorist act conducted by the opposition served to jolt workers and followers of the movement out of any realm of complacency they may have entered. The desire to enjoy and even bask in the afterglow of the march is completely understandable, especially if one considers that prior to this unprecedented multiracial gathering the movement had been involved with such emotionally taxing struggles as the *Brown v. the Board of Education of Topeka* decision in 1954, the Emmett Till murder of 1955, the Montgomery bus boycott of 1955 and 1956, and the Little Rock crisis of 1957 and 1958. In addition, the following decade brought about the Freedom Rides of 1961, James Meredith's enrollment in the University of Mississippi in 1962, sit-in demonstrations and Dr. King's arrest in Birmingham in 1963 (where King penned his famous "Letter from a Birmingham Jail"), as well as other events that literally served to alter the course of American history and race relations.

Months before Chambliss and others laced the Sixteenth Street Baptist Church with explosives, Birmingham had also been the site where Eugene "Bull" Connor, director of public safety and later sheriff, unleashed police dogs and fire hoses on a peaceful group of black children and young adult marchers. Photographs and videotaped footage of this brutality were widely published and broadcast, garnering the movement increased visibility and substantially more empathy, particularly from whites in the North. While all of these struggles and confrontations resulted in either minor or major victories, they all exacted tremendous individual, group, and community tolls. For many, the euphoria and cathartic release that resulted from the March on Washington had been in the making for at least a decade. Then came the Birmingham explosion, which reminded the nation of how little the terrorists respected black life and culture, including the places they gathered to worship and commune.

The innocence of the murdered girls was in part responsible for much of the disgust that followed the bombing. Dudley Randall captures this sense of innocence in "Ballad of Birmingham" by structuring his poem as a rhythmic dialogue between one of the young girls and her mother. Readers are given a daughter–mother, question–response conversation for the first half of the poem. While the mother prevents her daughter from participating in a "Freedom March" out of fear for her safety (amid possible attacks from police dogs and fire hoses), she is unable to protect her from harm and tragedy at church (from a Sunday morning bomb).

Raymond Patterson's "Birmingham 1963" also depends upon the innocence of preparing for and going to church on a Sunday morning. He leaves the reader with the extremely agonizing description of one of the daughters "amid the rubble, amid the people / Who perish, being innocent" (23–24).

Similarly "Birmingham Sunday" by Langston Hughes is grounded in the immediate circumstances surrounding the bombing. Hughes appropriately relies heavily on church and Christian imagery and references to capture the anger and frustration caused by the explosion. The poem's conclusion suggests the possibility of or hope for racial understanding "someday soon" but concedes that solidarity is "yet unfelt" in the American South (25, 27).

"Suffer the Children" by Audre Lorde warns against allowing the girls' deaths to be forgotten. Published in *Negro Digest* the year following the explosion, the poem also mentions the indifference and callousness of racists to the deaths of the children.

Indifference, or at least the potential for it, also informs Jean Valentine's "September 1963" and Edith Segal's "Ballad for Four Children and a President." Valentine juxtaposes typical childhood frivolity and the agonizing news of the church bombing. By the poem's end, however, there is the sense not only that whites and blacks live in separate worlds, but that whites are either uninformed or indifferent to the plight of blacks. Segal's poem shares some of the same sentiments, but does so by combining the murders of the four little girls and the assassination of President John F. Kennedy, which occurred approximately two months later. The poem asks repeatedly and adamantly, "How long can free world freedom wait?" The question is intended to highlight America's failure to live up to its ideals, especially those involving liberty and equality.

President Kennedy is also at the center of John Beecher's "Escort for a President," but Beecher's ultimate goal is to associate Kennedy's death with the deaths of Medgar Evers, the four girls who died in the bombing, and the two boys, Virgil Ware and Johnny Robinson, who were murdered in the aftermath of the bombing. Beecher is intent on not allowing the African American victims of 1963 to be forgotten or overshadowed by the assassination of President Kennedy.

:::::

Escort for a President

I

Rapt to our screens we watch him borne inert
and casketed into the plane he stepped
from a few hours ago invulnerable,
serene and radiant. Young Zeus he seemed
at breakfast, brandishing his thunderbolts
and vaunting of the billions he'd dispensed
to Texans slavering for contracts. Votes
he angled for with grisly bait but was
first casualty of his dread TFX
although the instrument which took his life
was obsolete as bow and arrow. Lord,
Thine irony is more cruel than Thy wrath.

II

The land's sad face averts itself, now bleak
and sere that's starred with blue bonnets in spring
and Dallas underwing diminishes,
the azure shafts that oil and cattle built,
the marts where Santa holds his blazing court.
Small Jesús flattens nose upon plate glass
but José's out of work and so is Maria.

III

Assumed into a myth more speedily
than Lincoln was or Roosevelt he floats

across the fabled river so far down
it seems the life-line on some ancient palm.
Mortality is sloughed in upper air
above the Mississippi. Brooding here
another myth circles on eagle wings
biding its time. Crossed hairs upon a back
as on a head brought to a baleful term
two young men's lives. Medgar, here's company.

IV

Now swarming up the air with cries like doves
or angels come black girls from Birmingham
with blood upon their Sunday finery
and faces blown away. Here also wheel
two black boys slain in cleanlier wise by bullets
upon that Sabbath day. May they escort
a president upon his journey home?

John Beecher, 1963

:::::

American History

Those four black girls blown up
in that Alabama church
remind me of five hundred
middle passage blacks,
in a net, under water
in Charleston harbor
so *redcoats* wouldn't find them.
Can't find what you can't see
can you?

Michael S. Harper, 1970

Here Where Coltrane Is

Soul and race
are private dominions,
memories and modal
songs, a tenor blossoming,
which would paint suffering
a clear color but is not in
this Victorian house
without oil in zero degree
weather and a forty-mile-an-hour wind;
it is all a well-knit family:
a love supreme.
Oak leaves pile up on walkway
and steps, catholic as apples
in a special mist of clear white
children who love my children.
I play "Alabama"
on a warped record player
skipping the scratches
on your faces over the fibrous
conical hairs of plastic
under the wooden floors.

Dreaming on a train from New York
to Philly, you had out six
notes which become an anthem
to our memories of you;
oak, birch, maple,
apple, cocoa, rubber.
For this reason Martin is dead;
for this reason Malcolm is dead;
for this reason Coltrane is dead;
in the eyes of my first son are the browns
of these men and their music.

Michael S. Harper, 1971

Birmingham Sunday

(September 15, 1963)

Four little girls
Who went to Sunday School that day
And never came back home at all
But left instead
Their blood upon the wall
With spattered flesh
And bloodied Sunday dresses
Torn to shreds by dynamite
That China made aeons ago—
Did not know
That what China made
Before China was ever Red at all
Would redden with their blood
This Birmingham-on-Sunday wall.

Four tiny girls
Who left their blood upon that wall,
In little graves today await
The dynamite that might ignite
The fuse of centuries of Dragon Kings
Whose tomorrow sings a hymn
The missionaries never taught Chinese
In Christian Sunday School
To implement the Golden Rule.

Four little girls
Might be awakened someday soon
By songs upon the breeze
As yet unfelt among magnolia trees.

Langston Hughes, 1967

Suffer the Children

He is forever trapped
who suffers his own waste.
Rain leaching the earth   for lack
of roots to hold it
and children who are murdered
before their lives begin.

Who pays his crops to the sun
when his fields lie parched by drought
will mourn the lost water
waiting another rain.
But who shall disinter these girls
to love the women they were to become
or read the legends written beneath their skin?

We who love them remember their child's laughter.
But he whose hate robs him of their gold
has yet to weep at night about their graves.

Audre Lorde, 1964

:::::

Birmingham 1963

Sunday morning and her mother's hands
Weaving the two thick braids of her springing hair,
Pulling her sharply by one bell-rope when she would
Not sit still, setting her ringing,
While the radio church choir prophesied the hour
With theme and commercials, while the whole house tingled;
And she could not stand still in that awkward air;
Her dark face shining, her mother now moving the tiny buttons,
Blue against blue, the dress which took all night making,

That refused to stay fastened;
There was some pull which hurried her out to Sunday School
Toward the lesson and the parable's good news,
The quiet escape from the warring country of her feelings,
The confused landscape of grave issues and people.

But now we see
Now we see through the glass of her mother's wide screaming
Eyes into the room where the homemade bomb
Blew the room down where her daughter had gone;
Under the leaves of hymnals, the plaster and stone,
The blue dress, all undone—
The day undone to the bone—
Her still, dull face, her quiet hair;
Alone amid the rubble, amid the people
Who perish, being innocent.

Raymond Patterson, 1969

:::::

Ballad of Birmingham

(on the bombing of a church in Birmingham, Alabama, 1963)

"Mother dear, may I go downtown
Instead of out to play,
And march the streets of Birmingham
In a Freedom March today?"

"No, baby, no, you may not go,
For the dogs are fierce and wild,
And clubs and hoses, guns and jail
Aren't good for a little child."

"But, mother, I won't be alone.
Other children will go with me,

And march the streets of Birmingham
To make our country free."

"No, baby, no, you may not go,
For I fear those guns will fire.
But you may go to church instead
And sing in the children's choir."

She has combed and brushed her night-dark hair,
And bathed rose petal sweet,
And drawn white gloves on her small brown hands,
And white shoes on her feet.

The mother smiled to know her child
Was in the sacred place,
But that smile was the last smile
To come upon her face.

For when she heard the explosion,
Her eyes grew wet and wild.
She raced through the streets of Birmingham
Calling for her child.

She clawed through bits of glass and brick,
Then lifted out a shoe.
"O, here's the shoe my baby wore,
But, baby, where are you?"

Dudley Randall, 1963

Ballad for Four Children and a President

For the stones will cry from the wall,
and the limbs of the trees will testify.
— TALMUD

The Governor hailed the status quo
The hate men heiled *"We'll keep it so,"*
They crept with death-filled killer hands
To where your church now shattered stands.
Oh innocent, sweet brown-skinned girls
In Sunday dresses, bows and curls,
Death hurried you, but freedom's late!
How long can free world freedom wait?

How many stones and walls have cried?
How many trees have testified?
Now you lie dead, oh dead so young,
Your laughter gone, your song unsung.
And in the dark night of our shame
Your graves send forth a warning flame:
"Death hurried us with winds of hate!
How long can free world freedom wait?"

Your killers reign complacently
They flaunt the flag of slavery.
The Governor hails the status quo
The hate men heil *"We'll keep it so!"*
And all the world asks mournfully
"Is yours the homeland of the free?
Death hurried you, but freedom's late!
How long can free world freedom wait?"

November came — *death struck again!*
Behold! Our President was slain!
And all the world, bewilderedly,
Cried out once more *"It cannot be!"*

And in the dark night of our shame
Now glows another warning flame:
Redeem our land from death, from hate!
How long can free world freedom wait?

And Lincoln weeps in his stone chair.
In August we assembled there
Two-hundred-fifty-thousand strong
To ask our President *"How long?"*
And now he lies in Arlington
Our free world freedom not yet won.
Death hurried you, but freedom's late!
How long can free world freedom wait?

Three hundred years—a bitter score
To fight and die at freedom's door!
We mean to enter proud and bold,
The lynched, the bombed, the young, the old,
To sing in truth, oh land, of thee
The words *"Sweet land of liberty. . . ."*
We shall not ask again "Oh when?"
Our freedom time is now! Amen!

Edith Segal, 1969

:::::

September 1963

We've been at home four years, in a kind of peace,
A kind of kingdom: brushing your yellow hair
At the tower's small window,
Playing hop-scotch on the grass.

With twenty other Gullivers
I hover at the door,

Watch you shy through this riddle of primary colors,
The howling razzle-dazzle of your peers.

Tears, stay with me, stay with me, tears.
Dearest, go: this is what
School is, what the world is.
Have I sewed my hands to yours?

Five minutes later in the eye of God
You and Kate and Jeremy are dancing.

Glad, derelict, I find a park bench, read
Birmingham. Birmingham. Birmingham.
White tears on a white ground,
White world going on, white hand in hand,
World without end.

Jean Valentine, 1965

6

"What we have seen / Has become history, tragedy"

THE ASSASSINATION OF PRESIDENT JOHN F. KENNEDY, 22 NOVEMBER 1963

Although John F. Kennedy (1917–63) presided over one of the most racially tumultuous periods in U.S. history, his tenure as America's thirty-fifth president in 1961–63 was tragically brief. With respect to the civil rights movement, Kennedy's most significant act as president was his initiation in 1963 of the Civil Rights Act. Kennedy never lived to see the passage of the Civil Rights Act in 1964 which, in part, outlawed segregation in public places and prevented segregated public schools from receiving federal funding. However, the bill came about largely as a result of his stated belief in equal opportunity for all Americans and pressure from civil rights leaders. After Kennedy's assassination, Dr. King published a short yet poignant essay on Kennedy in *Transition* magazine. In the essay, which was published in 1964, King asserts that the Civil Rights Act "will be both a living and a lasting monument" to Kennedy. King also insists:

> It took courage to offer it at the moment and in the manner, he did. It illustrated that special difference which made John Kennedy unique. Many political leaders refuse to act when a mass movement is exploding with intensity. President Kennedy might have said, as had others, that he would not proceed under pressure; as if it were a virtue to ignore mass protest. Instead he frankly acknowledged that he was responding to mass demands and did so because he thought it was right to do so. This is the secret of the deep affection he evoked. He was responsive, sensitive, humble before the people, and bold on their behalf. (27–28)

The sensitivity and boldness King mentions were demonstrated when Kennedy sent the civil rights bill to Congress. During a memorable televised speech from the White House on 11 June 1963 Kennedy informed the nation, "One hundred years of delay have passed since President Lincoln freed the slaves, yet their heirs, their grandsons, are not fully free. They are not yet freed from the bonds of injustice. They are not yet freed from social and economic oppression. And this Nation, for all its hopes and all its boasts, will not be fully free until all its citizens are free" (Sorensen 194). The speech was delivered as a response to Governor George Wallace's infamous "stand in the doorway" earlier that day at the University of Alabama. Wallace's actions delayed the admission of Vivian Malone and James Hood, two black students attempting to enroll at the university. In January Wallace had proclaimed "segregation now, segregation tomorrow and segregation forever" for public educational institutions in the state. In response to Wallace's actions in June, the president federalized the Alabama National Guard and Wallace eventually stepped aside. (Kennedy took similar action one year earlier by federalizing Mississippi's National Guard to assist James Meredith in his quest to become the first black student at Ole Miss.) Unfortunately the president's speech, which served to counter Wallace's philosophy and actions, had little time to set in or be appreciated by most civil rights activists. Hours later Byron De La Beckwith, a pro-segregation terrorist, shot and murdered Medgar Evers of the NAACP in Jackson, Mississippi. This dizzying chain of events occurred in less than twenty-four hours and seemed to highlight the Scylla and Charybdis of Alabama and Mississippi, two of the most racist states in the nation.

Kennedy's assassination occurred on 22 November 1963, nearly three months after the March on Washington, which he initially opposed, purportedly due to fear of violence, and two months after the bombing of the Sixteenth Street Baptist Church of Birmingham, Alabama. Kennedy's vision of a "fully free" United States never materialized during his lifetime, for social and economic oppression were still in abundance at the time of his death. The nation nonetheless appeared to be moving in the right direction. After decades of neglect and indifference, Americans at the bottom of the socioeconomic ladder, especially African Americans, were beginning to receive positive attention from the White House. Kennedy's death left many leaders of the movement in a crisis. Although he did not act as fast and was not as forceful as his campaign rhetoric promised, he did entertain and give voice to some of the demands of the movement's leaders. His short time in office, even with the multiple civil rights challenges his administration faced on the domestic front, was largely defined by affairs abroad: the Bay of Pigs invasion of Cuba, the Cuban missile crisis, his standoff with the Soviet Union's Nikita Khrushchev, and the escalation of U.S. troops in Vietnam.

Kennedy was assassinated "down in Dallas" as the poet X. J. Kennedy writes, "with the nail of a rifle crack" and "on the cross of a rifle sight" (lines 4, 20). That tragic moment is captured in similar terms by Derek Walcott, who decades later would win the Nobel Prize for Literature: "What was willed / on innocent, sun-streaked Dallas, the beast's claw / curled round that hairspring rifle" (16–18).

Not surprisingly most of the poetry written about Kennedy shortly after his assassination revolves around unfulfilled potential—his and America's. The poems collected here are also filled with lingering, overwhelming grief, or "not that hurried grief," as Lorenzo Thomas recalls so clearly. Thomas's line evokes the suddenness of Kennedy's passing and how his televised funeral left many in an extended state of mourning for the Kennedys and for America, the type of prolonged remorse that Thomas describes as "a genuinely new emotion" (25). As a result, aside from a line of verse by John Berryman, poets here never directly address specific issues of public policy usually associated with Kennedy's abbreviated term in office. More often than not, poets picked up their pens to praise him.

"Elegy for JFK" by W. H. Auden recalls Kennedy as "a just man" whose murder left more questions than answers in its wake. Auden and other poets respected Kennedy for multiple reasons, but one of those reasons rests in the fact that the president respected and supported the arts and creative expression. This became evident to poets almost immediately, when Kennedy invited Robert Frost to read a poem during his 20 January 1961 inauguration.

Barbara Guest reflects on this connection between artists and the president when she laments, "As if one more / of our artists / has died" (61–63). Most poems articulate a deep belief in the president and sincere regret for his passing, perhaps in order to overcome what Marjorie Mir calls the "final disbelief" (6). The mixture of disbelief and regret, according to A. R. Ammons, "touches us and lifts us into tears" (31). Gwendolyn Brooks strikes a similar chord when she writes, "I hear things crying in the world. / . . . The tilt and jangle of this death" (1, 4). Lewis Turco's "November 22, 1963" connects Kennedy's life to the lifeblood of the poets themselves.

Several poems express concern and affection for the First Family, including Anselm Hollo's "Until Death Do Us Part," Will Inman's "Jacqueline," and Marvin Solomon's "Sonnet for John-John," the nickname of John F. Kennedy Jr., who was almost three when his father was killed.

Belief

1
drums gather and humble us beyond escape,
propound the single, falling fact:
time, suspended between memory and present,
hangs unmeasured, empty

2
erect,
disciplined by cadence into direction, the soldier
obeys the forms of rumor:
the riderless horse,
restive with the pressure of held flight,
tosses the hung bit,
worries the soldier's tameless arm—
sidling, prances the energy out

3
ahead, unalterable, the fact proceeds,
and the bit holds;
the fire-needle bites,
training the head on course

4
the light, determined rattle
of the caisson
breaking into sunlight
through the crystal black ribbons of trees!
the slack traces,
weightlessness at the shoulders of horses!

5
if we could break free
and run this knowledge out,
burst this energy of grief
through a hundred countrysides!
if black through the black night

we could outrun
this knowledge into a different morning!

6
belief, light as a drumrattle,
touches us and lifts us into tears.

A. R. Ammons, 1964

:::::

Elegy for JFK

Why *then*? Why *there*?
Why *thus*, we cry, did he die?
The Heavens are silent.

What he was, he was:
What he is fated to become
Depends on us.

Remembering his death,
How we choose to live
Will decide its meaning.

When a just man dies,
Lamentation and praise,
Sorrow and joy are one.

W. H. Auden, 1964

Formal Elegy

I

A hurdle of water, and O these waters are cold
(warm at outset) in the dirty end.
Murder on murder on murder, where I stagger,
whiten the good land where we have held out.
These kills were not for loot,
however Byzantium hovers in the mind:
were matters of principle — that's worst of all —
& fear & crazed mercy.
Ruby, with his mad claim
he shot to spare the Lady's testifying,
probably is sincere.
No doubt, in his still cell, his sits pure.

II

Yes, it looks like a wilderness — pacem appellant.
Honour to Patrolman Tippit. Peace to the rifler's widow.
Seven, I believe, play fatherless.

III

Scuppered the yachts, the choppers, big cars, jets.
Nobody goes anywhere,
lengthened (days) into TV.
I am four feet long, invisibly.
What in the end will be left of us is a stare,
Underwater.
If you want me to join you in confident prayer, let's
not.
I sidled in & past, gazing upon it,
the bier.

IV

Too Andean hopes, now angry shade —
I am an automobile. Into me climb
Many, and go their ways. Onto him climbed
a-many and went his way.

For a while we seemed to be having a holiday
off from ourselves — ah, but the world is wigs,
as sudden we came to feel
and even his splendid hair kept not wholly real
fumbling & falsing in & out of the Bay of Pigs,
the bad moment of this excellent man,
suffered by me as a small car can.
Faithful to course we stayed.

V

Some in their places are constrained to weep.
Stunned, more, though.
Black foam. A weaving snake. An invulnerable sleep.
It doing have to come so.
All at once, hurtles, in the tide of applause
& expectation. I write from New York
where except for a paraplegic exterminator —
a gracious & sweet guy —
nobody has done no work
lately

VI

It's odd perhaps that Dallas   cannot after their crimes
criminals protect or Presidents.
Fat Dallas, a fit set.
I would not perhaps have for him next time.
Images of Mr. Kennedy blue the air,
who is little now, with no chance to grow great,
but who have set his touch across the State,
true-intended, strong

VII

My breath comes heavy, does my breath.
I feel heavy about the President's death.

VIII

I understand I hear I see I read
schoolgirls in Dallas when the white word came

or slammed, cheered in their thoughtful grades,
brought-up to a loving tone.
I do not sicken but somewhat with shame
I shift my head an inch; who are my own.
I have known a loving Texas woman in parades
and she was boastful & treacherous.
That boringest of words, whereas here I blush,
"education," peters to a nailing of us.

IX

An editor has asked me in my name
what wish or prophecy I'd like to state
for the new year. I am silent on these occasions
steadily, having no love for a fool
(which I keep being) but I break my rule:
I do all-wish the bullets swim astray
sent to the President, and that all around
help, and his heart keep sound.
I have a strange sense
he's about to be the best of men.
Amen.

X

It's quiet at Arlington. Rock Creek is quiet.
My primers, with Mount Auburn. Everybody should
have his sweet boneyards. Yet let the young not go,
our apprentice King! Alas,
muffled, he must. He seemed good:
brainy in riot, daring, cool.
So
let us abandon the scene of disorder. Drop
them in shattered bodies into tranquil places,
where moulder as you will. We compose our face
cold as the cresting water; ready again.
The waters break.
All black and white together, stunned, survive
the final insolence to the head of you;
bow.

Overwhelmed-un, live.
A rifle fact is over, pistol facts
almost entirely are too.
The man of a wise face opened it to speak:
Let us continue.

John Berryman, 1964

:::::

The Assassination of John F. Kennedy

> *... this Good, this Decent, this Kindly man ...*
> —SENATOR MANSFIELD

I hear things crying in the world.
A nightmare congress of obscure
Delirium uttering overbreath
The tilt and jangle of this death.

Who had a sense of world and man,
Who had an apt and antic grace
Lies lenient, lapsed and large beneath
The tilt and jangle of this death.

The world goes on with what it has.
Its reasoned, right and only code.
Coaxing, with military faith,
The tilt and jangle of this death.

Gwendolyn Brooks, 1964

On Not Writing an Elegy

My friend told me about kids in a coffee house
who laughed and celebrated the killing. Another friend
didn't care, sick at his own divorce,
drinking martinis with a delicate hand,
saying he couldn't care when I said I cried
like everybody. Still, I am the vain one,
a bullet in my shoulder, six seconds to go
before another burns in my head. Trying
to write about the thing, I always end
by feeling I have been shot. My brain, my spine
gone, and with time winding foolishly,
I am raced, tabled, cleaned out, boxed, flown,
Carried and lowered in. I have had this done
On a shiny day with my wife and bodyguards
and everyone there to cry out, and I have cried
without trying and without a clear thought.
This death has had me where I cannot write
or hate or love, numb as a coined face
fallen where all flames have only to burn
down. Lost where I must only lose my place,
I mourn the glories of our blood and state.

Richard Frost, 1964

:::::

At the Brooklyn Docks

November 23, 1963

In the morning air, the freighter *Havskar,*
From Oslo, lies drawn up at her Brooklyn pier.
The light breaks on her masts and ropes, and shows
Their endless tents and triangles that crowd

In the white air, and rise and ride each other.
A man waves, and a boom descends; a shout,
And a crate is hoisted up from dock to decks.
It swings and lands, and the men on board take it away.
Near me, above the ships, the workmen spread
Tar on the roofs, black in the early sun.
The smell of sea water and tar is thick;
It stings in the nostrils, and, like coffee, wakes me.

Wakes me to what I see and what I know.
Where the light strikes, there is the thrust of sadness,
Up the white spars and ropes, the shapes of day,
Along the decks, and on the *Havskar*'s flag,
At half-mast, like her neighbor's and my own.
Is work as old as grief? Watching, I feel
The slow and wounded groping of my senses
Toward my old life. Here, in my neighborhood,
Under the flags lost among ropes, the men
Cry out, crates swing in the silence after,
Under the watchful eyes the burden lands.
All down the shore, the day changes and moves.

Dorothy Gilbert, 1964

:::::

Verba in Memoriam

How to speak of it
when words today go
rapidly downhill to hide
under the grasses,

To let the stanza
on its miraculous wheels

convey
what was man
and existed as the warm road
we still ride
and run after.

Deciding, after all, it is the land
that goes on expanding,
contracting, a place
that is green
or sandy, that is marsh
or mountain
very like words.

I am going to use
these words
they were always usable
and useful to this man.

He would not object
to phrases
hiding themselves
under the grasses

He has found them there.

The earth is now
more constant
to him
than are we who need
the upper air.

What he had planned
had something of the classic in it
i.e. to say he thought in marble

We understood
Despite those turns

of elegiac
that he wished

Where he lived
Where he *once* lived
to be consecrated
to *Demos*

Despite his welcome
to princes
his reading of their scrolls.

This was youthful
and proper
for one who desired
an heroic name

To be inscribed
on his tomb
and so it was.

But the inscription
must include
our names
Who lived in his time.

Who now can be said
to be a lonely
generation

As if one more
of our artists
had died

And there were only
a few
who remained

Admiring the columns
the temple still standing
the grasses
fresh as a cupful
of light

The way
a new word strikes
the tender skin.

Barbara Guest, 1964

:::::

Until Death Do Us Part

To think of them
from afar
to think of the distance, that air
its broken voices
                thousands of miles, the sea
                and the rivers, returning
                the sun also rising
                                        but then

it was less: the distance
two hundred yards! They were moving
into the sights, they were moving

                into the eye, wide open,
                opened in the earth
                his earth, to let him in

the suddenly opened eye
the windscreen meshed
into a honeycomb of light—

To think of them
as close: as he was

his head in her lap, her arm
across his chest
as they were floating, floating

wherever it was
we were going, we cannot stay
on the road

yet must drive on
and out of their sight who try
who tried to think of us, as we entered
the dark city

to be encased in a light
of diamonds and death,
dead center of stillness

where there is
no fear
out of their sights
each into his
her night, now shared
forever.

Anselm Hollo, 1964

:::::

A Night Picture of Pownal

For JFK

Thanks to the moon,
Branches of our trees are coral

Fans, cast on the lanky snow
Which, crusted though,

Takes impressions
As Matthew Brady's eye received
The desperation of Civil War;
He was its retina

And watched history
Rise and set. Above its kilt
Of steel-blue air the moon turns,
A circle leans

To stare down fissures
Of space to that black forest set
Like matchsticks on the white hillside;
All sound has died.

Our apple tree
Prints its own photograph, its strong
Branches espaliered on the snow
Fading, will not go

From our minds, the clean
Etching of dark on white, each detail
Tuned to the whole; in its precision
Enduring as bone.

What we have seen
Has become history; tragedy
Marks its design upon the brain—
We are stained by its stain.

Barbara Howes, 1964

Before the Sabbath

The man is gone on a Friday.
Good father of silence,
give us peace of the Sabbath
with promises you grow in your blood.
Gone on a Friday before the Sabbath
of rest, his blood on stretchers
and on surgical instruments,
nowhere growing a promise,
the instruments cold, the forehead mute.
Good father of emptiness,
you keep saying over and over
in the birth of children
that we are not born to die,
but the mind is dulled,
for the man is gone on a Friday
before the Sabbath of the world remade.
Smiling, he is dead,
too quickly to explain.

By a hand in defiance
the fine, warm sun has been extinguished,
by one of us, talking of anger
and frustration. In the sudden darkness
the structures going up stand agape.
In unfinished corners we huddle,
growing cold.

David Ignatow, 1964

Jacqueline

And when she strides
soul uplifted
with unbrazen eyes,
his coffin cannot contain him,
her footsteps deliver him
in rhythms of dignity
down the avenues of our pulsedrums
that, mourning, we receive,
and, accepting his death, we
take unto us the living
flesh of his meanings.

Will Inman, 1964

:::::

Down in Dallas

Down in Dallas, down in Dallas
Where the shadow of blood lies black
Lee Oswald nailed Jack Kennedy up
With the nail of a rifle crack.

The big bright Cadillacs stomped on their brakes
And the man in the street fell still
When the slithering gun like a tooth of sin
Coiled back from the window sill.

In a white chrome room on a table top,
Oh, they tried all a scalpel knows
But they couldn't spell stop to that drop-by-drop
Till it bloomed to a rigid rose.

Down on the altar, down on the altar
Christ blossoms in bread and wine
But each asphalt stone where the blood dropped down
Is burst to a cactus spine.

Oh down in Dallas, down in Dallas
Where a desert wind walks by night
Lee Oswald nailed Jack Kennedy up
On the cross of a rifle sight.

X. J. Kennedy, 1964

:::::

In Arlington Cemetery

In the city of memorials,
among tombstones and small
headstones, I look through the cold
not for a monument
but for a grave with ferns
and evergreens lent
from the season past. A flame burns
in the air, not a leaf
to shelter it, blown like our grief,
variable and new, endless and old.

Uphill, over open ground,
on the wind's edge are coming
echoes of drummers drumming
on tight-stretched skin,
tattooing the stillness
to the funeral sound
of hoofs at the hobble,
unharnessed, held in

to the ritual pace;
and of wheels on the cobble.

The carriage circles a green park
with its temple, the dark
porch where the Form in his chair
sheds a marble tear
for what is fated like him:
statues for whom
there are robes of stone.
Love waves in her car
while Hate takes aim
Through a lens from far-
off, and History bleeds, an old charade,
and Madmen fly
the line of parade
down empty walks, and from the shocked
state the Actor's shout
is driven out.
Still, in those marble eyes
deepgrained as memory,
the barns are burning, the streets are blocked,
while motorcade and obsequies

through iron gates
to somber guns and horn's last notes
continually come.
For this to end, for the drum
to be stilled at last,
more than this green bough
will be cut and cast.

The flame leaps up. Fresh as our vow,
it makes a gentle monument at night
with the simplicity of light.

Stanley Koehler, 1964

Four Days in November

In late autumn sun
This coldness without season.
Strangers asking how.

A long rain today,
Cold against the face, has quenched
Final disbelief.

No movement of hours
Disturbs this room or betrays
The sly leap of pain.

Once restless as wind,
His quickness borne in slow march.
Nothing in its time.

Marjorie Mir, 1964

:::::

Sonnet for John-John

My father died in nineteen thirty-four,
When I was ten. It too was sudden; while
He turned in bed, a blood clot touched his heart.
Not bullets, but an old wound of the world
Unhealed, surprised him dead. And relatives
Ate heavy meals, and cried, and ate and cried
Again. Remembering but token love—
And most, hot temper, heavy beatings—I
Was quiet, and enjoyed my cousins. I
Must tell you this, somehow, because of wounds
That never heal. Our fathers die and die

Again in aching graves of withheld words
They did not say. While we re-live the pain
Of severance from the sons we might have been.

Marvin Solomon, 1964

:::::

Not That Hurried Grief, for John F. Kennedy

1

You were only a grainy face in the newspapers
A briefly passionate figure of speech
During breakfast   The voice of the radio at the end
Of my hand, your reputation

Didn't gleam as much as the fork in my hand
Such memorial! Your life was nothing
To me your death though an inscrutable mark on the lintel,
The same world I live in

I think of the popular word "transitory"
Your funeral, watching it on tv
I think the cathode overburdened, the gray lines strained
Your funeral lost in air

Our world so badly fitted for permanence
Or sorrow, your widow lost in air
Your name lonely on highways and airports   At least
You did not die to be a battleship

2

What kind of poverty becomes me, a callous wretch
I think of the popular word "transitory"
And I am saddened for you   Oh, we stinge on ourselves
I think of the word "callous"

And I know it's antique   I watched your funeral, your
          Widow moving
Like a Gloucester woman across the small screen
The jet planes our gesture of reverence,
And I was strangely moved, a genuinely new emotion, not
That hurried grief
                    flags drooping in the dark
As I walked along East 70th street
The night you died prim doormen bland and perfectly usual
Such memorial! Your death an oblique fact
You do not come to mind on the street
The airport has only a dim recollection, the times you
          landed there
And we are not ashamed
The airport your memorial has no eyes, no mouth
My mouth fallow as grief is plains in the western movie
          the night you died
What is this "I am going to the movies"
Barbara crying that afternoon and you flying back to Washington
Now we are sitting alone in our strange world, our
          curiosities assuaged
By scientific films of growing flowers in the southwest
Forgive the distance that couldn't fit me to appropriate weeds
The weeds on your grave, my replacement

Lorenzo Thomas, 1964

:::::

November 22, 1963

Weeping, I write this. You are dead. The dark
animal of the heart, the beast that bides
stilly in its web of flesh, has stolen
flight again out of the air. What is there
to say? That I wish we were gods? That the

mind of man were equal to its lust? It
is not—not yet. You were a man, but more:
you were an idea dreamt in a sweet
hour while the spider slept. We make our
web: its habitant makes greatness of its
prey. We are ourselves victim and victor.
You were and are ourselves. In killing you
We murder an emblem of what we strive
to be: not men, but Man. In mourning you,
good Man, we grieve for what we are, not what
we may become.
Sleep, my heart. We will try
Once more. Sleep, sleep, John. We will try again.

Lewis Turco, 1964

:::::

The Gulf

[for Jack and Barbara Harrison]

I

The airport coffee tastes less of America.
Sour, unshaven, dreading the exertion of
tightening, racked nerves fuelled with liquor,

some smoky, resinous bourbon,
the body, buckling at its casket hole,
a roar like last night's blast racing its engines,

watches the fumes of the exhausted soul
as the trans-Texas jet, screeching, begins
its flight and friends diminish. So, to be aware

of the divine union the soul detaches
itself from created things. "We're in the air,"
the Texan near me grins. All things: these matches

from LBJ's campaign hotel, this rose
given me at dawn in Austin by a child,
this book of fables by Borges, its prose

a stalking, moonlit tiger. What was willed
on innocent, sun-streaked Dallas, the beast's claw
curled round that hairspring rifle is revealed

on every page as lunacy or feral law;
circling that wound we leave Love Field.
Fondled, these objects conjure hotels,

quarrels, new friendships, brown limbs
nakedly moulded as these autumn hills
memory penetrates as the jet climbs

the new clouds over Texas; their home means
an island suburb, forest, mountain water;
they are the simple properties for scenes

whose joy exhausts like grief, scenes where we learn,
exchanging the least gifts, this rose, this napkin,
that those we love are objects we return,

that this lens on the desert's wrinkled skin
has priced our flesh, all that we love in pawn
to that brass ball, that the gifts, multiplying,

clutter and choke the heart, and that I shall
watch love reclaim its things as I lie dying.
My very flesh and blood! Each seems a petal

shrivelling from its core. I watch them burn,
by the nerves' flare I catch their skeletal
candour! Best never to be born,

the great dead cry. Their works shine on our shelves,
by twilight tour their gilded gravestone spines,
and read until the lamplit page revolves

to a white stasis whose detachment shines
like a propeller's rainbowed radiance.
Circling like us; no comfort for their loves!

II

The cold glass darkens. Elizabeth wrote once
that we make glass the image of our pain;
I watch clouds boil past the cold, sweating pane

above the Gulf. All styles yearn to be plain
as life. The face of the loved object under the glass
is plainer still. Yet, somehow, at this height,

above this cauldron boiling with its wars,
our old earth, breaking to familiar light,
that cloud-bound mummy with self-healing scars

peeled of her cerements again looks new;
some cratered valley heals itself with sage,
through that grey, fading massacre a blue

lighthearted creek flutes of some siege
to the amnesia of drumming water.
Their cause is crystalline: the divine union

of these detached, divided states, whose slaughter
darkens each summer now, as one by one,
the smoke of bursting ghettos clouds the glass

down every coast where filling station signs
proclaim the Gulf, an air, heavy with gas,
sickens the state, from Newark to New Orleans.

III

Yet the South felt like home. Wrought balconies,
the sluggish river with its tidal drawl,
the tropic air charged with the extremities

of patience, a heat heavy with oil,
canebrakes, that legendary jazz. But fear
thickened my voice, that strange, familiar soil

prickled and barbed the texture of my hair,
my status as a secondary soul.
The Gulf, your gulf, is daily widening,

each blood-red rose warns of that coming night
when there's no rock cleft to go hidin' in
and all the rocks catch fire, when that black might,

their stalking, moonless panthers turn from Him
whose voice they can no more believe, when the black X's
mark their Passover with slain seraphim.

IV

The Gulf shines, dull as lead. The coast of Texas
Glints like a metal rim. I have no home
as long as summer bubbling to its head
boils for that day when in the Lord God's name
the coals of fire are heaped upon the head
of all whose gospel is the whip and flame,

age after age, the uninstructing dead.

Derek Walcott, 1968

7

"Deep in the Mississippi thicket / I hear the mourning dove"

THE SEARCH FOR JAMES CHANEY, ANDY GOODMAN, AND MICHAEL SCHWERNER, 1964

After a tumultuous 1963 that included the assassination of Medgar Evers, the death of four girls in the Sixteenth Street Baptist Church, and the assassination of President John F. Kennedy, several civil rights organizations launched Freedom Summer, formerly known as the Mississippi Summer Project in 1964. Under the Council of Federated Organizations (COFO) CORE, SNCC, SCLC, and the NAACP united to assist blacks in Mississippi who had been systematically locked out of the electoral process. Part of COFO's strategy consisted of recruiting young whites, especially white college students, to take part in Freedom Summer alongside young black workers. Not only would those students provide valuable assistance, but they would also, because of their race, generate increased media attention and federal protection. According to Dave Dennis, who helped organize Freedom Summer with Bob Moses, "The Idea was not only to begin to organize for the Democratic Convention, but also to get the country to begin to respond. . . . They were not gonna respond to a thousand blacks working in that area. They would respond to a thousand young white college students" (Raines 273).

Andrew Goodman and Michael "Mickey" Schwerner were two of the young whites who volunteered to help bring change to Mississippi. Goodman, twenty, was a student at Queens College in New York City; Schwerner, twenty-four and already a member of CORE, was a social worker from New York. The two men, along with James Chaney, a twenty-two-year-old African American activist from Meridian, Mississippi, were investigating the bombing of Mount Zion Methodist Church in Neshoba County on the evening of 21 June 1964 when Deputy Sheriff Cecil Ray Price pulled them over, ostensibly for a traffic violation. Price arrested, jailed, and later released the three men. Shortly after their discharge, and as they were driving back to Meridian, Price pulled them over again. This time, however, he was not alone. In tow were two carloads of Klansmen who ordered Chaney, Goodman, and Schwerner out of the blue station wagon they had borrowed from Dave Dennis and CORE. As Sara Bullard recalls in *Free at Last*, "One by one, the three young men were taken out of the car and shot at point-blank range. Their bodies were deposited at a nearby farm where an earthen dam was under construction. The bulldozer operator who had been hired by the Klan scooped out a hole for the bodies, and built the dam above them" (70–71). Although a massive federal search was initiated almost immediately, the three victims remained buried beneath the dam for forty-four days. A team of FBI agents eventually located the bodies on 4 August after receiving a tip from an anonymous informant. The discovery led the poet Armand Schwerner, Michael's cousin, to write, "Mickey I think of you, I think of you / . . . in the loam of a dam between Philadelphia and Meridian" (lines 60, 63). After autopsies were conducted, it was determined that Chaney had been shot in the back, abdomen, and head, Goodman in the right chest, and Schwerner in the left lung (Morris 172).

Three years later, in October 1967, Deputy Sheriff Price and six other Klansmen were convicted, not for murder but for violating the victims' civil rights. Six others were acquitted or freed due to a hung jury. While the convictions of the seven defendants were historic — they marked the first time in Mississippi history that a jury found Klansmen guilty of contributing to the death of an African American or a civil rights activist—the sentences were light given the nature of the crime, ranging from three to ten years (Bullard 72). In an attempt to justify the lenient sentences the presiding federal judge, William Harold Cox, explained, "They killed one nigger, one Jew, and a white man. I gave them all what I thought they deserved" (Cagin and Dray 452). Not until 2005 would one of the men who contributed to the deaths of the civil rights workers be charged with murder. Edgar Ray "Preacher" Killen, now eighty, was charged with three counts of murder in January 2005 for planning the murders and giving orders to the Klansmen who carried out the crime. Killen, a Baptist minister, was convicted and sentenced to sixty years in prison on three counts of manslaughter on 21 June, exactly forty-one years after Chaney, Goodman, and Schwerner were shot and killed.

The last lines of Raymond Patterson's "Schwerner, Chaney, Goodman" seem to sum up the sentiments of the poems in this section as a whole: "Three lives / In deathless constellation." Not surprisingly the poems also make note of the ever-present sense of danger experienced by civil rights workers. For instance, the all-pervading presence of opposition to social transformation informs Marjorie Mir's "Mississippi, 1964." "Local faces serve their warning," Mir states, later adding, "The muffled breath of danger / cannot be hushed away" (4, 7–8).

In "When Black People Are" A. B. Spellman reveals to readers a psyche traumatized by the prevalence of racial violence, a psyche that often in solitude entertains visions of whites and blacks attacking and killing each other. The poem is a testament to the frequency and intensity of potentially debilitating visions. But these early declarations of violence and paranoia are trumped later in the poem by images of a white army "mass producing beautiful / black corpses & stealing them away" (22–23).

Margaret Walker's "For Andy Goodman, Michael Schwerner, and James Chaney" is dominated by references to the trinity and nature, and for the most part the poem is solemnly elegiac. However, midway through, Walker asks a succession of questions that not only alters the tone of the poem but also acknowledges the sacrifices of the three civil rights workers. The poem eventually calls for others to join the martyrs, either spiritually or physically.

Gregory Orr commences "The Demonstration" with the following lines: "They bob above us all afternoon— / three giant charcoal portraits / of Goodman, Schwerner and Chaney" (1–3). Set at the Democratic National Convention of August 1964, Orr's poem is an autobiographical account of his first civil rights demonstration. Orr joined CORE as a white seventeen-year-old because he believed the movement belonged to a "world of meaning" (*The Blessing* 149–50). He marched at the Convention to support the Mississippi Freedom Democratic Party's attempt to unseat the traditional delegation that excluded black participation. "One man. One vote," he and the other protesters chanted outside "on the dilapidated boardwalk" of Atlantic City (*The Caged Owl* 23, 25). By poem's end the specter of Chaney, Goodman, and Schwerner remains, reminding the demonstrators of the type of violence often visited upon activists, and of the need "to protect themselves from demons" or "the crowd's hostility" (lines 28, 20).

:::::

A Commemorative Ode

For the 60th Anniversary of the Beecher Memorial United Church
of Christ in New Orleans, Louisiana, October 25, 1964

Old church with the same name as my own
you and I were born the same year
It has taken two generations to bring us together
Now here we are in New Orleans
meeting for the first time
I hope I can say the right thing
what the man you are named for
might have said on one of his better days
He was my great-great-uncle
but come to think of it
he was instrumental in my founding too
Rolled in a tube at home I have a certificate
signed by Henry Ward Beecher
after he had united my grandfather and grandmother
in the holy bonds of matrimony

at Plymouth Church in Brooklyn
The year was 1858
and James Buchanan was President
The South was riding high
Making the North catch and send back its escaped Negroes
and it looked to most people
as if slavery were going to last forever
but not to Henry Ward Beecher
which I suppose is why you named your church for him
He certainly helped to change all that
together with his brother Edward and his sister
whose name was Harriet
and Mr. Lincoln and General Ulysses S. Grant
and a large number of young men
who wound up under the long rows of crosses
at Gettysburg Chickamauga Cold Harbor and such places

Nineteen hundred and four was a better year
than 1858
and the building of this church was a sign of it
It was no longer a crime to meet and worship by yourselves
with your own preacher
your own beautiful songs
with no grim-lipped regulators to stand guard over you
nobody breaking up your services with a bull-whip
Yes this was some better
Booker T. Washington was in his hey-day
the apostle of segregation
"We can be in all things social as separate as the fingers"
he said and Mr. Henry Grady the Atlanta editor
applauded him to the echo
as did all the other good white folks around
and they said
"This boy Booker has a head on his shoulders
even if it is a nappy one"
Dr. Washington was 48 years old at the time
but you know how southern whites talk

a man is a boy all his life if he's black
Dr. Washington was a pragmatist
and settled for what he could get
When they announced that dinner was served in the dining car
he ate his cindery biscuits out of a paper bag
and when George the porter made up berths in the Pullman
he sat up all night in the Jim Crow coach
Because of his eminently practical attitude
Dr. Washington was successful in shaking down
the big white philanthropists
like C. P. Huntington the railroad shark
or was it octopus
and Negro education was on its way

Old church
since 1904 you and I have seen some changes
slow at first
now picking up speed
I have just come from Mississippi
where I saw churches like this one
burned to the ground
or smashed flat with bombs
almost like Germany when I was there in 1945
only these Negroes were not beaten people
they sang in the ashes and wreckage
such songs as *We Shall Overcome*
and *Let My Little Light Shine*
O Freedom! They sang
Before I'll be a slave
I'll be buried in my grave
and go home to my Lord and be free
They sang *I'm going to sit at the welcome table*
I'm going to live in the Governor's mansion
One of these days
I heard three mothers speak
who had made the President listen
and "almost cry, or he made like he was about to cry"

when they told him
how their homes had been dynamited
"It's not hard to be brave"
one of these mothers said
"but it's awful hard to be scared"
I expect to see her statue on a column in the square
in place of the Confederate soldier's
one of these days

Remember
slavery looked pretty prominent in 1858
when it had just five years to go
and now in 1964
the White Citizen's Councils and the Ku Klux Klan
think they can keep their kind of half-slave South forever
Their South isn't on the way out
It's already dead and gone
only they don't know it
They buried it themselves
in that earthwork dam near Philadelphia Mississippi
when they thought they were getting rid of the bodies

John Beecher, 1964

:::::

Mississippi, 1964

In memory of Michael Schwerner,
James Chaney, and Andrew Goodman

Do young men ever truly doubt
morning is sure to come?

Like the walls of old towns,
local faces serve their warning,
stone supporting stone.

Night fears of shadowed corners,
the muffled breath of danger
cannot be hushed away.
We wake to find them true.

Small among the mourners,
Ben, the little brother,
lifts his face to the music,
weeps and sings.

Marjorie Mir, 1964

:::::

The Book of Job and a Draft of a Poem to Praise the Paths of the Living

in memory of Mickey Schwerner

image   the images   the great games therefore the locked

the half-lit jailwinds

in the veins the lynch gangs

simulate blows   bruise   the bones
breaking   age

of the world's deeds this is the young age   age

of the sea's surf   image   image

of the world its least rags
stream among the planets   Our
lady of poverty the lever the fulcrum
the cam and the ant
hath her anger and the emmet
his choler the exposed

belly of the land
under the sky
at night and the windy pines unleash
the morning's force what is the form
to say it there is something
to name Goodman   Schwerner   Chaney
who were beaten not we
who were beaten   children
not our
children   ancestral
children rose in the dark
to their work there grows
there builds there is written
a vividness   there is   rawness
like a new sun the flames
tremendous the sun
itself ourselves ourselves
go with us *disorder*

so great the tumult wave

upon wave this traverse

this desert   extravagant
island of light

*

the long road
going north

on the cliffs   small
and numerous

the windows

look out on the sea's simulacra
of self-evidence   meaning's

instant   wild-
eyed as the cherry
tree blossoms

in that fanatic glass from our own
homes our own
rooms we are fetched out   we

the greasers
says yesterday's

slang in the path of tornado the words

piled on each other   lean
on each other dance

with the dancing

valve stems   machine glint
in the commonplace the last words

survivors, will be tame
will stand near our feet
what shall we say   they have lived their lives
they have gone feathery
and askew
in the wind from the beginning   carpenter
mechanic   o we
impoverished we hired
hands that turn the wheel   young
theologians of the scantlings   wracked
monotheists of the   weather-side sometimes I imagine
they speak

*

luxury, all
said Bill, the fancy things   always

second hand but in extreme
minutes guilt

at the heart
of the unthinkable hunger   fear   enemy

world   briefly shame

of loneliness all that has touched
the man

touches him
again arms and dis-

arms him meaning
in the instant

tho we forget

the light

*

precision of place the rock's place in the fog we suffer
          loneliness painlessly not without fear the common breath
                    here at extremity

obsolescent as the breathing
of tribespeople   fingers cold

early in the year cold and windy on the sea the wind
          still blows thru my head in the farmhouse

weather of the camera's click
lonely as the shutter closing
over the glass lens weathered mountains
of the hurrying sea the boat in these squalls sails
          like a sparrow a wind blown
sparrow on the sea some kite string

taut in the wind green
and heavy the masses of the sea weeds move
and move in rock shelters share marvelous games

*

inshore,   the rough grasses
rooted on the dry hills or to stand still

like the bell buoy   telling

tragedy so wide
spread so

shabby a north sea salt
tragedy 'seeking a statement

of an experience of our own' the bones of my hands

bony   bony   lose me the wind cries   find
yourself   I?

this?   the road
and the traveling   always

undiscovered
country forever

savage *the river*
was a rain and flew
with the herons   the sea
flies in the squall

*

        backward
over the shoulder
now the wave
of the improbable
drains from the beaches the heart of the hollow
tree singing bird note bird rustle we live now
in dreams all
wished to tell him we are locked
in ourselves   That is not
what they dreamed

in any dream they dreamed the weird morning
of the bird waking mid continent

mid continent iron rails
in the fields and grotesque
metals in the farmer's heartlands a sympathy
across the fields
and down the aisles
of the crack trains
of 1918 the wave
of the improbable
drenches the galloping carpets in the sharp
edges in the highlights
of the varnished tables we ring
in the continual bell
the undoubtable bell found music in itself
of itself speaks the word
actual heart breaking
tone row it is not ended
not ended the intervals
blurred ring
like walls
between floor
and ceiling the taste
of madness in the world birds
of ice Pave
the world o pave
the world carve

thereon . . .

George Oppen, 1973

The Demonstration

Democratic National Convention
Atlantic City, New Jersey, 1964

They bob above us all afternoon—
three giant charcoal portraits
of Goodman, Schwerner and Chaney.
civil rights martyrs whose tortured
bodies have just been found
in the red clay wall
of a dam in rural Mississippi.

Staring up at their flat, larger-
than-life faces, I envy the way
they gaze at the gray ocean
and the gray buildings
with the calm indifference
of those whose agonies are over.
Myself, I'm a frightened teenager
at my first demonstration.
carrying a placard that demands
the seating of a mixed delegation
from a Southern state.

No one
prepared me for the crowd's hostility.
the names we're called.

Still, we chant the slogan reason
proposed: "One man, one vote."
And still it holds—the small shape
we make on the dilapidated boardwalk—
reminding me now of the magic circles
medieval conjurers drew
to protect themselves from demons
their spells had summoned up.

Gregory Orr, 1964

Schwerner, Chaney, Goodman

Behind you, now,
Your final pain,
Your dreams,
The search in darks
Toward friendless hands,
The violent men you could have saved,
Your loved and fumbling nation.

Before us, now,
Your deeds to do again.
The darkness around this world engraved:
Three lives
In deathless constellation.

Raymond Patterson, 1969

:::::

Speech for LeRoi

In memory of my cousin Mickey Schwerner
(written for and read at a benefit for LeRoi Jones' defense fund, in 1967)

common cause
common cause
come come come come
remission of sins is not in question
Jefferson is not in question
fear is in question 10:30 is in question hunger is in question
come to the anxiety fair
common sauce reasons of soup and meat terrible
anger and the noose of news
like wolf's jaw
              tightening

friends laugh
in metal
in ropes
in distrust
to make common cause
with the time nothing is
enough or quite right, all activity forgets
ends in the exercise of being, absolutes
leap into usefulness to comfort the grave-
diggers.
The coolest is the most obsessed the ownership of souls
newly patented every month.
                                        We live,
think of it, establishing
nourishment from solid
anger,
          that is left,
like the wolf toward mirages
                                        and we stand
a little too straight.
                              Yes I live
in a dark time, belief in the poem
requires a major transplant every morning, I imagine
on my cheek, on my cornea, behind
my knee connective tissue hardening
in death, simple local answers
to the pressures in the body of the world,
                                                            come
belief, passion
                    come, come
sweet poem, or sour, or
broken is best;
                    to come sweetly
is evidence of the body letting up
on itself, falling into images.
                                        But I know of men in an art

in an endless whip of fury, their angry certainty.
Whoever possessed by Justice selects Holy and Holier
and cries Artifact at flesh
forgets nothingness
and walks at the funeral of the whole human race.
If you took the road
through my cranial suture, through the dura matter,
what an allegorical fool you would find,
fat and weary
from too much time passing too fast, the right arm
paralyzed, and left holding up the pennant holding
the pennant of poetry.

Mickey I think of you, I think of you
into my body,
jelly tissue beginnings soft parts
in the loam of a dam between Philadelphia and Meridian
I think about reasons for getting up this morning
and the commonness of tissue
and the violence of gravediggers and the violence
of my wish for an end

Armand Schwerner, 1967

:::::

When Black People Are

when black people are
with each other
we sometime fear ourselves
whisper over our shoulders
about unmentionable acts
& sometimes we fight & lie
These are some things we sometimes do

& when alone I sometimes walk
from wall to wall fighting visions
of white men fighting me
& black men fighting white men
& fighting me & i lose my
self between walls &
ricocheting shots & can't say
for certain who I have killed
or been killed by

it is the fear of winter passing
& summer coming & the killing
i have called for coming
to my door saying
hit it a. b., you're in it too

& the white army moves like thieves
in the night mass producing beautiful
black corpses & then stealing them away
while my frequent death watches me
from orangeburg on cronkite &
i'm oiling my gun & cooking my food
& saying "when the time comes"
to myself, over & over, hopefully

but i remember driving from Atlanta
to Birmingham with stone & Featherstone
& cleve & feather talked
about dueling a pair of klansmen
& cleve told how they hunted chaney's
schwerner's & goodman's bodies
in the haunted hours of the silver nights
in the mississippi swamp while a runaway survivor
from orangeburg slept between wars
on the back seat

times like this
are times when black people

are with each other & the strength flows
back & forth between us like
borrowed breath

A. B. Spellman, 1968

:::::

For Andy Goodman, Michael Schwerner, and James Chaney

Three Civil Rights workers murdered in Mississippi on June 21, 1964
Poem written after seeing the movie, Andy in A.M.

Three faces . . .
    Mirrored in the muddy stream of living . . .
young and tender like
quiet beauty of still water,
    sensitive as the mimosa leaf,
    intense as the stalking cougar
    and impassive as the face of rivers;
The sensitive face of Andy
The intense face of Michael
The impassive face of Chaney.

Three leaves . . .
    Floating in the melted snow
    Flooding the Spring
    oak leaves
    one by one
    moving like a barge
    across the seasons
    moving like a breeze across the windowpane
    winter . . . summer . . . spring
When is the evil year of the cricket?
When comes the violent day of the stone?
In which month
do the dead ones appear at the cistern?

Three lives . . .
    Turning on the axis of our time
    Black and white together
    turning on the wheeling compass
    of a decade and a day
    The concerns of a century of time
. . . an hourglass of destiny

Three lives . . .
    ripe for immortality of daisies and wheat
    for the simple beauty of a hummingbird
    and dignity of a sequoia
    of renunciation and
    resurrection
For the Easter morning of our Meridians.

Why should another die for me?
Why should there be a calvary
A subterranean hell for three?
In the miry clay?
In the muddy stream?
In the red misery?
In mutilating hatred and in fear?
The brutish and the brazen
without brain
without blessing
without beauty . . .
They have killed these three.
They have killed them for me.

Sunrise and sunset . . .
Spring rain and winter windowpane . . .
I see the first leaves budding
The green Spring returning
I mark the falling
of golden Autumn leaves

and three lives floating down the quiet stream
Till they come to the surging falls. . . .

The burned blossoms of the dogwood tree
tremble in the Mississippi morning
The wild call of the cardinal bird
troubles the Mississippi morning
I hear the morning singing
larks, robins, and the mockingbird
while the mourning dove
broods over the meadow
Summer leaf falls never turning brown

Deep in the Mississippi thicket
I hear the mourning dove
Bird of death singing in the swamp
Leaves of death floating in their watery grave

Three faces turn their ears and eyes
sensitive
intense
impassive
to see the solemn sky of summer
to hear the brooding cry
of the mourning dove

Mississippi bird of sorrow
O mourning bird of death
Sing their sorrow
Mourn their pain
And teach us death,
To love and live with them again!

Margaret Walker, 1970

8

“We are not beasts and do not / intend to be beaten”

RIOTS, REBELLIONS, AND UPRISINGS, 1964–1971

In many areas of the country during the civil rights era, police were viewed as neighborhood overseers with a mandate to protect whites and their property by mistreating blacks. The volatile combination of segregation, economic injustice, police transgressions, and chronic inhumane treatment forced repressed anger and resentment to the surface. Some of the more well-known rebellions of the period and the frustration and unrest that fueled them were documented in verse, including those in Harlem (1964), Watts (1965), and Newark and Detroit (1967). Poems were also written in response to the Orangeburg Massacre of 1968 and the prisoner revolt at the Attica Correctional Facility in New York in 1971.

On 16 July 1964 (less than a month after the disappearance of Chaney, Goodman, and Schwerner in Mississippi), James Powell, a black fifteen-year-old, was fatally shot by Thomas

Gilligan, a white off-duty New York City police lieutenant. Two nights later violence erupted in Harlem and hundreds of people took to the streets, transforming the neighborhood into a chaotic scene for three days. The uprising later spread to the Bedford-Stuyvesant section of Brooklyn and lasted two days, 24–25 July.

The Watts riots of the following summer were ignited on 11 August 1965 after a police officer stopped twenty-one-year-old Marquette Frye and his twenty-two-year-old brother Ronald for suspicion of drunk driving. Additional officers arrived on the scene of the Los Angeles neighborhood, as did the brothers' mother, Rena Frye. An altercation between the officers and the Fryes ensued, and the family was arrested. Frustrations spiraled that evening between officers and angry bystanders and did not dissipate until six days later. By that time no fewer than sixteen thousand law enforcement officers had been called to the scene, including the National Guard. The riot in Watts became the most extreme display of urban racial unrest in American history.

The Newark riots started on 12 July after John Smith, a black taxi driver, was physically abused while in custody for an alleged traffic violation. When news of Smith's treatment reached the black community it was accompanied by the false rumor of his death at the hands of police officers. The National Guard was eventually called in, but violence continued from 14 through 17 July. (One of the injured and arrested was the poet Amiri Baraka, who was badly beaten by police officers and taken into custody on weapons charges and for resisting arrest.)

The riots in Detroit only six days later would prove to be more devastating than the destruction in Newark. Caused primarily by a police raid on an after-hours drinking establishment, the 5-day Detroit riots resulted in 43 deaths, 1,189 injuries, more than 7,000 arrests, and approximately $22 million worth of property damage. Three of the 43 victims were found dead from police gunfire inside the Algiers Motel on the night of 26 July 1967 (see Michael S. Harper's "A Mother Speaks: The Algiers Motel Incident, Detroit").

In 1968 students at South Carolina State College, along with others, attempted to desegregate the All Star Bowling Lanes in Orangeburg. The students' efforts were met with resistance, eventually leading to three tense evenings in the city. On the fourth night, 8 February, students and community members demonstrated near campus while officers patrolled the area. South Carolina highway patrolmen eventually opened fire on the demonstrators, killing two SCSC students and one high school student. Twenty-seven others were wounded.

Cultural differences and long-standing claims of inhumane treatment eventually led to a rebellion at Attica Correctional Facility in upstate New York. Prisoners at Attica had complained about various aspects of their treatment before the riot, but to no avail. On 9 September 1971 they set fires inside the prison, then captured more than three dozen outnumbered guards and civilians, holding them hostage for four days. Governor Nelson Rockefeller called more than five hundred National Guard to the scene, resulting in at least thirty-five deaths and eighty-three wounded inmates.

Maya Angelou in "Riot: 60's" and Karl Carter in "Heroes" reference the Harlem confrontations as part of a series of similar riots. David Henderson provides a more direct and elaborate account in "Keep On Pushing." The poem's narrator comes across as a sociopolitical journalist with an eye for detail—"Even in a group / the sparse Negro cop walks alone" (lines 45–46)—and as someone familiar with the community.

In the poem "Watts," Ojenke (Alvin Saxon) depicts buildings in flames as "Senile edifices crying like lumberjacks: 'Timber!'" and the neighborhood itself as "Streets of dwellings wrapped in cellophane / of negligence" (5–7). In the second half of the poem, Socrates and Diogenes visit the city. Both quickly become disappointed in the physical, social, and political chaos of the community. In fact Socrates finds nothing to live for, and Diogenes, in a display of hopeless frustration, casts his storied lantern of honesty to the "barren soil" (34). "Watts" paints an unmistakable portrait of urban unrest and neglect.

In a similar vein Charles Bukowski, a famed writer and resident of Los Angeles during the riots, wrote "finish" because he detested the type of violence that transpired in Watts. The poem, one of Bukowski's favorites at the time (Pleasants 148), later became part of his collection, *The Days Run Away Like Wild Horses over the Hills*, published in 1969. Early in the poem Bukowski writes, "Men murder each other in the streets / without reason" (lines 25–26). Not only does the poem condemn police brutality; it censures humankind as well ("we have done this to ourselves, we / deserve this"). Bukowski is suggesting that our failure as humans to be civil and humane to each other has led to this outburst of violence.

The Newark uprising is at the heart of Julius Lester's poem "On the Birth of My Son, Malcolm Coltrane." Lester suggests that the uprising should be viewed as a demand by a neglected and oppressed community for human and civil rights. The Detroit riots inform "A Mother Speaks: The Algiers Motel Incident, Detroit" by Michael S. Harper. Harper's poem is in many ways a poetic distillation of John Hersey's investigation, *The Algiers Motel Incident*, which was originally published in 1968.

The title of Denise Levertov's "The Gulf" serves as a metaphor for what the poem sees as current and future racial divisions in Detroit. The speaker of the poem, presumably white, as is the poet, offers images of two contrasting scenes. The first speaks to leisure, growth, and nurturing; the second depicts a young male looter who finds no satisfaction in the flowers he has stolen or in existence as a whole. Indeed the poem paints him, in the end, as trapped, with no outlet for his frustrations and no hope of attaining the quality of life the speaker enjoys.

Philip Levine's "Coming Home, Detroit, 1968" takes stock of the physical and racial landscapes of Detroit one year after the riots. In fact the two terrains become intertwined during the course of the poem. Levine offers readers imagery of the local blue-collar automobile and alcohol industries by way of a narrative about a presumably white driver who comes face-to-face with a black child at a traffic signal. A year after the riot polarizations remain, suggesting little or no progress, leaving the poem's narrator to conclude, "We burn this city every day" by way of division and neglect (21). This last line, with its imagery of fire and destruction, reminds readers of the poem's first line, "A winter Tuesday, the city pouring fire." Taken together the two lines hold the driver and child in a smoldering crucible, as if to remind both communities of their interconnectedness and the need for increased unity.

Karl Carter in "Heroes" and Charles Lynch in "If We Cannot Live as People" allude to what has since become known as the Orangeburg Massacre. Denise Levertov also mentions the tragedy in "The Day the Audience Walked Out on Me and Why" (see chapter 11). While Carter, Lynch, and Levertov commemorate the deaths in Orangeburg as part of broader commentaries on American culture, A. B. Spellman's poem is written primarily about the tragedy. "In Orangeburg My Brothers Did" focuses on the bonfire the demonstrators created prior to the arrival of the police. The poem suggests sarcastically that the flames conjured the officers and was all the justification they needed to fire on the crowd.

Keith Baird in "Attica—U.S.A.," June Jordan in "Poem against the

State (of Things): 1975," and Charles Lynch in "If We Cannot Live as People" reflect on the spirit and details surrounding the Attica uprising. During the uprising approximately 4,500 rounds of ammunition were fired at prisoners and hostages, resulting in at least 43 deaths.

:::::

Riot: 60's

Our
YOUR FRIEND CHARLIE pawnshop
was a glorious blaze
I heard the flames lick
then eat the trays
of zircons
mounted in red gold alloys

Easter clothes and stolen furs
burned in the attic
radios and teevees
crackled with static
plugged in
only to a racial outlet

Some
thought the FRIENDLY FINANCE FURNITURE CO.
burned higher
When a leopard print sofa with gold leg
(which makes into a bed)
caught fire
an admiring groan from the waiting horde
"Absentee landlord
you got that shit"

Lighting: a hundred Watts
Detroit, Newark and New York

Screeching nerves, exploding minds
lives tied to
a policeman's whistle
a welfare worker's doorbell
finger.

Hospitality, southern-style
corn pone grits and you-all smile
whole blocks novae
brand new stars
policemen caught in their
brand new cars
Chugga chugga chigga
git me one nigga
lootin' n burnin'
he won't git far

Watermelons, summer ripe
grey neck bones and boiling tripe
supermarket roastin' like the
noon-day sun
national guard nervous with his shiny gun
goose the motor quicker
here's my nigga picka
shoot him in the belly
shoot him while he run.

Maya Angelou, 1969

:::::

Attica—U.S.A.

We will not seek to soothe with comfortable words,
No, we'll tell it like it is, will speak
The truth and name the devils.

They are criminals, they who hold our dungeon keys,
And make our misery free enterprise.
(Better to state this bitter existential fact
Than feign the lie, aiming to please the foe, and fooling self.)
By what act of mental shuffle, shuck and jive
Can we accept our plight, and stoop and scrounge and scuffle,
For mere survival? Must we abide this spiteful dooming
  of black destinies? No! this we say:
While Caesar slays our people for his profit
And for our right and proper protest would destroy us,
We come to bury Caesar, not to praise him.

Keith E. Baird, 1971

:::::

finish

the hearse comes through the room filled with
the beheaded, the disappeared, the living
mad.
the flies are a glue of sticky paste
their wings will not
lift.
I watch an old woman beat her cat
with a broom.
the weather is unendurable
a dirty trick by
God.
the water has evaporated from the
toilet bowl
the telephone rings without
sound
the small limp arm petering against the
bell.

I see a boy on his
bicycle
the spokes collapse
the tires turn into
snakes and melt
away.
the newspaper is oven!hot
men murder each other in the streets
without reason.
the worst men have the best jobs
the best men have the worst jobs or are
unemployed or locked in
madhouses.
I have 4 cans of food left.
air-conditioned troops go from house to
house
from room to room
jailing, shooting, bayoneting
the people.
we have done this to ourselves, we
deserve this
we are like roses that have never bothered to
bloom when we should have bloomed and
it is as if
the sun has become disgusted with
waiting
it is as if the sun were a mind that has
given up on us.
I go out on the back porch
and look across the sea of dead plants
now thorns and sticks shivering in a
windless sky.
somehow I'm glad we're through
finished—
the works of Art
the wars
the decayed loves
the way we lived each day.

when the troops come up here
I don't care what they do for
we already killed ourselves
each day we got out of bed.
I go back into the kitchen
spill some hash from a soft
can, it is almost cooked
already
and I sit
eating, looking at my
fingernails.
the sweat comes down behind my
ears and I hear the
shooting in the streets and
I chew and wait
without wonder.

Charles Bukowski, 1969

:::::

Heroes

Sometimes I sit up at night
Listening to myself cry
My sobs for those we lost
In the battle with the beast,
And thoughts flash my mind
Realizing that I am somewhere between battles
Counting those we lost;
        Rap five years in the internal concentration
                camps,
        Cleve five years in the belly of the beast,
        Stokely silenced by the belchings of racism,
        Dan Massey paralyzed by a racist cop's shot
            gun blast in the back in Nashville,

Malcolm by an assassin's bullet
Martin the same
Places come back like shadow figures upon a darkened
stage and bodies lie strewn there
soaking the ground red with their blood;
Orangeburg, Jackson, Memphis,
New York, Nashville,
The funeral pyres of an era breathe forth their stench
And I sit lost myself weeping inwardly
Riding somewhere in my mind with Eldridge Cleaver
Through the streets of Nashville on an April night
During a riot

Karl Carter, 1969

:::::

Revolutionary Letter #3

store water; make a point of filling your bathtub
at the first news of trouble : they turned off the water
in the 4th ward for a whole day during the Newark riots;
or better yet make a habit
of keeping the tub clean and full when not in use
change this once a day, it should be good enough
for washing, flushing toilets when necessary
and cooking, in a pinch, but it's a good idea
to keep some bottled water handy too
get a couple of five gallon jugs and keep them full
for cooking

store food—dry stuff like rice and bean stores best
goes farthest. SALT VERY IMPORTANT : : its health and
energy
healing too, keep a couple pounds
sea salt around, and, because we're spoiled, some tins

tuna, etc. to keep up morale—keep up the sense
of 'balanced diet' 'protein intake' remember
the stores may be closed for quite some time, the trucks
may not enter your section of the city for weeks, you can cool it
indefinitely
with 20lb brown rice
20lb whole wheat flour
10lb cornmeal
10lb good beans—kidney or soy
5lb sea salt
2 qts good oil

dried fruits and nuts
add nutrients and a sense of luxury
to this diet, a squash or coconut
in a cool place in your pad will keep six months

remember we are all used to eating less
than the 'average American' and take it easy
before we
ever notice we're hungry the rest of the fold will be starving
used as they are to meat and fresh milk daily
and help will arrive, until the day no help arrives
and then you're on your own.

hoard matches, we aren't good
at rubbing sticks together any more
a tinder box is useful, if you can work it
don't count on gas stove, gas heater
electric light
keep hibachi and charcoal, CHARCOAL STARTER a help
kerosene lamp and candles, learn to keep warm
with breathing
remember the blessed American habit of bundling

Diane di Prima, 1971

A Mother Speaks: The Algiers Motel Incident, Detroit

It's too dark to see black
in the windows of
Woodward or Virginia Park.

The undertaker pushed his body
back into place with plastic and gum
but it wouldn't hold water.

When I looked for marks or lineament or fine stitching
I was led away without seeing
this plastic face they'd built
that was not my son's.

They tied the eye torn out
by shotgun into place
and his shattered arm cut away
with his buttocks that remained.

My son's gone by white hands
though he said to his last word—
"Oh I'm so sorry, officer,
I broke your gun."

Michael S. Harper, 1970

:::::

Keep On Pushing

(Harlem Riots / Summer / 1964)

The title taken from a recent hit recording (Summer, '64) by the famous rhythm & blues trio, Curtis Mayfield and The Impression.

I

Lenox Avenue is a big street
The sidewalks are extra wide—three and four times

the size of a regular Fifth Avenue or East 34th
Street sidewalk—and must be so to contain the
unemployed vigiling Negro males, the picket lines
and police barricades.
Police Commissioner Murphy can
muster five hundred cops in fifteen minutes.
He can summon extra
tear gas, bombs, guns, ammunition
within a single call
to a certain general alarm.
For Harlem
reinforcements come from the Bronx
just over the three-borough Bridge.
a shot a cry a rumor
can muster five hundred Negroes
from idle and strategic street corners
bars stoops hallways windows
Keep on pushing.

II
I walk Harlem
I see police eight per square block
crude mathematics
eight to one
eight for one
I see the store owners and keepers—all white
and I see the white police force
The white police in the white helmets
and white proprietors in their white shirts
talk together and
look around.
I see Negro handymen put to work because of the riots
boarding up smashed storefronts
They use sparkling new nails
The boards are mostly fresh-hewn pine
and smell rank fresh.
The pine boards are the nearest Lenox Avenue will ever have

to trees.
        Phalanxes of police
march   up   and   down
They are dispatched   and   gathered   helmet heads
Bobbing white black and blue.
They walk around—squadroned & platooned.
groups of   six   eight   twelve.
Even in a group
the sparse Negro cop walks alone
or with a singular
talkative
white buddy.
                    Keep on pushing
        Am I in the 1940's?
        Am I in Asia? Batista's Havana?
where is Uncle Sam's Army? The Allied Forces
when are we going to have the plebiscite?

III

I walk and the children playing frail street games seem
like no other children anywhere
they seem unpopular   foreign
as if in the midst of New York civilization existed
a cryptic and closed society.
        Am I in Korea?
I keep expecting to see
companies of camouflage-khakied marines
the Eighth Army
Red Crosses—a giant convoy
Down the narrow peopled streets
jeeps with granite-face military men
marching grim champions of the Free World
Trucks dispensing Hershey bars   Pall Malls
medical equipment
nurses doctors drugs serums to treat
the diseased and the maimed
and from the Harlem River
blasting whistles horns

volleying firebombs against the clouds
the 7th Fleet . . .

but the prowling Plymouths
and helmeted outlaws from Queens
persist.
Keep On A 'Pushing

IV

I see the plump pale butchers pose with their signs:
"Hog maws 4 pounds for 1 dollar"
"Pig ears 7 pounds for 1 dollar"
"Neckbones   chitterlings   6 pounds for 1"
Nightclubs,   liquor stores   bars 3, 4, 5 to one block
3 & 4 shots for one dollar
I see police eight to one
in its entirety Harlem's 2nd law of Thermodynamics
Helmet
nightsticks bullets to barehead
black reinforced shoes to sneaker
Am I in Korea?

V

At night Harlem sings and dances
And as the newspapers say:
they also pour their whiskey on one another's head.
They dog and slop in the bars
The children monkey in front of Zero's Records Chamber
on 116th and Lenox
They mash potatoes and Madison at the Dawn Casino,
Renaissance Ballroom, Rockland Palace, and the Fifth
Avenue Armory
on 141st and the Harlem River.

— Come out of your windows

dancehalls, bars and grills   Monkey   Dog   in the street
like Martha and the Vandellas

Dog for NBC
The Daily News and *The New York Times*
Dog for Andrew Lyndon Johnson
and shimmy a bit
for "the boys upstate"
and the ones in Mississippi

Cause you got soul
Everybody knows . . .
Keep on Pushin'

VI

This twilight
I sit in Baron's Fish and Chip Shack
Alfonso (the counterman) talks of ammunition
The *Journal-American* in my lap
headlines promise EXCLUSIVE BATTLE PHOTOS
by a daring young photographer they call Mel Finkelstein
through him they insure "The Face of Violence—The
Most Striking Close-up" /
WWRL the radio station that serves
the Negro community
tools along on its rhythm n blues vehicle
The colorful unison announcers
declare themselves "The most soulful station in the nation"
Then the lecture series on Democracy comes on
The broadcaster for this series doesn't sound soulful
(eight to one he's white, representing management)
We Negroes are usually warned of the evils of Communism
and the fruits of Democracy / but this evening he tells us
that / in this troubled time we must keep our heads
and our Law
and our order (and he emphasizes order)
he says violence only hurts (and he emphasizes hurts)
the cause of freedom and dignity / He urges the troubled
restless residents of Harlem and Bedford-Stuyvesant to stay in
their homes, mark an end to the tragic and senseless violence
a pause

then he concludes
"Remember
        this is the land of the free"
and a rousing mixed chorus ends with the majestic harmony of
        "AND THE HOME OF THE BRAVE . . ."

Alfonso didn't acknowledge
he hears it every hour on the hour.
The Rhythm n Blues returns
a flaming bottle bursts on Seventh Avenue
and shimmies the fire across the white divider line
helmets
and faces white as the fluorescence of the streets
bob by
Prowl cars speeding wilding wheeling
the loony turns of the modulating demodulating sirens
climb the tenements window by window
Harlem moves in an automatic platform
The red fish lights swirl the gleaming storefronts
there will be no Passover this night
and then again the gunfire high
in the air   death static
        over everything . . .
ripped glass
shards sirens gunfire
down towards 116th
        as Jocko scenes radio WWRL
late at night Jocko hustles wine: Italian Swiss Colony Port
sherry and muscatel. Gypsy Rose and Hombre "The
        Man's Adult Western Wine"
but by day and evening
his raiment for Harlem's head is different
zealous Jocko coos forward
his baroque tongue
snakes like fire
                "Headache?
                        . . . take Aspirin

Tension?
. . . take Compoz!"

Keep on pushin'
Someway somehow
I know we can make it
With just a little bit of soul.

David Henderson, 1970

:::::

Poem against the State (of Things): 1975

I

wherever I go (these
days)
the tide seems low
(oh) wherever I go (these
days)
the tide seems very
very low

ATTICA!
ALLENDE!
AMERIKA!

Welcome to the Sunday School
of outfront machineguns
and secretive
assassinations

EVERYBODY WELCOME!

Almighty

Multinational
Corporate
Incorporeal
Bank of the World
The World Bank
Diplomacy
        and Gold

This is the story:
This is the prayer:
                Rain fell
                Monday the thirteenth
                1971
                Attica
                coldstone covered by a cold moon-
                light hidden by the night
                when fifteen hundred Black
                Puerto Rican
                White (one or two)
                Altogether Fifteen Hundred Men
                plus
                thirty-eight hostages
                (former keepers of the keys
                to the ugliest
                big
                house of them all)
                Fifteen Hundred and Thirty
                Eight
                Men
                lay sleeping in a long
                wait
                for the sun
                and not one with a gun
                not one with a gun

(oh) wherever I go
the tide seems low

Fifteen Hundred and Thirty
Eight
prisoners in prison
at Attica / they
lay sleeping in a long
long wait
for the sun
and not one with a gun
not one with a gun

But they were not really alone:

ATTICA!
ALLENDE!
AMERIKA!

Despite
the quiet of the cold moon-
light on the coldstone
of the place
Despite
the rain that fell
transforming the D-yard
blankets and tents
into heavyweight, soggy
and sweltering hell

The Brothers were hardly alone:

on the roofs
on the walkways
in turrets
and tunnels
from windows
and whirlybirds

overhead

The State
Lay in wait

Attica Attack Troops
wearing masks
carrying gas containers
and proud to be white
proud to be doing
what everyone can
for The Man
Attica Attack Troops
lay armed
at the ready
legalized killers
hard
chewing gum
to master an all-American impatience
to kill
to spill blood
to spill blood of the Bloods

and not one with a gun

the State
lay in wait

Attica Attack Troops
carrying pistols and
big-game / .270 rifles and
Ithaca Model 37 shotguns
with double-o buckshot
and also
shotguns appropriate
for "antivehicle duty"
or shotguns appropriate
for "reducing a cement block wall

to rubble"
they were ready

for what?

(oh) wherever I go (these
days)
the tide seems low

Fifteen Hundred and Thirty Eight
Prisoners
lay waiting for the next
day's sun
Fifteen Hundred and Thirty Eight
Brothers
asleep
and not one with a gun
not one with a gun

II
Why did the Brothers revolt
against Attica?

why were they there?

What did they want?

a response
recognition
as men
"WE are MEN!" they
declared:
"WE are MEN!
We are not beasts and do not
intend to be beaten
or driven as such."

ATTICA!
ALLENDE!
AMERIKA!

The State
lay in wait.

III

Black woman weeping at the coldstone wall
Rain stops. And blood begins to fall

"JACKPOT ONE!" was the animal
cry of The State
in its final
reply
"JACKPOT ONE!!"
was the cry
9:26 A.M.
Monday the thirteenth
September, 1971
Police
State Troopers
prison guards
helicopters / The Attica Attack Troops
terrified the morning
broke through
to the beasts within them
beasts
unleashed by the Almighty
Multination
Corporate
Incorporeal
Bank of the World
Despoilers
of Harlem
Cambodia
Chile
Detroit
the Philippines
Oakland
Montgomery
Dallas

South Africa
Albany
Attica
Attica
The Attica Killers
The Almighty State shot /
murdered / massacred
forty three men
forty three men
The other Brothers / they
were gassed and
beaten
bleeding or not
still clubbed and beaten:

"Nigger! You should
have got it through the head!
Nigger! You gone wish that you were
Dead!   Nigger!   Nigger!

Monday the Thirteenth
September, 1971
Attica
Blood fell on the Brothers: Not one with a gun.
Black women weeping into coldstone.

IV

wherever I go (these
days)
the tide seems low
(oh) wherever I go (these
days)
the tide seems very
very low

God's love has turned away
from this Almighty place
But

I will pray
one prayer while He yet grants me
time and space:

NO MORE AND NEVER AGAIN!
NO MORE AND NEVER AGAIN!
A-men.
A-men.

June Jordan, 1975

:::::

On the Birth of My Son, Malcolm Coltrane

at the time of Newark Rebellion, July 12, 1967

Even as we kill,
let us
not
forget
that it is only so we may be
more human.

Let our
exaltation not be
for the blood that
flows in the gutters,
but for the
blood that
may more freely flow through our bodies.

We must
kill
in order to live,
but let us never
enjoy the

killing
more than the
new life,
the only reason for the killing.

And if we forget,
then those who come
afterward
will have to kill us
(will have to kill us)
for the
life that we,
in our killing,
failed
to give them.

Julius Lester, 1967

:::::

The Gulf

(During the Detroit Riots, 1967)

Far from our garden at the edge of a gulf,
where we calm our nerves in the rain,

(scrabbling a little in earth to pull weeds
and make room for transplants—

dirt under the nails, it
hurts, almost, and yet feels good)

far from our world the heat's on.
Among the looters a boy of eleven

grabs from a florist's showcase (the Times says)
armfuls of gladioli, all he can carry,

and runs with them. What happens?
I see him

dart into a dark entry where there's no one
(the shots, the shouting, the glass smashing

heard dully as traffic is heard).
Breathless he halts to examine

the flesh of dream: he squeezes
the strong cold juicy stems, long as his legs,

tries the mild leafblades—they don't cut.
He presses his sweating face

into flower faces, scarlet and pink and purple,
white and blood red, smooth, cool—his heart is pounding.

But all at once an absence
makes itself known to him—it's like

a hole in the lungs,
life running out. They are without

perfume!
          Cheated, he drops them.
White men's flowers.

They rustle in falling,
lonely he stands there, the sheaves

cover his sneakered feet . . .
                                        There's no place to go
with or without his prize.

Far away, in our garden he cannot imagine,
I'm watching to see if he picks up the flowers

at least or goes,
leaving them lie.

But nothing happens.
He stands there.

He goes on standing there,
Useless knowledge in my mind's eye.

Nothing will move him.
We'll live out our lives

in our garden on the edge of a gulf,
and he in the hundred years' war ten heartbeats long

unchanging among the dead flowers,
no place to go.

Denise Levertov, 1970

:::::

Coming Home, Detroit, 1968

A winter Tuesday, the city pouring fire,
Ford Rouge sulfurs the sun, Cadillac, Lincoln,
Chevy gray. The fat stacks
of breweries hold their tongues. Rags,
papers, hands, the stems of birches
dirtied with words.
                                        Near the freeway
you stop and wonder what came off,
recall the snowstorm where you lost it all,
the wolverine, the northern bear, the wolf
caught out, ice and steel raining
from the foundries in a shower
of human breath. On sleds in the false sun
the new material rests. One brown child

stares and stares into your frozen eyes
until the lights change and you go
forward to work. The charred faces, the eyes
boarded up, the rubble of innards, the cry
of wet smoke hanging in your throat,
the twisted river stopped at the color of iron.
We burn this city every day.

Philip Levine, 1968

:::::

If We Cannot Live as People

> *If we cannot live as people,*
> *we will at least try to die like men*
> —AN ATTICA INMATE

Inspire our sons to seek their man-shadows
gauntleted, spread-eagled, mired in blood
seeping beneath walls six-feet deep
where Attica attacked no Attucks,
but nobly raging brothers
white-washed chronicles shall give
no plaque, no wreath,

no amnesty   for truth massacred
by orderlies of law slinking
along the parapets of hate,
goose-stepping to shatter flesh gasping
at the gate of non-negotiable slaughter.

Black death will not be defined by murder
(ignoble beast that charged through war-zone D).
Illicit blood sanctifies life again, again again again:

generations of Sharpeville, Orangeburg, Attica,
reckoning peoplehood,
shadowing the shadow-men.

Charles Lynch, 1972

:::::

Kuntu

I

I am descended from Drum
I am descended from Drum
from that which first formed
from that which first formed
descended from Drum.
The First that formed
The First that formed
am from the first that formed
the pulse that formed
the pulse that formed
the pulse that formed the Word
the pulse that formed the Word
and the Word informing the Universe
and the Word informing the Universe
and the Word informing the pulse
Word and pulse and Universe
Word and pulse and Universe
The First that formed to link, to link
Word and Act
to link Word and Substance
to link Word and desire.

II

Word, Act, and Universe
the First form out of the Earth

Drum's Earth and Black Earth Faces
Drum's Song and Black Earth Song
Drum's first Song in the Black of Olorun—the Universe.
in Olorun the Universe, I formed
the Word and the Earth and linked them in the Dance.
the first form was formless sound
the first Word was Drum's word
am descended from Drum
The Drum's words informed us, giving us flesh,
and flesh shaped the Word; I say and flesh
shaped the Word, linked the Song, linked the Earth to Sky.

No wonder we float so lightly in Summer
we float high, drifting on the rhythms of Drum,
do air-dances O so lightly,
the Drum informing our lives, our wars.

III

Drum was there on the Amistead.
Drum was there in Jamestown.
Drum was there in Watts.
Drum was there in Newark.
Drum was there in Detroit
behind the crackle of ghetto fires,
He informed the flames
pushing the rhythms,
sending us back into our time, our most powerful time
our time
our time
our time
back into most powerful time
Drum running down some mean shit
to all the Brothers and Sisters
all the Brothers and Sisters
listening to Drum, my Old Man.

Larry Neal, 1969

Watts

1

From what great sleep
lightning jumps from an amber sky
causing famine,
assassinating tin people and whole grass-blades?

Senile edifices crying like lumberjacks: "Timber!"
Streets of dwellings wrapped in cellophane
of negligence,
where old wind-winded wisemen in oversized coats
and baggy trousers soliloquize a jungle futility.
And a baby warbles a milk-dry cry
to a mother's wiry ear who sits ice-eyed
with frozen pain like icicles in her heart.

What great sleep,
resonant with nightmares,
causes a man to awaken gap-eyed?

2

Diogenes came with a burning lamp
searching for honest men, but his beautiful light
fell only upon the shadow people
and those who found meaning in the penumbral days
meted out in marijuana's fantasy
and the half-bliss of the prostitute's bed.

Socrates came with nebulous knowledge
to make a liar of the Oracle of Delphi,
but found only
schoolrooms of metal and wood carvings
and those who escape into
some kind of intoxicant—running from
some too-true truth.

Against what false fantasy
the children ball on their golden slides,
bouncing balls, and putty clay—
and Socrates, horrid-eyed, gulped the hemlock
while weeping Diogenes hurled his flame
to the barren soil.

Ojenke (Alvin Saxon), 1967

:::::

In Orangeburg My Brothers Did

in Orangeburg my brothers did
the african twist around a bonfire they'd built
at the gate to keep the hunkies out. the day
before they'd caught one shooting up
the campus like the white hunter
he was. but a bonfire? only conjures
up the devil. up popped the devil from behind a bush
the brothers danced the fire
danced the bullets cut their flesh
like bullets. black death
black death black death black
brothers black sisters black me with no white blood on my hands
we are so beautiful
we study our history backwards
& that must be the beast's most fatal message
that we die to learn it well.

A. B. Spellman, 1969

9

"Prophets were ambushed as they spoke"

THE ASSASSINATION OF MALCOLM X, 21 FEBRUARY 1965

The assassination of Malcolm X left an immeasurable void in the struggle for black liberation in America. Born Malcolm Little on 19 May 1925 in Omaha, the charismatic leader provided an alternative to the traditional methods of the civil rights movement. He was also viewed by admirers and detractors alike as a threat to America's racial status quo.

Malcolm X felt that the treatment blacks received in America was a matter not so much of civil injustice as human injustice. Seeking to internationalize the plight of African Americans and to connect their struggle with those of people of color around the world, he pressured, albeit unsuccessfully, the United Nations to charge America with human rights violations. According to Malcolm, an insistence upon civil rights did not speak adequately to the treatment endured by blacks in America. In

"The Ballot or the Bullet," a speech given in 1964, he presented the difference between civil and human rights in the following manner:

> You can take Uncle Sam before a world court. But the only level you can do it on is the level of human rights. Civil rights keeps you under his restrictions, under his jurisdiction. Civil rights keeps you in his pocket. Civil rights means you're asking Uncle Sam to treat you right. Human rights are something you were born with. Human rights are your God-given rights. Human rights are the rights that are recognized by all nations of this earth. And any time any one violates your human rights, you can take them to the world court. (Breitman 35)

The U.S. government, Malcolm asserted, did not possess the requisite objectivity to treat blacks as equals or to view itself as committing human rights violations. His stance was controversial, as were many of his opinions on race relations, but it was a stance that segments of the black population admired and respected.

His ascent from a criminal past undoubtedly led to his appeal in a community that has traditionally valued perseverance, forgiveness, and redemption. Malcolm X himself sought forgiveness from civil rights leaders and others for previous comments about integration after his hajj to Mecca. During his trip he witnessed people from various races and backgrounds working and worshipping together, something he had not experienced in the United States. Upon his return he stated publicly that he would work to help achieve integration in America, which was a departure from his earlier views on the subject.

Ossie Davis, the late actor and civil rights activist, may have unwittingly influenced several poets when he delivered Malcolm X's eulogy on 27 February 1965 inside Harlem's Faith Temple Church of God. Near the end of his tribute, Davis crystallized his appreciation for the former Nation of Islam leader by asserting, "Malcolm was our manhood, our living, black manhood! This was his meaning to his people. And, in honoring him, we honor the best in ourselves" (Randall and Burroughs 121). Davis's comments were intended to draw attention to America's denial of black selfhood, including manhood, dating to the days of master–slave relations. Several poets, male and female, would later write elegies for Malcolm

X that contained a similar theme, often referencing Malcolm's embodiment of black manhood. "Rich-robust" is how Gwendolyn Brooks recalls Malcolm, before adding, "We gasped. We saw the maleness / We saw the maleness . . . making guttural the air" (lines 3, 5–6). Sonia Sanchez in "malcolm" says solemnly:

> this man
> this dreamer
> thick-lipped with words
> will never speak again. (8–11)

In the context of civil rights and black power, Davis's use of "living, black manhood" takes on a more profound meaning. The phrase is used to characterize Malcolm as someone devoted to eradicating impediments to a black cultural revolution in America, by any means necessary. This meant standing up to and vociferously and articulately castigating structures of power intent on maintaining the status quo. Malcolm eschewed pacifism and the brand of nonviolent social protest espoused by Dr. King, although both worked toward the same goal. Like King, Malcolm was not a proponent of violence, but he was an advocate of self-defense. His advocacy of striking back against segregationists who initiate violence undoubtedly led to his designation as a "man" by Davis and many of the poets gathered here.

Poets addressed the death of Malcolm X from multiple angles, but most chose to praise him for serving as a role model for the black community, especially black men. For example, Amiri Baraka in "A Poem for Black Hearts" encourages black men to carry themselves with the type of dignity Malcolm displayed. Similarly Marvin X (Marvin E. Jackmon) implies in "That Old Time Religion," that Malcolm was able to engender a high level of influence and respect from the community because he was "nothing but a man, who threw fear away" (5). Not only does this line suggest that other black males should cast fear aside as well (and stop "stuttering and shuffling," as Baraka's poem would have it), but the words "nothing but a man" also intimates that Malcolm was a common man, down-to-earth and personable. In "If Blood Is Black Then Spirit Neglects My Unborn Son" Conrad Kent Rivers also invokes the term "manhood" when he claims that Malcolm, while in the process of not allowing fear to govern his choice of subject or words, was "articulating complete manhood" (21).

A Poem for Black Hearts

For Malcolm's eyes, when they broke
the face of some dumb white man, For
Malcolm's hands raised to bless us
all black and strong in his image
of ourselves, For Malcolm's words
fire darts, the victor's tireless
thrusts, words hung above the world
change as it may, he said it, and
for this he was killed, for saying,
and feeling, and being / change, all
collected hot in his heart, For Malcolm's
heart, raising us above our filthy cities,
for his stride, and his beat, and his address
to the grey monsters of the world, For Malcolm's
pleas for your dignity, black men, for your life,
black man, for the filling of your minds
with righteousness, For all of him dead and
gone and vanished from us, and all of him which
clings to our speech black god of our time.
For all of him, and all of yourself, look up,
black man, quit stuttering and shuffling, look up,
black man, quit whining and stooping, for all of him,
For Great Malcolm a prince of the earth, let nothing in us rest
until we avenge ourselves for his death, stupid animals
that killed him, let us never breathe a pure breath if
we fail, and white men call us faggots till the end of
the earth.

Amiri Baraka, 1965

For Malcolm: After Mecca

My whole life has been a chronology of—*changes.*

You lie now in many coffins
in a parlor where your name
is dropped more heavily even than Death
sent you crashing to the stage
on which you had exorcised your shame.

In little rooms they gather now
bringing their own memories of your pilgrimage
they come and go
speaking of revolution
without knowing as you learned
how static hate is
without recognizing the man you were
lay in our shame
and your growth into martyrdom.

Gerald W. Barrax, 1970

:::::

Malcolm X

(for Dudley Randall)

Original.
Ragged-round.
Rich-robust.

He had the hawk-man's eyes.
We gasped. We saw the maleness.
The maleness raking out and making guttural the air
and pushing us to walls.

And in a soft and fundamental hour
a sorcery devout and vertical
beguiled the world.

He opened us—
who was a key,

who was a man.

Gwendolyn Brooks, 1968

:::::

Judas

How does Judas look when he is black?
Does he scratch his head?
Shuffle his feet?
Lay his body before cars in the street?
How does Judas look when he is black?
Is he a "Tom"?
What does he do?
Is he the Afro-American sitting next to you?
Is he visible or out of sight?
Is he a blackman whose mind is white?
How does Judas look when he is black?
If he is the enemy within we need to attack,
How do we prevent him from stabbing us in the back?
Who was Judas?
What did he do?
Jesus was the man that Judas slew
Malcolm was the man that we sold too.

Karl Carter, 1969

malcolm

nobody mentioned war
but doors were closed
black women shaved their heads
black men rustled in the alleys like leaves
prophets were ambushed as they spoke
and from their holes black eagles flew
screaming through the streets

Lucille Clifton, 1972

:::::

El-Hajj Malik El-Shabazz

(Malcolm X)

O masks and metamorphoses of Ahab, Native Son

I

The icy evil that struck his father down
and ravished his mother into madness
trapped him in violence of a punished self
struggling to break free.

As Home Boy, as Dee-troit Red,
he fled his name, became the quarry of
his own obsessed pursuit.

He conked his hair and Lindy-hopped,
zoot-suited jiver, swinging those chicks
in the hot rose and reefer glow.

His injured childhood bullied him.
He skirmished in the Upas trees
and cannibal flowers of the American Dream—

but could not hurt the enemy
powered against him there.

II

Sometimes the dark that gave his life
its cold satanic sheen would shift
a little, and he saw himself
floodlit and eloquent;

yet how could he, "Satan" in The Hole,
guess what the waking dream foretold?

Then false dawn of vision came;
he fell upon his face before
a racist Allah pledged to wrest him from
the hellward-thrusting hands of Calvin's Christ—

to free him and his kind
from Yakub's white-faced treachery.
He rose redeemed from all but prideful anger,

though adulterate attars could not cleanse
him of the odors of the pit.

III

Asalam Alaikum!

He X'd out his name, became his people's anger,
exhorted them to vengeance for their past;
rebuked, admonished them,

their scourger who
would shame them, drive them from
the lush ice gardens of their servitude.

Asalam alaikum!

Rejecting Ahab, he was Ahab's tribe.
"Strike through the mask!"

IV

Time. "The Martyr's time," he said
Time and the karate killer,
knifer, gunman. Time that brought
ironic trophies as his faith

twined sparking round the bole,
the fruit of neo-Islam.
"The martyr's time."

But first, the ebb time pilgrimage
toward revelation, hejira to
his final metamorphosis;

Labbayak! Labbayak!

He fell upon his face before
Allah the raceless in whose blazing Oneness all
were one. He rose renewed renamed, became
much more than there was time for him to be.

Robert Hayden, 1967

:::::

Portrait of Malcolm X

(for Charles Baxter)

He has the sign
of the time shining
in his eyes the high sign

His throat moans
Moses on Sinai and cracks
stones

His lips lay full and flowered
by the breast of Mother Africa

His forehead is red
and sacrosanct and
smooth as time and
love for you

Etheridge Knight, 1968

:::::

Malcolm X—An Autobiography

I am the Seventh Son of the Son
who was also the Seventh.
I have drunk deep of the waters of my ancestors
have traveled the soul's journey towards cosmic harmony,
the Seventh Son.

Have walked slick avenues
and seen grown men fall, to die in a blue doom
of death and ancestral agony;
have seen old men glide, shadowless, feet barely
touching the pavements.

I sprung out of the Midwestern plains
the bleak Michigan landscape, the black blues of Kansas
City, these kiss-me-nights;
out of the bleak Michigan landscape wearing the slave name—
Malcolm Little.

Saw a brief vision in Lansing when I was seven, and in
my momma's womb heard the beast cry of death,
a landscape on which white robed figures ride, and my
Garvey father silhouetted against the night-fire, gun in hand
form outlined against a panorama of violence.

Out of the Midwestern bleakness, I sprang, pushed eastward,
past shack on country nigger shack, across the wilderness
of North America.
I hustler. I pimp. I unfulfilled Black man
bursting with destiny.
New York City Slim called me Big Red,
and there was no escape, close nights of the smell of death.
Pimp. Hustler. The day fills these rooms.
I am talking about New York. Harlem.
Talking about the neon madness.
Talking about ghetto eyes and nights
Talking about death protruding across the room.
Talking about Small's Paradise.
Talking about cigarette butts, and rooms smelly with white
sex flesh, and dank sheets, and being on the run.
Talking about cocaine illusions.
Talking about stealing and selling.
Talking about these New York cops who smell of blood and money.
I am Big Red, tiger, vicious, Big Red, bad nigger, will kill.

But there is rhythm here.
Its own special substance:
I hear Billie sing, no Good Man, and dig Prez, wearing the Zoot
suit of life, the Porkpie hat tilted at the correct angle.
Through the Harlem smoke of beer and whiskey, I understand the
mystery of the signifying monkey,
in a blue haze of inspiration, I reach for the totality of Being.
I am at the center of the swirl of events.
War and death.
Rhythm.
Hot women.
I think life a commodity bargained
for across the bar in Small's.
I perceive the echoes of Bird
and there is a gnawing in the maw
of my emotions.

And then there is jail.
America is the world's greatest jailer,
and we all in jails. Black spirits contained like magnificent
birds or wonder. I now understand my father urged on by the
ghost of Garvey,
and see a small brown man standing in a corner. The cell. cold.
dank. The light around him vibrates. Am I crazy? But to under-
stand is to submit to a more perfect will, a more perfect order.
To understand is to surrender the imperfect self.
For a more perfect self.

Allah formed black man, I follow
and shake within the very depth of my most imperfect being,
and I bear witness to the message of Allah
and I bear witness—all praise is due Allah!

Larry Neal, 1969

:::::

At That Moment

When they shot Malcolm Little down
On the stage of the Audubon Ballroom,
When his life ran out through bullet holes
(Like the people running out when the murder began)
His blood soaked the floor
One drop found a crack through the stark
Pounding thunder—slipped under the stage and began
Its journey: burrowed through concrete into the cellar,
Dropped down darkness, exploding like quicksilver
Pellets of light, panicking rats, paralyzing cockroaches—
Tunneled through rubble and wrecks of foundations,
The rocks that buttress the bowels of the city, flowed
Into pipes and powerlines, the mains and cables of the city:

A thousand fiery seeds.
At that moment,
Those who drank water where he entered . . .
Those who cooked food where he passed . . .
Those who burned light while he listened . . .
Those who were talking as he went, knew he was water
Running out of faucets, gas running out of jets, power
Running out of sockets, meaning running along taut wires—
To the hungers of their living. It is said
Whole slums of clotted Harlem plumbing groaned
And sundered free that day, and disconnected gas and light
Went on and on and on . . .
They rushed his riddled body on a stretcher
To the hospital. But the police were too late.
It had already happened.

Raymond Patterson, 1967

:::::

If Blood Is Black Then Spirit Neglects My Unborn Son

For Malcolm X in Substance

You must remember structures beyond cotton plains
filled
by joes voting for godot,
stealing the white man's thunder,
avarice,

Songs of silence parade your dead body
Distracted by housemaids' bending backs
Gold dusted, not sinned in the angry silence
Surrounding fetid breaths and heavy sighs
As your actor friend tells of tall trees
Addressing that tenth talented mind

Bowing for recognition under the sun shining
Cameras shaping your body

You must remember that and this second whirl of
care
while black brothers grieve
your unbroken Upanishads passing the white
man's understanding of your new peace
without hate.
Your new love with sweet words
articulating complete manhood,
directly questioning the whole and famous
words you said.
Let my women mourn for days
in flight.

Conrad Kent Rivers, ca. 1965

:::::

malcolm

do not speak to me of martyrdom
of men who die to be remembered
on some parish day.
i don't believe in dying
though i too shall die
and violets like castanets
will echo me.

yet this man
this dreamer,
thick-lipped with words
will never speak again
and in each winter
when the cold air cracks

with frost, i'll breathe
his breath and mourn
my gun-filled nights.
he was the sun that tagged
the western sky and
melted tiger-scholars
while they searched for stripes.
he said, "fuck you white
man. we have been
curled too long. Nothing
is sacred now. not your
white faces nor any
land that separates
until some voices
squat with spasms."

do not speak to me of living.
life is obscene with crowds
of white on black.
death is my pulse.
what might have been
is not for him / or me
but what could have been
floods the womb until i drown.

Sonia Sanchez, 1965

:::::

For Malcolm Who Walks in the Eyes of Our Children

He had been coming a very long time,
had been here many times before
in the flesh of other persons
in the spirit of other gods

His eyes had seen flesh turned to stone,
had seen stone turned to flesh
had swam within the minds
of a billion great heroes,

had walked amongst builders
of nations, of the Sphinx, had built
with his own hands those nations,

had come flying across time a cosmic spirit,
an idea, a thought wave transcending
flesh fusion spirit of all centuries,
had come soaring like a sky break

above ominous clouds of sulphur
in a stride so enormous it spanned
the breadth of a people's bloodshed,

came singing like Coltrane breathing life
into stone statues formed from lies

Malcolm, flaming cosmic spirit who walks
Amongst us, we hear your voice
Speaking wisdom in the wind,
we see your vision in the life / fires of men,
in our incredible young children
who watch your image
flaming in the sun

Quincy Troupe, 1967

For Malcolm X

All you violated ones with gentle hearts
You violent dreamers whose cries shout heartbreak;
Whose voices echo clamors of our cool capers,
And whose black faces have hollowed pits for eyes.
All you gambling sons and hooked children and bowery bums
Hating white devils and black bourgeoisie,
Thumbing your noses at your burning red suns,
Gather round this coffin and mourn your dying swan.

Snow-white moslem head-dress around a dead black face!
Beautiful were your sand-papering words against our skins!
Our blood and water pour from your flowing wounds.
You have cut open our breasts and dug scalpels in our brains.
When and Where will another come to take your holy place?
Old man mumbling in his dotage, or crying child, unborn?

Margaret Walker, 1966

:::::

That Old Time Religion

Malcolm.
The Saint
          behind our skulls
in the region of fear and strength
Nothing but a man, who threw fear away
and caught something greater . . . life
And the price of life is death
protect ourselves from the beast
and he went unprotected
by the will of allah
most merciful

a lost leader
though we have found his spirit
        behind our skulls
        in the region of fear and strength
Malcolm held our manhood
        he said what we knew but feared
        we feared to name the beast
        who is a man; who has a number
        and the number is 666 spoken of
        in Revelations of the Bible.
        Ready or not . . . God is here
        LET THERE BE BLACKNESS OVER THIS LAND
        LET BLACK POWER SHINE AND SHINE.

Marvin X, 1968

10

"In the panic of hooves, bull whips and gas"

SELMA-TO-MONTGOMERY VOTING RIGHTS MARCH, 1965

Eight days after the funeral of Malcolm X in Harlem, civil rights marchers gathered in Selma, Alabama, to protest the murder of a local activist and to demonstrate against unjust voter registration practices. Although civil rights advocates already had a presence in Selma, especially for the sake of improving voting conditions for blacks, the murder of Jimmy Lee Jackson (also widely referred to as Jimmie) prompted leaders to intensify their presence and efforts. Jackson, an unarmed twenty-six-year-old African American, was shot by the Alabama State Trooper James Bonard Fowler in Marion on the evening of 18 February 1965 after a protest march had been raided and disrupted by local police and state troopers. Jackson, his mother, and his eighty-two-year-old grandfather were attempting to evade the officers when Fowler opened fire and struck Jackson in the abdomen. Jackson died the following week. Fowler was eventually questioned about and arraigned for Jackson's death—more than forty years after he pulled the trigger.

Activists assembled on 7 March 1965 for a fifty-four-mile eastward march to neighboring Montgomery, the state capital, for what would become known as "Bloody Sunday." Nearly six hundred people advanced along the streets of Selma to the crest of the arch-shaped Edmund Pettus Bridge. Blue-helmeted and uniformed Alabama state troopers stood at the bottom of the other side of the bridge. In addition Sheriff James G. Clark positioned behind the troopers dozens of local armed men. Troopers struck marchers with clubs and fired C-4 tear gas. As clouds of smoke began to form, troopers in gas masks advanced against the marchers, swinging nightsticks as they swept through the crowd. Clark's "posse" advanced as well, many of them mounted on horses and carrying clubs and whips. The melee continued, with horses galloping over fallen and choking marchers. Troopers clubbed, stomped, and bloodied as many men and women as they could reach, all in plain view of cameramen and reporters.

Televised images of the unprovoked attacks angered Americans across the country, and many of them supported or participated in the two additional marches that followed. The second occurred on 9 March, the Tuesday following "Bloody Sunday," and the third took place on Sunday, 21 March. The second march amounted to a symbolic or ceremonial demonstration, primarily due to a court order preventing the march from taking place. In compliance with the order, Dr. King led approximately fifteen hundred marchers to the Edmund Pettus Bridge, stopped, conducted a brief prayer meeting, and returned to Brown's Chapel, where the marchers had originally assembled. Although the activities of the day were largely uneventful, the events that transpired that evening resulted in more violence. Clark Olsen, Orloff Miller, and James Reeb, three white Unitarian Universalist ministers who participated in the march (more than four hundred white clergy were present for the march), were attacked after they left a soul food restaurant in Selma and walked past the Silver Moon Café, a known hangout for white racists. Reeb, thirty-eight, died two days later; he had suffered a blow to the head with a club. Reeb's murder resulted in even more demonstrations throughout the country. While civil rights leaders mourned Reeb's death, many wondered why the country didn't have a similar reaction when Jimmy Lee Jackson was murdered (Williams 275). The deaths of whites in the movement, such as Reeb, Goodman, and Schwerner, usually received significantly more media attention than the deaths of blacks.

The third march drew more demonstrators than the first two marches combined. With the aid of federal protection provided by President Johnson, the number of protesters swelled to thirty-two hundred by the time marchers reached Montgomery on 25 March. Dr. King, the marchers, and their supporters rallied on the steps of the state capitol, having succeeded after the viciousness that had taken place over the past weeks. The march became one of the defining moments of the civil rights era, not only because it illustrated the courage and determination of the participants, but also because it led directly to the signing of the Voting Rights Act of 1965 by President Johnson on 6 August. The legislation made illegal discriminatory voting practices like the literacy tests administered in Dallas County.

The murder of Jimmy Lee Jackson, which led to the escalation of civil rights activities in Selma, is recalled by Jim "Arkansas" Benston in "Ode to Jimmy Lee." The poem, which personally addresses its subject in the opening line ("I did not know you, Jimmy Lee"), is written with the hope of making sure that others *do* get to know or learn about Jackson, his sacrifice, and his contribution to the struggle in Selma.

June Brindel's "The Road to Selma" shares a similar goal. She too invokes and links Jackson's name to other activists, including Reeb, whose presence is the most dominant in the poem. As the poem progresses readers come to realize that Brindel is constructing a fantasy wherein the two men come in contact with Evers, Chaney, Goodman, Schwerner, Emmett Till, the four young victims of the Sixteenth Street Baptist Church bombing, and Abraham Lincoln. Brindel also acknowledges those who died with little or no recognition.

The speaker in Thich Nhat Hanh's poem finds himself preoccupied with notions of freedom in the U.S. while stationed in Vietnam. Nhat Hanh, a Vietnamese Buddhist monk who was nominated for the Nobel Peace Prize by Dr. King in 1967, writes "The Sun of the Future" from the perspective of an African American soldier. The speaker struggles with issues of race, humanity, and justice while attempting to kill the Vietcong.

He is unable to reconcile the purpose of the war in Vietnam with the struggle for civil rights back in the United States. Selma and other cities are listed as places more deserving of his time and of U.S. dollars.

Questions of conflict and aggression also haunt Maria Varela, who offers an autobiographical perspective on the struggle in Selma. In "Crumpled Notes (found in a raincoat) on Selma," she asks, "What does a man do / In this kind of war?," referring to the "slashed and gassed, / trampled and beaten" protesters who participated in the "Bloody Sunday" march (lines 69–70, 67–68).

:::::

Ode to Jimmy Lee

I did not know you, Jimmy Lee,

But I came to watch you lowered to the Earth in highest homage
As though a king, or chief, or priest of Sacred Truth.

I was a one of four thousand sad, and scared, and seething Souls
Who trekked the miles from Marion in pouring rain
that holy Alabama Sunday so long ago,
Washing away our tears;
replacing even our fears and anger
With a determination no tide of reaction or terror could stem.

Perhaps it was not my own blood upon the jacket I wore thereafter
But Yours, Sheyanne's, Martin's,
That of Annie Lee, & Brother Reeb, and young Saint Jonathan of Daniel.

We mixed blood by day, and laughter by night
and tears before the dawn.

The Shack rocked and rang with the footsteps of our dancing
{Song medley interlude with "Shotgun," "When a Man Loves a Woman," "Change Gonna Come."}

the Shack rocked and rang with the footsteps of our dancing. The silent streets echoed
with the pounding of our Hearts.
Love came easily—as did conflict—and rode away with the next carload to Atlanta
Perhaps never to return that terrible and wondrous winter before the Dawn

I know not how many years I grew that month before the Spring
But, fleeting decades since scarce have left so true a mark upon my Soul.

From afar they do not remember your name—
Those who came to carry on the torch you passed into their hands;
As they do remember Daisy, and Medgar, and Andy, and Mickey, and Jim.
But we who stood by your side
And heard your final verdict pronounced:
"Died of massive internal infection."
We, we who stood the Cause we know.
And when we met the horses on the Bridge,
The gas, the clubs, the whips, the angry shouts and flaming eyes of hatred
Yes!   We Knew!

From that moment we were certain that Our Cause "should not have died in vain,"
That we would march on, to Montgomery,
Affront the eyes of All the World
And seal one mighty victory forever
Along the never-ending trial-trail for Freedom

The Struggle the Task   the Prayer   the Song of Human Dignity.

And you, dear Jimmy Lee Jackson, age 26, of Marion, Alabama,
Footnote of history,

As You rose to protect your grandfather from the vicious clubs of
  hatred that February night,
    and thereby gave your life,
You helped to lead us on.
    And we, we who stood by your side
    We REMEMBER

Jim "Arkansas" Benston, 1965

:::::

The Road to Selma

The road from Selma stretches in the rain
white as a shroud, rimmed with stiff troopers.

The marchers stand bowed, hands joined, swaying gently
their soft strong song stilled.

Then up from a Birmingham bed
rises a gentle Boston man, Jim Reeb,
steps softly back to Selma
and moves among the stilled marchers.

The troopers stir, link arms,
close ranks across the road
stretching from Selma in the rain
white as a shroud.

The Boston man, Jim Reeb, walks toward the troopers
and they straighten and stand guard tight as death.
But someone moves behind them, waves his hand.
"That you, Jackson?" Jim Reeb peers ahead.
"That's right, Reverend. Come on through."

The troopers tighten guard, straight as death
But Jim Reeb doesn't stop.

He goes on through,
right through the stiff ranked troopers
white as a shroud
rimming the road from Selma.

And Jimmie Lee Jackson takes him by the arm
and they march down the road to the courthouse.

Over in Mississippi Medgar Evers stands,
three young men rise up from a dam in Neshoba County
and they all go down the road
and walk right through the tight stiff trooper line
and down the road from Selma.

And from all over there's a stirring sound.
Emmett Till jumps up and runs laughing like any boy
through the stiff white rim.
Four small girls skip out of a church in Birmingham
and the tall old man in Springfield gets up
and goes to Selma.

And down from every lynching tree
and up from every hidden grave
come men, women, children, heads carried high,
passing a moment among the bowed, stilled troopers
and down the white road from Selma.

Until the age long road is packed
black with marchers streaming to the courthouse.

And the bowed stilled group in Selma
raise their heads, hands joined,
swaying gently, in soft strong song
that goes right through the stiff ranked troopers
white as a shroud
barring the road from Selma.

June Brindel, 1965

Selma, Alabama, 3/6/65

For Wendell Rivers

Racist, Jew, fanatic, gentile,
Apologist, Southerner, Anglophile—
I am all these things today,
Things that curse, things that pray,
Things that don't know what to say
Or think or dream. My mind kneels
In dusty roads. My knees know fatigue,
And I can't even whimper.

I want to vote, like other things
That qualify as human beings.
I tell myself that I'm a man.
I face the lies of democracy,
Am singed by its senseless fires.
I cry sometimes in my separate room,
Where birth and death are inseparable
And equal, but they do not heed
What I need to say and dream and do.
They claim that *be* and *seem*
Are not the same, that *ought*
And *should* could only be bought
At a cost they'd never pay.

But we'll meet at the church,
Where the road joins the birch copse,
Half a mile from town.
We'll wear our brown skin,
Our black skin, inside out
And ignore their shouts,
For to fight back would be wrong,
Would make us part of the throng
Of innocent ignorance
That preys behind every tree.
We can't submit to the hordes

That disgrace themselves,
Knowing they sow scornful seeds
In the soil of all men's dignity.

We'll march while the sun's in hiding,
Start running as it rises to shadows.
What other way is there to say
That we're not just fractional things,
Unless all men be puppeteers'
String-moved slaves?

Let's march now. Let's run now.
I don't know how to whimper anymore.
Let us bow and pray,
Then walk, march, run that race
With the sun. We'll arise today
From the centuries of disgrace
To soothe the sweaty brows
Of children who'll take these vows.

Louis Daniel Brodsky, 1965

:::::

The Sun of the Future

Sitting in a wet trench
a whole afternoon,
I hold my gun down
and wait for Victor,
Victor Charlie
the yellow-skinned Vietcong.

How sorrowful is the cry of the monkey
in this Asian mountain.
How sorrowful is this country called Vietnam.

How do these forests and mountains differ
from the forests and mountains of Africa?

My gun, barking and spitting fire,
has the eyes of Victor Charlie—
his eyes,
whether black skin or yellow skin,
what do the eyes say?—
his eyes, the sorrow of Asia.
I have heard somewhere a poet
expressing the
sorrow of Africa.
It doesn't matter whether he is black or white.
Why do I have to hate you,
Victor Charlie?

Our money has been flowing into Vietnam
while my poor, black brothers
bear the burden of racism and discrimination.
Detroit, Selma, Chicago, Birmingham, Watts
are already engaged in the struggle.
My brothers and sisters have started to leave
the land of suffering.

We have taken a stand—
thirty billion dollars
for the war in 1967.
Three million dollars
for each hour of the war—
my wife and children in Chicago,
still caught in the net of poverty.
Two billion dollars for each month of the war,
more than the yearly budget to help the poor
in our country, the great America.
To support half a million immigrant families,
education,
children's programs,

housing,
and health care,
to meet the yearly budget for all of that,
we only need to stop the war for eight hours.

Why are we in Vietnam,
the forests and mountains of Asia?

Victor Charlie,
when did we sow the first seed of hatred and anger?
This is not what we meant to do!
They hid the truth from us.
They did not tell us the limits.
The sun of the future
is hidden
behind the forests and mountains.
At the foot of the Asian continent,
the Earth is trembling.
And she is trembling
under the African continent as well.

Thich Nhat Hanh, 1967

:::::

Race Relations

for D.B.

I sang in the sun
of my white oasis
as you broke stone

Then I sang and paraded
for the distant martyrs
loving the unknown

They lay still in the sun
of Sharpeville and Selma
while you broke stone

When you fled tyranny
facedown in the street
signing stones with your blood

Far away I fell silent
in my white oasis
ringed with smoke and guns

Martyred in safety
I sighed for lost causes
You bled on   You bled on

Now I recommence singing
in a tentative voice
loving the unknown

I sing in the sun
and storm of the world
to the breakers of stone

You are sentenced to life
in the guilt of freedom
in the prison of memory

Haunted by brothers
who still break stone
I am sentenced to wait

And our love-hate duet
is drowned by the drum
of the breakers of stone

Carolyn Kizer, 1970

Alabama Centennial

They said, "Wait." Well, I waited.
For a hundred years I waited
In cotton fields, kitchens, balconies,
In bread lines, at back doors, on chain gangs,
In stinking "colored" toilets
And crowded ghettos,
Outside of schools and voting booths.
And some said, "Later."
And some said, "Never!"

Then a new wind blew, and a new voice
Rode its wings with quiet urgency,
Strong, determined, sure.

"No," it said. "Not 'never,' not 'later.'
Not even 'soon.'
Now.
Walk!"

And other voices echoed the freedom words,
"Walk together, children, don't get weary,"
Whispered them, sang them, prayed them, shouted them.
"Walk!"
And I walked the streets of Montgomery
Until a link in the chain of patient acquiescence broke.

Then again: Sit down!
And I sat down at the counters of Greensboro.
Ride! And I rode the bus for freedom.
Kneel! And I went down on my knees in prayer and faith.
March! And I'll march until the last chain falls
Singing, "We shall overcome."

Not all the dogs and hoses in Birmingham
Nor all the clubs and guns in Selma
Can turn this tide.

Not all the jails can hold these young black faces
From their destiny of manhood,
Of equality, of dignity,
Of the American Dream
A hundred years past due.
Now!

Naomi Long Madgett, 1965

:::::

On a Highway East of Selma, Alabama

As the sheriff remarked: I had no business being there. He was
right, but for the wrong reasons. Among that odd crew of volunteers
from the North, I was by far the most inept and least effective.
I couldn't have inspired or assisted a woodchuck to vote.
    In fact, when the sheriff's buddies nabbed me on the highway east of Selma,
I'd just been released from ten days of jail in Mississippi. I was fed up and terrified; I was
actually fleeing north and glad to go.

*

In Jackson, they'd been ready for the demonstration. After the
peaceful arrests, after the news cameras recorded us being quietly
ushered onto trucks, the doors were closed and we headed for
the county fairgrounds.
    Once we passed its gates, it was a different story: the truck
doors opened on a crowd of state troopers waiting to greet us
with their nightsticks out. Smiles beneath mirrored sunglasses
and blue riot helmets; smiles above badges taped so numbers
didn't show.
    For the next twenty minutes, they clubbed us, and it kept up
at intervals, more or less at random, all that afternoon and into
the evening.

Next morning we woke to new guards who did not need to conceal their names or faces. A little later, the FBI arrived to ask if anyone had specific complaints about how they'd been treated and by whom.

But late that first night, as we sat bolt upright in rows on the concrete floor of the cattle barn waiting for mattresses to arrive, one last precise event: A guard stopped in front of the ten-year-old black kid next to me. He pulled a FREEDOM NOW pin from the kid's shirt, made him put it in his mouth, then ordered him to swallow.

*

That stakeout at dusk on Route 80 east of Selma was intended for someone else, some imaginary organizer rumored to be headed toward their dismal, godforsaken town. Why did they stop me?

The New York plates, perhaps, and that little bit of stupidity: the straw hat I wore, a souvenir of Mississippi.

Siren-wail from an unmarked car behind me — why should I think they were cops? I hesitated, then pulled to the shoulder. The two who jumped out waved pistols, but wore no uniforms or badges. By then, my doors were locked, my windows rolled. Absurd sound of a pistol barrel rapping the glass three inches from my face: "Get out, you son of a bitch, or we'll blow your head off."

When they found pamphlets on the backseat they were sure they'd got the right guy. The fat one started poking my stomach with his gun, saying, "Boy, we're gonna dump you in the swamp."

*

It was a long ride through the dark, a ride full of believable threats, before they arrived at that hamlet with its cinderblock jail.

He was very glad to see it, that adolescent I was twenty years ago. For eight days he cowered in his solitary cell, stinking of dirt and fear. He's cowering there still, waiting for me to come back and release him by turning his terror into art. But consciously or not, he made his choice and he's caught in history.

And if I reach back now, it's only to hug him and tell him to be brave, to remember that black kid who sat beside him in the Mississippi darkness. And to remember that silence shared by guards and prisoners alike as they watched in disbelief the darkness deepening around the small shape in his mouth, the taste of metal, the feel of the pin against his tongue.

It's too dark for it to matter what's printed on the pin; it's too dark for anything but the brute fact that someone wants him to choke to death on its hard shape.

And still he refuses to swallow.

Gregory Orr, 1965

:::::

Crumpled Notes (found in a raincoat) on Selma

I

you asked me
to tell you what i saw
that gray sunday morning
of the first attempt to march on Montgomery.

there was that pile
of rolled-up blankets,
taken off beds and wrapped up
with belts, or old ties, or string.

remember how we had laughed and said,
"and where will 'de lawd' get 10,000
blankets to sleep his multitude—
will He multiply them like loaves and fishes?"

there they were
in the corner by the altar—
a patchwork mountain of rolled-up trust.

they were a rebuke—
a mountain of faith
that we had not fathomed
and that He would soon use.

"we are going"
"WE ARE GOING"
spoke that patchwork mountain
in its unvalued dignity
(the 'dignity' that week
came from the cameras
and microphones
and press-carded vultures)

"WE ARE GOING"
but in the strategy sessions
in the back office
they couldn't hear:
"no,
don't bother putting up that
50 mile radio antenna . . .
they won't make it past the bridge."

(i should have put it up—
it would have been my bedroll)

"No,
He won't be here,
but we'll take them down,
and they'll probably get gassed,
and that will be the victory
then we'll bring them back to the church."
(they didn't hear the old woman,
"No
i guess we won't get too far,
but I'm going anyway,
we've got to start sometime.")

(i wonder what happened to that lady,
in the panic of hooves, bull whips and gas?)

"We are going" said the brown paper bags,
and toothbrushes
and sturdy old shoes.

but they couldn't hear
in those medical committee meetings.
not that they didn't want to—
but i couldn't tell from the detached,
clinical descriptions being professionally
murmured, whether they knew
what this war was like.

How did that quiet morning briefing . . .
"we can expect tear gas,
and mustard acid gentlemen,
you know the treatment . . ."
match up to the afternoon's screaming horror
of body after body after body
slashed and gassed,
trampled and beaten.

(what does a man do
In this kind of war?)

II

HE DIDN'T COME.
They never said exactly why.

(and when He finally came
on the week anniversary
of Selma's humiliation on
the Edmund Pettus Bridge,
He never said WHY . . .
WHY he wasn't there.
He said, instead,
"just tell them,
the mayor and sheriff and all,
just tell them that Ralph and martin are back.")

He didn't come
and they went without him.
Picked up their bedrolls,

umbrellas (we had laughed about
what 'de lawd' would do
if it rained)
and brown paper sacks with toothbrushes.

They lined up
and went to their red sea . . .
only this time there was no god
to part the sea of posse
and moses didn't show up.

i wonder would it have been different
had he been there?

Would they have touched him,
Would they have touched him,
his head anointed by the Powers
and their press?

but no matter . . .
a *man* is allowed his weak moments
and other christs always seem to rise up
to take their place.
many hundred did that day.

III

There's only one last thing i remember.
i remember the man,
trembling in anger and rage
over the children seen under hooves,
the women standing, cowering under whips,
the men breaking and running in humiliation.

The man screamed for a march
on the courthouse — right then,
NOW, he said,
LET'S SHOW THEM WE'RE NOT AFRAID
LET'S ALL GO
LET'S ALL MARCH ON THE COURTHOUSE.

And the first to reach his side
and quiet him
was not the sheriff
or the posse,
but a Man of the Word.

“That’s not the Way
my son,
we’ve got to be disciplined, now.
Our leaders will tell us when to go.”

Quietly,
he turned to that Man of God
and said, “I’m gonna get my gun”
and disappeared into the crowd.

Maria Varela, 1965

11

"Set afire by the cry of / BLACK POWER"

THE BIRTH AND LEGACY OF THE BLACK PANTHER PARTY

Huey P. Newton and Bobby Seale founded the Black Panther Party for Self-Defense on 15 October 1966 in Oakland, California, in response to hostile, abusive practices by local police. The two men developed a ten-point platform for the Panthers. By now those ten points have been widely read and critiqued, but a summary of them bears repeating. They essentially boil down to what Newton and Seale agreed to in their tenth point: the desire for land, bread, housing, education, clothing, justice, and peace for the black community (Seale 61). They would go on to set up free breakfast programs and liberation schools for children and health clinics for the black community. The two men, citing the Second Amendment, advocated armed self-defense to help achieve their goals. This proved to be a highly controversial decision, especially with respect to local and eventually federal law officials. In less than three years J. Edgar Hoover, director of the

FBI, would deem the Panthers America's greatest internal security risk, presumably due to the guns they carried.

Newton was arrested in 1967 for allegedly murdering Oakland Patrolman John Frey. He spent nearly three years in prison before being released as a result of a legal technicality. During his incarceration "Free Huey" became the rallying cry for Panthers and those who sympathized with their cause.

On 20 May 1969 a Black Panther recruit and suspected FBI informant named Alex Rackley was tortured and murdered near New Haven, Connecticut. The crime occurred during a period of intense COINTELPRO operations against the Party, many of which led to paranoia among the ranks of Black Panthers. Several leaders suspected that government informants had infiltrated the Party, and efforts were taken to identify and expel those individuals. Rackley's case became one of the most controversial in the history of the organization. Three Panthers were eventually arrested for direct involvement in Rackley's murder, but Bobby Seale, Ericka Huggins, and others were also arrested for possible involvement or conspiracy in the murder.

As the trials of Seale and Huggins approached in New Haven the following year, approximately fifteen thousand Yale students, community members, writers, and activists from across the country, including the beat poet Allen Ginsberg, gathered for a May Day rally for the Panthers on Yale's campus. Ginsberg read "May King's Prophecy" at the rally, a poem written specifically for the occasion (P. Bass and Rae, "The Panther and the Bulldog").

Months after Rackley's death Chicago police officers raided an apartment occupied by several Panthers well before daybreak on 4 December 1969. Fred Hampton and Mark Clark were shot to death in their sleep. In all, the officers fired between eighty-two and two hundred rounds of ammunition into the apartment as part of an ongoing nationwide campaign against the Panthers and other militant black organizations (Zinn 463).

Angela Davis was also arrested in 1970 on charges of murder, as well as kidnapping and conspiracy. Davis was thought to have supplied the weapons used in a courtroom kidnapping. Jonathon Jackson, the younger brother of the prisoner and author George Jackson, attempted to take hostages in Marin County, California, on 7 August 1970, in exchange for the release of his brother and other prisoners. George published *Soledad*

Brother in 1970 and was killed the following year in an alleged escape attempt from Soledad Prison. (Melvin Newton, Huey's older brother, wrote "We Called Him the General" in his honor.) The weapons used by Jonathon Jackson, who was killed outside the courthouse, would later be traced to Davis, who had registered the weapons after purchasing them for protection. Davis eluded capture until October 1970, when she was arrested and placed in jail for approximately a year and a half before her trial began. In the meantime she became a cause célèbre among American and international activists. "Free Angela" campaigns, similar to those for Huey Newton, were mobilized. Davis was freed two years later when a jury acquitted her of all charges.

The Black Panther Party and poetry are not usually uttered in the same breath, but the relationship between the Panthers, their sympathizers, and poetry is substantive. Huey Newton himself wrote poetry and published with Ericka Huggins a nearly forgotten slim volume titled *Insights and Poems* with City Lights Books in 1975. Selflessness and sacrifice for the sake of black liberation are the subjects of their respective poems in this collection. "By surrendering my life to the revolution / I found eternal life" Newton writes in "Revolutionary Suicide" (lines 7–8). Huggins cautions, "Let the fault be with the woman / who places emphasis on comfort of the body / rather than on stability of the mind" (3–5).

In addition to Newton and Huggins, other members of the Black Panther Party wrote poetry, including Kathleen Cleaver, who served as the Party's communications secretary and was the first woman to join the Party's Central Committee, the primary decision-making body of the organization. Cleaver's "The Black Mass Needs but One Crucifixion" ties the need for firearms to the struggle to free Huey Newton after his arrest in 1967.

On 6 April, less than a month after Cleaver's poem appeared, Eldridge Cleaver, her husband and the former minister of information for the Panthers, was involved in a shootout with Oakland police, for which he was arrested. After his release on bail Cleaver fled the country; he stayed away for nearly a decade, living at different times in Cuba, Algeria, North Korea, and Paris. Meanwhile his collection of essays, *Soul on Ice*, published in 1968, increased his international reputation as a radical black liberation leader. His stature as well as his problems with the legal system inspired Craig Randolph Pyes and Adrienne Rich to invoke him in their respective poems.

Denise Levertov and Haki Madhubuti recall the Chicago raid that left Hampton and Clark dead. "Hampton was murdered in his bed" as Denise Levertov writes in "The Day the Audience Walked Out on Me, and Why" (14). In "One-Sided Shoot-Out" Madhubuti seeks answers to troubling questions about the officers' ability to locate and penetrate the apartment with ease, raising the possibility of an informant's assistance.

Michael S. Harper's "Newsletter from My Mother" chronicles a similar raid against the Panthers in California just four days after the murders of Hampton and Clark in Chicago. More than 140 law enforcement officers invaded the group's Los Angeles headquarters, presumably in an attempt to capture Geronimo Pratt, a Vietnam veteran who had risen up the ranks of the local Party. The officers, who were operating from information supplied by the infiltrator Melvin "Cotton" Smith, and Panthers engaged in a four-hour gun battle that resulted in thirteen arrests but no deaths (Churchill and Wall 82). Pratt would later receive international attention for his arrest on murder charges in 1970 that were eventually overturned, but not before he had served twenty-seven years in prison.

The Black Mass Needs but One Crucifixion

Malcolm X died for us

We will have no more religious executions
    no more political assassinations
    no more murdering of black men
        in the streets of Babylon

The black mass needs but one crucifixion

And in that death

On the cross of America

We all received a new birth

For in us awoke a new life

    Set afire by the cry of

        BLACK POWER

That burned in Watts, that burned in Newark, that
burned in Detroit

And that burns in Huey's soul

Brought alive by Malcolm, brought awake by Stokely,
we will be brought to motion by Huey P. Newton

Move to defend ourselves against the massive onslaught

Of cracker killers who hate and fear us

Of coward white men with lynch mobs after us

Ritualizing their insanity and inhumanity

with castration and death by fire

By police squad

By unemployment and starvation

By white-only torture

In the black streets of stench and filth and mire

Up against a wall of fear and hatred and bloodshed

Chained to our blackness like slaves on
a plantation

Although we are supposedly free

To go to school and give birth and get married and
drive Cadillacs

But the pain involved and the struggle required

Just to live in this madness for one more day

Is more than a man can say

He must just pick up the gun

Refuse to run

Stand on his feet

And act like a man

Demand that he be free

By any means necessary, demand that he be free

And take his freedom by any means necessary

If death in the gas chamber stares him in the face

Malcolm told us that he would be killed

And when he died his words came true

Huey told us to defend our lives

To stop this tide of genocide

The gas chamber will not be his fate

By any means necessary

HUEY P. NEWTON MUST BE SET FREE!

The black mass needs but one
crucifixion.

Kathleen Cleaver, 1968

:::::

apology

(to the panthers)

i became a woman
during the old prayers
among the ones who wore
bleaching cream to bed
and all my lessons stayed

i was obedient
but brothers i thank you
for these mannish days

i remember again the wise one
old and telling of suicides
refusing to be slaves

i had forgotten and
brothers i thank you

i praise you
i grieve my whiteful ways

Lucille Clifton, 1972

:::::

Revolutionary Letter #20

(for Huey Newton)

I will not rest
till men walk free & fearless on the earth
each doing in the manner of his blood
& tribe, peaceful in the free air

till all can seek, unhindered
the shape of their thought
no black cloud fear or guilt
between them & the sun, no babies burning
young men locked away, no paper world
to come between flesh & flesh in human
encounter

till the young women
come into their own, honored & fearless
birthing strong sons
loving & dancing

till the young men can at last
lose some of their sternness, return
to young men's thoughts, till laughter
bounces off our hills & fills
our plains

Diane di Prima, 1971

For Angela

1.

When you were
A baby in diapers
Or even before you made
Your first yelp into life
Our own black Richard had
Penned "The God that failed."
Even if you didn't
Listen to his voice
Or those of others
Yours was the right to move
To the drumming of
Your own beating heart.

2.

Yes, some stoked
Their paths in fire,
Others in blood—
In Watts, in Howe,
In Detroit
And in Newark.
Remember the "Algiers" dead?
Some knew
The whip of Bull Connors,
The dogs and the hose.
In Birmingham we still
Remember the children.
Huey Newton and Cleaver
Fred Hampton and Clark
Martin and Malcolm
Evers and the
Mississippi three.
The line is long
And painful.
The line is endless.

Must we go on
To sanctify a point?

3.
So we evolve.
Each step, each
Link to link.
We evolve.
Some move to
Individual tunes,
Others to a whole
Orchestra playing.
Whatever your music, Angela
We embrace. We condone
And we evolve.

Zack Gilbert, 1971

:::::

May King's Prophecy

Spring green buddings, white blossom-
ing trees, Mayday picnic
        O Maypole Kings O Krishnaic Spring-
        time
O holy Yale Panther Pacifist Conscious
        populace awake alert sensitive tender
children's bodies—and a ring of
        quiet Armies round the town—
planet students cooking brown rice
        for scared multitudes—
Oh Souls all springtime prays your
        bodies

quietly pass mantric peace Fest
    grass freedom thru our nation
    thru your holy voices' prayers
your bodies here so tender & so
    wounded with Fear
Metal gas fear, the same fear
    Whales tremble war conscious-
    Ness
Smog City—Riot court paranoia—
    Judges, tremble, Armies weep
    your fear—
O President guard thy sanity
Attorneys General & Courts obey
    the Law
and end your violent War Assemblage
O Legislatures pass your Creeds of
    Order
& end by proper law illegal war!
Now man sits Acme Conscious over
    his gas machine covered Planet—
Springtime's on, for all your sacred
    & Satanic Magic!
Ponds gleam heaven, Black voices
    chant their ecstasy on car radio
Oh who has heard the scream of death
    in Jail?
Who has heard the quiet Om under
    Wheel-whine and drumbeat
outside railyards on wire tower'd
    outroads from New Haven?

Allen Ginsberg, May 1, 1970

Black Power

For all the Beautiful Black Panthers East

But the whole thing is a miracle — See?

We were just standing there
talking — not touching or smoking
Pot
When this cop told
Tyrone
Move along buddy — take your whores
outta here

And this tremendous growl
From out of nowhere
Pounced on him

Nobody to this very day
Can explain
How it happened

And none of the zoos or circuses
Within fifty miles
Had reported
A panther
Missing

Nikki Giovanni, 1968

Newsletter from My Mother:
8:30 a.m., December 8, 1969

for Katherine Johnson Harper

"1100 Exposition
4115 South Central
and some place on 55th Street
were all subject to a siege
at 5:30 this morning.
The police arrived with search warrants.

"At the present time
1100 Exposition
and the house on 55th Street
have fallen.

"4115 South Central
is still resisting;
they have sandbagged
the place and are wearing
bullet-proof vests,
tear gas masks;

"the whole area is cordoned off,
Wadsworth School is closed;
the police are clearing a hotel
next door to get a better vantage.

"The police deny this is part
of a nationwide program to wipe
out the Panther Party;
one of the fellows here at work,
who lives in the area,
says that they were clearing the streets
last night, arresting people
on any pretext,
and that the jails are full.

"(I have to wait until my boss
starts her class in the conference
room so I can turn on the radio
and get the latest news.)

"10 A.M.
The Panthers are surrendering
1 at a time."

Michael S. Harper, 1971

:::::

[let the fault be with the man]

let the fault be with the man
whose desires overwhelm his humanness

let the fault be with the woman
who places emphasis on comfort of the body
rather than on stability of the mind

let the fault be with those who judge one's
                                        character
by one's ability to be "polite"

let the fault be with those who fear the nature of
development
rather than those whose development is natural,
                                                open, real.

if we are revolutionaries, then what is correct
must be that which provides for our survival.

if we should struggle
then let it be for real reasons / not for
                                        reasons derived
from fear.

we can only for so long as we live
remain the people that we are — fighting,
living, dying,

in the long run it will be those whose
character is steadfast who will make us win.

let the fault be then with the man or woman
whose views create our failure.

Ericka Huggins, 1972

:::::

The Day the Audience Walked Out on Me, and Why

(May 8th, 1970, Goucher College, Maryland)

Like this it happened:
after the antiphonal reading from the psalms
and the dance of lamentation before the altar,
and the two poems, "Life at War" and "What Were They Like,"
I began my rap,
and said:

Yes, it is well that we have gathered
in this chapel to remember
the students shot at Kent State,

but let us be sure we know
our gathering is a mockery unless
we remember also
the black students shot at Orangeburg two years ago,
and Fred Hampton murdered in his bed
by the police only months ago.

And while I spoke the people
— girls, older women, a few men —

began to rise and turn
their backs to the altar and leave.

And I went on and said,
Yes, it is well that we remember
all of these, but let us be sure
we know it is hypocrisy
to think of them unless
we make our actions their memorial,
actions of militant resistance.

By then the pews were almost empty
and I returned to my seat and a man stood up
in the back of the quiet chapel
(near the wide-open doors through which
the green of May showed, and the long shadows
of late afternoon)
and said my words
desecrated a holy place.

And a few days later
when some more students (black) were shot
at Jackson, Mississippi,
no one desecrated the white folks' chapel,
because no memorial was held.

Denise Levertov, 1971

:::::

One Sided Shoot-out

(for brothers fred hampton & mark clark, murdered 12/4/69
by chicago police at 4:30 a.m. while they slept)

only a few will really understand:
it won't be yr / mommas or yr / brothers & sisters or even me,

we all think that we do   but we don't.
it's not *new*   and
under all the rhetoric the seriousness is still not serious.
the national rap deliberately continues, "wipe them niggers
    out."
(no talk do it, no talk do it, no talk do it, notalk notalk notalk
    do it)

& we.
running circleround getting caught in our own cobwebs,
in the same old clothes, same old words, just new adjectives.
we will order new buttons & posters with: "remember fred"
    & "rite-on mark."
& yr / pictures will be beautiful & manly with the deeplook /
    the accusing look
to remind us
to remind us that suicide is not black.

the questions will be asked & the answers will be the new
    clichés.
but maybe,
just maybe we'll finally realize that "revolution" to the real-
  world
is international 24hours a day and that 4:30 AM is like
    12:00 noon,
it's just darker.
but the evil can be seen if u look in the right direction.
were the street lights out?
did they darken their faces in combat?
did they remove their shoes to *creep* softer?
could u not see the whi-te of their eyes,
the whi-te of their deathfaces?
didn't yr / look-out man see them coming,   coming,   coming?
or did they turn into ghostdust and join the night's fog?

it was mean.
& we continue to call them "pigs" and "muthafuckas"
    forgetting what all

black children learn very early: "sticks & stones may break
my bones but names can
never hurt me."
it was murder.
& we meet to hear the speeches / the same, the duplicators.
they say that which is expected of them.
to be instructive or constructive is to be unpopular (like: the
leaders only
sleep when there is a watchingeye)
but they say the right things at the right time, it's like a
stageshow:
only the entertainers have changed.
we remember bobby hutton. the same, the duplicators.

the seeing eye should always see.
the night doesn't stop the stars
& our enemies scope the ways of blackness in three bad
shifts a day.
in the AM their music becomes deadlier.
this is a game of dirt.

only blackpeople play it fair.

Haki Madhubuti (Don L. Lee), 1969

:::::

Revolutionary Suicide

By having no family
I inherited the family of humanity.
By having no possessions
I have possessed all.
By rejecting the love of one
I received the love of all.

By surrendering my life to the revolution
I found eternal life.
Revolutionary Suicide.

Huey P. Newton, 1975

:::::

We Called Him the General

The sky is blue,
Today is clear and sunny.

The house that George once
lived in headed for the
grave,
While the Panthers spoke
of the spirit.
I saw a man move catlike
across the rooftops,
Glide along the horizons,
Casting no shadow,
only chains into the sea,
using his calloused hands
and broken feet to
smash and kick down
barriers.
The angels say his name
is George Lester Jackson—

El General.

All the people went home to
their hovels,
He to the world of gods,

heroes, tall men, giants.
He went like the rushing
wind, the rolling tide;
The thunder's roar,
The lightning's flash;
Smashing all challengers·
and devils in his path,
While caressing the leaves,
sand and sky.

Melvin Newton, 1973

:::::

The Panther / After Rilke

> *Sein Blick ist vom*
> *Vorübergehn der Stabe*
> *so müd geworden, dass*
> *er nichts mehr halt.*
> RILKE

> A slave who dies of
> natural causes cannot
> balance two dead flies
> in the Scales of Eternity.
> ELDRIDGE CLEAVER

This is not a solid wall
the iron ribs
          are only half as much
as the spaces in between them
                                        pacing
stopping occasionally to put his hand
through the bars
extending his reach
to the next set of bars

his fingertips leave messages
on the cold iron
bars
his body backs up against the wall
and in a black radius
circles
the
cell again.
Each revolution is a sign of strength
inking the perimeters of endurance
with bloody history

captivity is drained from the body
his ribs are momentarily resilient
causing him to flex, he takes
a free

breath
and feels the bars become rigid in his chest.

Craig Randolph Pyes, 1969

:::::

From "Ghazals: Homage to Ghalib"

A dead mosquito, flattened against a door;
his image could survive our comings and our goings.

LeRoi! Eldridge! listen to us, we are ghosts
condemned to haunt the cities where you want to be at home.

The white children turn black on the negative.
The summer clouds blacken inside the camera-skull.

Every mistake that can be made, we are prepared to make;
anything less would fall short of the reality we're dreaming.

Someone has always been desperate, now it's our turn—
we who were free to weep for Othello and laugh at Caliban.

I have learned to smell a *conservateur* a mile away:
they carry illustrated catalogues of all that there is to lose.

Adrienne Rich, 1968

12

"America, self-destructive, self-betrayed"

THE ASSASSINATION OF MARTIN LUTHER KING JR., 4 APRIL 1968

Dr. King's participation in the civil rights movement began in 1955, when at the age of twenty-six he was chosen to lead the Montgomery Bus Boycott. The eloquent young minister would later encounter personal threats and attacks, including the bombing of his home, from terrorist-minded organizations that were threatened by his popularity, nonviolent protests, and calls for integration. King's far-reaching appeal was also viewed as a threat by his own government. Through wiretaps and surveillance the FBI monitored many of King's activities as if he were plotting a violent overthrow of the country's leadership. It is also no exaggeration to claim that J. Edgar Hoover, the director of the agency, did not care if King lived or died. For instance, there were occasions when Hoover, who once referred to King in private as a "burrhead," had reason to suspect that gunmen were plotting to kill King but ordered agents not to share the information with the civil rights leader and to provide no protection for him (Branch, *Canaan's Edge* 63). In spite of it all, King's efforts and successful marches, boycotts, and protests placed him at the forefront of America's struggle to overcome centuries-old racial disparities and eventually earned him international acclaim, including the Nobel Peace Prize in 1964.

King was assassinated on 4 April 1968. On the evening of his murder more than a hundred cities across America experienced racial upheaval. His death, reportedly at the hands of a white gunman, James Earl Ray, led to a rash of fatal racial confrontations. Federal troops had to be activated in Washington, D.C., Baltimore, and Chicago, where death and injury tolls were the highest in the country. Eleven people were killed and 1,113 injured in D.C., while six were killed and nine hundred wounded in Baltimore. In Chicago nine people died and five hundred suffered injuries (Berry 179).

In "Amos, 1963," Margaret Walker describes King as a leader "Preaching social justice to the Southland / Preaching to the poor a new gospel of love" (3–4). These lines, written after the historic March on Washington for Jobs and Freedom (28 August 1963), during which King delivered his "I Have a Dream" speech, capture the essence of King's life and legacy. He was a minister committed to nonviolent social transformation for the purpose of improving the lives of the downtrodden and oppressed. His "new gospel of love" was informed by the philosophy of Mahatma Gandhi and the tradition of prophetic religious teachings which encouraged him to not only preach but to put his ideologies to work in real-world situations. For King, this largely meant addressing the issues of racism, segregation, and the relegation of African Americans to second-class citizenship in the United States, particularly in the Southland, as Walker terms it.

While Walker's "Amos, 1963" is set during King's lifetime, most of the poems that honor him were written after his death and are retrospective in tone, though no less laudatory. In fact many of the poems were written on or soon after 4 April 1968. Naturally there is a sense of immediacy in several of the poems, many of them containing emotions that overtook some Americans as well as individuals abroad. The poems gathered here reflect the frustration, resignation, and reverence undoubtedly experienced by millions worldwide upon hearing the news of King's death.

Indignation and anger are clearly evident in poems by Nikki Giovanni, Ebon Dooley, Donald L. Graham, and Harry Edwards. "What can I, a poor Black woman, do to destroy America?" Nikki Giovanni asks in the opening line of "Reflections on April 4, 1968," a wide-ranging poem that reads at times like random or disjointed thoughts jotted down in a personal journal. The poem's cohesive tissue is the combination of the poet's fury, specifically directed at white racists, and her quest for guidance and answers in a post-King America. The poem seeks violent retaliation, calls for a Black Revolution, suggests police or government complicity in King's murder, and closes with a variation on a traditional Christian hymn. The poem also insists, "God will not love us unless we share with others our / suffering," clearly expressing a philosophical shift that had been in the works for years in the black community, from nonviolent protest to self-defense and physical retribution (lines 53–54).

Further evidence of this shift can be found in Ebon Dooley's "A Poem to My Brothers Killed in Combat or Something about a Conversation with My Father after Rev. King Was Killed." Dooley's poem first appeared in *Negro Digest* in February 1969. In the poem the father's voice is enraged and wary: "They want to kill us all, son / they want to kill us all!" (21–22).

The major themes expressed by Giovanni and Dooley are echoed in Donald L. Graham's "April 5th." The poem begins on a somber note and later recalls the tragic bombing of the Sixteenth Street Baptist Church of Birmingham (1963) and the murders of Malcolm X (1965), Medgar Evers (1963), and Emmett Till (1955). Like Giovanni's "Reflections on April 4, 1968," Graham's "April 5th" concludes with an appeal to Christ. Graham revisits and rephrases an utterance Christ makes on the cross in the Book of Luke, but whereas Christ calls for forgiveness, "April 5th" pleads for vengeance.

Vengeance also serves as the impetus for "How to Change the U.S.A." by Harry Edwards. Missing entirely from Edwards's poem is the sentiment of nonviolent protest and social change that Dr. King and others popularized and used to great effect. Violent retribution is the focal point of the poem. The narrator calls on the federal government and local police officers ("pigs in blue") to send a message to the racist "crackers" who murdered King and others by dismembering them with dull axes at midday on national television "as a gesture / of good faith" (23–24). While

Edwards's intentionally hyperbolic poem comes across as a revenge fantasy more than a call to action, it does give voice to those frustrated by acts of violence aimed at innocent Americans and the slow pace of social change.

Not every poem written after King's assassination seeks retributive justice. Several poets, including Robert Lowell and Robert Mezey, express grief, denial, or reverence in their elegies. Haki Madhubuti's "Assassination" and Victor Manuel Rivera Toledo's "Black Thursday" incorporate vivid and memorable imagery of the murder as a way of processing the magnitude of the tragedy.

The Chicago-based poet Gwendolyn Brooks composed a three-part meditation on the outbreak of violence in her city after King's assassination. "Riot" details an imaginary uprising of blacks against European culture, as represented by the English explorer John Cabot in part 1. The middle section addresses, in part, the riot in 1968 with direct and symbolic phrasings, while part 3 suggests the need for strengthening the spirit and determination of the black community in the wake of King's death and the subsequent riots.

Lucille Clifton's "the meeting after the savior gone" addresses how the country, especially the black community, should proceed in the absence of King's leadership. A meeting is convened, and amid an overwhelming sense of resignation everyone agrees that self-preservation (as well as the notion of being one's own savior) is the best way forward.

•

Martin Luther King, Jr.

A man went forth with gifts.

He was a prose poem.
He was a tragic grace.
He was a warm music.

He tried to heal the vivid volcanoes
His ashes are
    reading the world.
His Dream still wishes to anoint
    The barricades of faith and control.

His word still burns the center of the sun,
    Above the thousands and the
    Hundred thousands.

The word was Justice. It was spoken.

So it shall be spoken.
So it shall be done.

Gwendolyn Brooks, 1968

:::::

Riot

> Riot
> *A riot is the language of the unheard.*
> —MARTIN LUTHER KING

John Cabot, out of Wilma, once a Wycliffe,
all whitebluerose below his golden hair,
wrapped richly in right linen and right wool,

almost forgot his Jaguar and Lake Bluff;
almost forgot Grandtully (which is The
Best Thing That Ever Happened To Scotch); almost
forgot the sculpture at the Richard Gray
and Distelheim; the kidney pie at Maxim's,
the Grenadine de Boeuf at Maison Henri.

Because the Negroes were coming down the street.

Because the Poor were sweaty and unpretty
(not like Two Dainty Negroes in Winnetka)
and they were coming toward him in rough ranks.
In seas. In windsweep. They were black and loud.
And not detainable. And not discreet.

Gross. Gross. *"Que tu es grossier!"* John Cabot
itched instantly beneath the nourished white
that told his story of glory to the World.
"Don't let It touch me! the blackness! Lord!" he whispered
to any handy angel in the sky.

But in a thrilling announcement, on It drove
and breathed on him: and touched him. In that breath
the fume of pig foot, chitterling and cheap chili,
malign, mocked John. And, in terrific touch, old
averted doubt jerked forward decently,
cried "Cabot! John! You are a desperate man,
and the desperate die expensively today."

John Cabot went down in the smoke and fire
and broken glass and blood, and he cried "Lord!
Forgive these nigguhs that know not what they do."

The Third Sermon on the Warpland

Phoenix

"In Egyptian mythology, a bird which lived for
five hundred years

and
then consumed itself in fire, rising renewed from
the ashes."—
Webster

The earth is a beautiful place.
Watermirrors and things to be reflected.
Goldenrod across the little lagoon.

The Black Philosopher says
"Our chains are in the keep of the Keeper
in a labeled cabinet
on the second shelf by the cookies,
sonatas, the arabesques . . .
There's a rattle sometimes.
You do not hear it who mind only
cookies and crunch them.
You do not hear the remarkable music—'A
Death Song For You Before You Die.'
If you could hear it
you would make music too.
The *black*blues."

West Madison Street.
In "Jessie's Kitchen"
nobody's eating Jessie's Perfect Food.
Crazy flowers
cry up across the sky, spreading
and hissing *This is*
it

The young men run.

They will not steal Bing Crosby but will steal
Melvin Van Peebles who made Lillie
a thing of Zampoughi a thing of red wiggles and trebles
(and I know there are twenty wire stalks sticking out of her head
as her underfed haunches jerk jazz).

A clean riot is not one in which little rioters
long-stomped, long-straddled, BEANLESS
but knowing no Why
go steal in hell
a radio, sit to hear James Brown
and Mingus, Young-Holt, Coleman, John, on V.O.N.
and sun themselves in Sin.
However, what
is going on
is going on.

Fire.
That is their way of lighting candles in the darkness.
A White Philosopher said
"It is better to light one candle than curse the darkness."
These candles curse—
inverting the deeps of the darkness.

GUARD HERE, GUNS LOADED.
The young men run.
The children in ritual chatter
scatter upon
their Own and old geography.

The Law comes sirening across the town.

A woman is dead.
Motherwoman.
She lies among the boxes
(that held the haughty hats, the Polish sausages)
In newish, thorough, firm virginity
As rich as fudge is if you've had five pieces.
Not again shall she
partake of steak
on Christmas mornings, nor of nighttime
chicken and wine at Val Gray Ward's
nor say
of Mr. Beetley, Exit Jones, Junk Smith

nor neat New-baby Williams (man-to-many)
"He treat me right."

That was a gut gal.

"We'll do an us!" yells Yancey, a twittering twelve.
"Instead of your deathintheafternoon,
kill 'em, bull!
kill 'em, bull!

The Black Philosopher blares
"I tell you, *exhaust*ive black integrity
would assure a blackless America. . . ."

Nine die, Sun-Times will tell
and will tell too
in small black-bordered oblongs "Rumor? check it
at 744–4111."

A Poem to Peanut.
"Coooooool!" purrs Peanut. Peanut is
Richard—a Ranger and a gentleman.
A Signature. A Herald. And a Span.
This Peanut will not let his men explode.
And Rico will not.
Neither will Sengali.
Nor Bop nor Jeff, Geronimo nor Lover.
These merely peer and purr,
and pass the Passion over.
The Disciples stir
And thousandfold confer
with ranging Rangermen;
mutual in their "Yeah!—
this AIN'T all upinheah!"

"But WHY do These People offend *themselves?*" say they
who say also "It's time.
It's time to help
These People."

Lies are told and legends made.
Phoenix rises unafraid.

The Black Philosopher will remember:
"There they came to life and exulted,
the hurt mute.
Then it was over.

The dust, as they say, settled."

An Aspect of Love, Alive in the Ice and Fire

Labohem Brown

In a package of minutes there is this We.
How beautiful.
Merry foreigners in our morning,
we laugh, we touch each other,
are responsible props and posts.

A Physical light is in the room.

Because the world is at the window
we cannot wander very long.

You rise. Although
genial, you are in yourself again.
I observe
your direct and respectable stride.
You are direct and self-accepting as a lion
in African velvet. You are level, lean, remote.

There is a moment in Camaraderie
when interruption is not to be understood.
I cannot bear an interruption.
This is the shining joy;
the time of not-to-end.

On the street we smile.
We go

in different directions
down the imperturbable street

Gwendolyn Brooks, 1969

:::::

the meeting after the savior gone

4/4/68

what we decided is
you save your own self.
everybody so quiet.
not so much sorry as
resigned.
we was going to try and save you but
now i guess you got to save yourselves
(even if you don't know
    who you are
    where you been
    where you headed)

Lucille Clifton, 1968

:::::

A Poem to My Brothers Killed in Combat or Something about a Conversation with My Father after Rev. King Was Killed

I

I cannot cry this time . . .
he said

and I nodded to agree.

I wept for Malcolm . . .
and wanted to kill
somebody
when Carrie's boy was shot.
(he was fifteen to be this spring)

and now you come
and tell me
King is dead.

head smashed
against the floor
and Love destroyed
by some murdering cracker's craze.

I refuse to cry!
and a single life
seems too small
a revenge to take . . .

and I nodded to agree.

II
they want to kill us all, son
they want to kill us all!

they're shooting us down
every day
in alleyways
and podiums
and cold grey balconies
in the South . . .

they're trying to kill us all!

III
King should be the last one!

the last hero.
the last martyr

poster / plastered against billboards and store-fronts
reminding us . . .

King should be the last one!

there should be
no more funerals
no more dirges
no more flowers
and tear-stained grave sites . . .

King should be the last one!

THEY should die!
not one at a time,
but in masses,
in churches,
in bleeding El trains
in the night,
they should die . . .

King will be the last one!

and I nodded to agree . . .

Ebon Dooley, 1968

:::::

How to Change the U.S.A.

For openers, the Federal government
  the honkies, the pigs in blue
must go down South
  and take those crackers out of bed,
the crackers who blew up
  those four little girls
in that Birmingham Church,

those crackers who murdered
Emmett Till, Jimmie Lee Jackson,
Medgar Evers, Viola Liuzzo and
the three Civil Rights workers,
those crackers who beat
Reverend Reeb to death and
Shot Martin Luther King—
they must pull them out of bed
and kill them with axes
in the middle of the street.
Chop them up with dull axes.
Slowly. One at a time.
At high noon
with everybody watching
on television, in color.
Just as a gesture
of good faith.

Harry Edwards, 1968

:::::

Reflections on April 4, 1968

What can I, a poor Black woman, do to destroy America? This is a question, with appropriate variations, being asked in every Black heart. There is one answer—I can kill. There is one compromise—I can protect those who kill. There is one cop-out—I can encourage others to kill. There are no other ways.

The assassination of Martin Luther King is an act of war. President johnson, your friendly uncandidate, has declared war on Black people. He is not making any distinction between us and negroes. The question—does it have rhythm? The answer—yes. The response—kill it. They have been known to shoot at the wind and violate the earth's gravity for these very reasons.

Obviously the first step toward peace is the removal of at least two fingers, and most probably three, from both hands of all white people. Fingers that are not controlled must be removed. This is the first step toward a true and lasting peace. We would also suggest blinding or the removal of at least two eyes from one of the heads of all albino freaks.

And some honkie asked about the reaction? What do you people want? Isn't it enough that you killed him? You want to tell me how to mourn? You want to determine and qualify how I, a lover, should respond to the death of my beloved?

May he rest in peace. May his blood choke the life from ten hundred million whites. May the warriors in the streets go ever forth into the stores for guns and tv's, for whatever makes them happy (for only a happy people make successful Revolution) and this day begin the Black Revolution.

How can one hundred and fifty policemen allow a man to be shot? Police were seen coming from the direction of the shots. And there was no conspiracy? Just as there was no violent reaction to his death. And no city official regretted his death but only that it occurred in Memphis. We heard similar statements from Dallas—this country has too many large Southern cities.

Do not be fooled, Black people. Johnson's footprints are the footprints of death. He came in on a death, he is presiding over a death and his own death should take him out. Let us pray for the whole state of Christ's church.

Zeus has wrestled the Black Madonna and he is down for the count. Intonations to nadinolia gods and a slain honkie will not overcome. Let america's baptism be the fire this time. Any comic book can tell you if you fill a room with combustible materials then close it up tight it will catch fire.

This is a thirsty fire they have created. It will not be squelched until it destroys them. Such is the nature of revolution.

America has called itself the promised land—and themselves God's chosen people. This is where we come in, Black people. God's chosen people have always had to suffer—to endure—to overcome. We have suffered and america has been rewarded. This is a foul equation. We must now seek our reward. God will not love us unless we share with others our suffering. Precious Lord—Take Our Hands—Lead Us On.

Nikki Giovanni, 1968

:::::

April 5th

non-violence is dead
it died last night
last night in color
i saw
Nbc tell me i saw
Abc tell me
the leader has fallen
pale newsmen cried
it seemed last night

Last night i thought
a lamb has fallen as
i heard him cry
aint gonna let no in
junction turn me round
aint gonna let no po
lice dogs turn me round
but I saw four little

girls malcolm X medgar evers
emmett till and the soft
touch I had die last night
from the corner
a white man read martin's
dream
but my sister moaned

Lord strike their ass
for they know what
they do.

Donald L. Graham, 1968

:::::

What Color?

> *His skin was black,*
> *but with the purest soul,*
> *white as the snow . . .*
> YEVGENY YEVTUSHENKO, IN A CABLE,
> ON THE ASSASSINATION OF MARTIN LUTHER KING, JR.

Such a white soul, they say,
that noble pastor had.
His skin so black, they say,
his skin so black in color,
was on the inside snow,
a white lily,
fresh milk,
cotton.
Such innocence.
There wasn't one stain
on his impeccable interior.
(In short, a handsome find:

"The Black whose soul was white,"
that curiosity.)

Still it might be said another way:
What a powerful black soul
that gentlest of pastors had.
What proud black passion
burned in his open heart.
What pure black thoughts
were nourished in his fertile brain.
What black love,
so colorlessly
given.

And why not,
why couldn't that heroic pastor
have a soul that's black?

A soul as black as coal.

Nicolás Guillén, ca. 1968

:::::

Words in the Mourning Time

I
For King, for Robert Kennedy,
destroyed by those they could not save,
for King for Kennedy I mourn.
And for America, self-destructive, self-betrayed.

I grieve. Yet know the vanity
of grief—through power of
The Blessed Exile's
Transilluminating word

aware of how these deaths, how all
the agonies of our deathbed childbed age
are process, major means whereby,
oh dreadfully, our humanness must be achieved.

II

Killing people to save, to free them?
With napalm lighting routes to the future?

III

He comes to my table in his hungry wounds
and his hunger. The flamed-out eyes,
their sockets dripping. The nightmare mouth.

He snatches food from my plate, raw
fingers bleeding, seizes my glass
and drinks, leaving flesh-fragments on its rim.

IV

Vietnam   bloodclotted name in my consciousness
Recurring and recurring
like the obsessive thought many midnights
now of my own dying

Vietnam   and I think of the villages
mistakenly burning   the schoolrooms devouring
their children   and I think of those who
were my students
                    brutalized   killing
wasted by horror
in ultimate loneliness
dying
            Vietnam Vietnam

V

Oh, what a world we make,
oppressor and oppressed.

Our world—
this violent ghetto, slum
of the spirit raging against itself.

We hate kill destroy
in the name of human good
our killing and our hate destroy.

VI

Lord Riot
        Naked
                In the flaming clothes
Cannibal ruler
               of anger's
                        carousals
      sing hey nonny no
terror
      his tribute
                  shriek of bloody glass
his praise
            sing wrathful sing vengeful

            sing hey nonny no
gigantic
        and laughing
                      sniper on tower
I hate
      I destroy
                I am I am
       Sing hey nonny no
       Sing burn baby burn

VII

voice in the wilderness

Know that love has chosen you
to live his crucial purposes.
Know that love has chosen you.

And will not pamper you nor spare;
demands obedience to all
the rigorous laws of risk,
does not pamper, will not spare.

Oh, master now love's instruments—
complex and not for the fearful,
simple and not for the foolish.
Master now love's instruments.

I who love you tell you this,
even as the pitiful killer waits for me,
I who love you tell you this.

VIII

Light and the
distortions
of light as
the flame-night
dawns
Zenith-time and the anger
unto death and the
fire-focused
image
of a man
invisible man
and black boy and native
son and the
man who
lives underground whose
name nobody
knows
harrowing havocking
running through
holocaust
seeking the
soul-country of his
meaning

IX

As the gook woman howls
for her boy in the smouldering,
as the expendable Clean-Cut Boys
From Decent American Homes
are slashing off enemy ears for keepsakes;

as the victories are tallied up
with flag-draped coffins, plastic bodybags,
what can I say
but this, this:

We must not be frightened nor cajoled
into accepting evil as deliverance from evil.
We must go on struggling to be human,
though monsters of abstraction
police and threaten us.

Reclaim now, now renew the vision of
a human world where godliness
is possible and man
is neither gook nigger honkey wop nor kike

but man

                    permitted to be man.

X

and all the atoms cry aloud

    I bear Him witness now
Who by the light of suns beyond the suns beyond
    the sun with shrill pen

    revealed renewal of
the covenant of timelessness with time, proclaimed
    advent of splendor joy

alone can comprehend
and the imperious evils of an age could not
withstand and stars

and stones and seas
acclaimed—His life its crystal image and
magnetic field.

I bear Him witness now—
Mystery Whose major clues are the heart of man,
the mystery of God:

Bahá'u'lláh:
Logos, poet, cosmic hero, surgeon, architect
of our hope of peace,

Wronged, Exiled One,
chosen to endure what agonies of knowledge, what
auroral dark

bestowals of truth
vision power anguish for our future's sake.
"I was but a man

"like others, asleep upon
My couch, when, lo, the breezes of the All-Glorious
Were wafted over Me. . . ."

Called, as in dead of night
a dreamer is roused to help the helpless flee
a burning house.

I bear Him witness now:
toward Him our history in its disastrous quest
for meaning is impelled.

Robert Hayden, 1970

Rites of Passage

To M.L.K., Jr.

Now rock the boat to a fare-thee-well.
Once we suffered dreaming
Into the place where the children are playing
Their child's games
Where the children are hoping
Knowledge survives if
Unknowing
They follow the game
Without winning.

Their fathers are dying
Back to the freedom
Of wise children playing
At knowing
Their fathers are dying
Whose deaths will not free them
Of growing from knowledge
Of knowing
When the game becomes foolish
A dangerous pleading
For time out of power.

Quick
Children kiss us
We are growing through dream.

Audre Lorde, 1970

Two Walls

[1968, Martin Luther King's Murder]

Somewhere a white wall faces a white wall,
one wakes the other, the other wakes the first,
each burning with the other's borrowed splendor—
the walls, awake, are forced to go on talking,
their color looks much alike, two shadings of white,
each living in the shadow of the other.
How fine our distinctions when we cannot choose!
Don Giovanni can't stick his sword through stone,
two contracting, white stone walls—their pursuit
of happiness and his, confident. . . .
At this point of civilization, this point of the world,
the only satisfactory companion we
can imagine is death—this morning, skin lumping in my throat,
I lie here, heavily breathing, the soul of New York.

Robert Lowell, 1968

:::::

Assassination

it was wild.
the
bullet hit high.
                    (the throat-neck)
& from everywhere:
          the motel, from under bushes and cars,
          from around corners and across streets,
          out of the garbage cans and from rat holes
          in the earth
they came running.
with

guns
drawn
they came running
toward the King—
                    all of them
                    fast and sure—
as if
the King
was going to fire back.
they came running,
fast and sure,
in the
wrong
direction.

Haki Madhubuti, 1968

:::::

April Fourth

I throw open the door
And someone like the night walks in

A moist wind in the doorway
A breath of flowers
In the wake of the august presence

I was sitting for hours
Watching the coal
Of the cigarette rising and falling
Finally one must do something

The evening I thought
The evening was the last evening
As usual

I was thinking of heroes
Whose knuckles shine as they curl round a rifle
I was thinking of my brother
Who brings me my head in a basket
What is there to do

Let me make myself empty
I can live without sleeping tonight

I can live without dreams of the King
Awash on his balcony
Half of his face and neck in another kingdom

In the morning I will not understand

Mountains surfacing from the mortal darkness
A scum of yellow flowers
The great oak crying with a thousand voices

All that
Wrinkles like heat and disappears into thin air.

Robert Mezey, 1968

:::::

Martin Luther King, Malcolm X

Bleeding of the mountains
the noon bleeding
he is shot through the voice
all things being broken

The moon returning in her blood
looks down   grows white
loses color
and blazes

. . . and the near star gone—

voices of cities
drumming in the moon

bleeding of my right hand
my black voice bleeding

Muriel Rukeyser, 1973

:::::

Elegy for Martin Luther King

(for jazz orchestra)

I

Who said I was stable in my mastery, black under scarlet and gold?
Who said that I, like the master of hammer and maul,
Master of dyoung-dyoung drums and tom-toms, leader of the dance,
Commanded the red Powers with my carved scepter
Better than camel drivers their long-distance dromedaries?
They bend so supplely, and the slow winds and fertile rains fall.
Who said, who said in the century of hate and the atom bomb,
When all power is dust and all force weak, that the Super Powers
Tremble in the night on their deep bomb silos and tombs,
When, at the season's horizon, I peer into the fever of sterile
Tornadoes of civil disorder? But tell me who said it?
Flanked by the orchestra's lead drum, eyes sharp and mouth white
Like the village idiot, I see the vision, I hear the style
And the instrument, but the words like a herd of stumbling buffaloes
Beat against my teeth and my voice opens up the void.
The last chord hushed, and I must begin again at zero,
Learn once again this language so strange and ambiguous,
And confront it with my smooth lance, confront the monster,
This sea-cow lioness, siren serpent in the labyrinth of cliffs.
Along the first chorus, at the first step on the pages of my loins,

I lost my lips, threw up my hands, and I tremble harshly.
And you speak of happiness when I am mourning Martin Luther King!

II

This night, this clear insomnia, I remember one year ago yesterday.
It was the eighth day, the eighth year of our circumcision,
The one-hundred-seventy-ninth year of our stillbirth in St. Louis.
St. Louis, St. Louis! I remember yesterday and the time before,
It was one year ago in the Center's Capital, on the prow
Of the cleaving peninsula, the bitter substance straight ahead.
On the long wide track, and like a victory hung red-gold flags
And the standards of clacking hope, splendid in the sun.
And under the embers of joy, a numberless black people
Celebrated their triumph in the stadiums of the Word,
The regained seat of its ancient presence. It was yesterday
In St. Louis during the Feast among the Lingueres and Signares,
The young women carrying loads, their dresses open on their long
Legs, among the haughty hairstyles and in the burst of teeth.
The mix of laughters and drinks. Suddenly, I remember feeling
A weight on my shoulders, my heart, the whole lead of the past.
I looked around and saw the faded, worn-out dresses
Under the smiling Signares and Lingueres.
I saw laughter stop and teeth become veiled with blue-black lips,
I saw Martin Luther King again, lying with a red rose at his neck.
And I felt in the marrow of my bones, voices and tears set down,
Ha! A blood deposit of four hundred years, four hundred million eyes,
Two hundred million hearts, two hundred million mouths,
Two hundred million useless dead.
Today my people, I feel that April 4, you are vanquished,
Twice dead in Martin Luther King.
Lingueres and Signares, my beautiful giraffes, what good
Are your handkerchiefs, your muslin, your flannels,
Your *fobines*, what good are your songs if not to magnify
MARTIN LUTHER KING, THE KING OF PEACE?
Burn your lantern floats, Signares, and pull off your wigs, Lingueres.
Handmaidens, and you my militant daughters, may you be ashes,
Close and lower your dresses so your ankles don't show.

Noble are women who nourish their people by their polished hands
And rhythmic songs. For you must fear God, but God has already
  struck
Us with his terrifying left hand, Africa harder than the others,
And Senegal harder than Africa. In nineteen hundred sixty-eight!

III

It is the third year, the third wound, as it was in our mother Egypt.
Lord, last year you were never so angry as during the Great Famine
And Martin Luther King was no longer here to sing your wrath
And appease it. In the sky were brief days of ashes, silent grey days
Upon the land. From the Almadies Point to the forts of Fongolimbi
And to the Flaming sea of Mozambique, to Cape Despair,
I say the bush is red and the fields white and the woods
Like bulging matchboxes. Like great waves of nausea, you have raised
Hunger from the depths of memories. See our lips without oil
And full of cracks, under the Harmattan and the marshland swamps.
The sap has run dry at its source, the wells are empty,
Ringing on the lips of buds, the sap has not risen
To sing the pascal joy of spring, but the *swi-mangas*
Weaken on flowers, absent leaves, and deadly bees.
God is an earthquake, a dry tornado roaring in the day of his fury
Like the Ethiopian lion. The volcanos have erupted in Eden,
Across three hundred kilometers, like fireworks celebrating
The festivals of sin and the feast of Seboim in Sodom and Gomorrah,
The volcanos have burned the lakes and plains. And the diseases,
And the herds and men with them, because we didn't come to his aid,
We haven't mourned Martin Luther King.
I say these are not the times of kapos, quartering, barreling, dogs
And quicklime, of crushed peppers and melted lard, the plunder,
Sling, and intrigues, buttocks exposed to the wind and fire,
No longer the bullwhip, powder up the ass, castration,
Amputation or cruxifixion. You are skinned delicately,
Your heart slowly, relentlessly burned.
It is the post-colonial war rotten with bubos, pity abolishes
The code of honor and war where the Super Powers napalm you
Through third parties who are relatives. In the hell of petroleum

There are two-and-a-half million wet corpses and not one satisfying
Flame to consume them all. And Nigeria, wiped off the face of the
Globe like Nigritia for seven times, yes seven times seventy years.
Lord let the voice of Martin Luther King
Fall on Nigeria and on Nigritia.

IV

It was the fourth of April, nineteen hundred and sixty eight,
A spring evening in a grey neighborhood, a district smelling
Of garbage, mud, where children played in the streets in Spring,
And Spring blossomed in the dark countryside where blue murmuring
Streams played, a song of nightingales in the ghetto night of hearts.
Martin Luther King chose then, the motel, the district,
The sanitation workers with the eyes of his heart in those
Spring days, those days of passion wherever the mud of flesh
Would have been glorified in the light of Christ.
It was the evening when light is clearest and air sweetest,
Before evening at the heart's hour, and its flowering of secrets
Mouth to mouth, and organ and rhythms and incense.
On the balcony now haloed in crimson where the air no longer
Is limpid, Martin Luther stands speaking pastor to pastor
"Brother do not forget to praise Christ in his resurrection
And let his name be praised!"
And now opposite him, in a house of prostitution, profanation
And perdition, yes, in the Lorraine Motel—Ah, Lorraine, ah
Joan, the white and blue woman, let our mouths purify you
Like rising incense. In that evil house of tom-cats and pimps
A man stands up, a Remington rifle in his hands.
James Earl Ray sees the Reverend Martin Luther King
Through his telescope, sees the death of Christ. "My brother,
Don't forget to praise Christ in his resurrection this evening."
Sent by Judas, he watches him, for we have made the poor into wolves
Of the poor. He looks through his spy glass, sees only the tender
Neck so black and beautiful. He hates that golden voice modulating
The angel's flutes. The voice of bronze which thunders on terrible
Sodom and on Adama. Martin looks ahead at the house in front, he sees
The skyscrapers of light and glass. He sees curly blond heads, dark

Kinky heads full of dreams like mysterious orchids, and the blue lips
And rose sing in a chorus like a harmonious organ.
The white man looks hard and precise as steel. James Earl aims
And hits the mark, touches Martin who withers like a fragrant flower
And falls. "My brother, sing His name clear, may our bones
Exult in the Resurrection!"

V

As the Reverend's heart evaporated like incense and his soul
Flew like a diaphanous rising dove, I heard behind my left ear
The slow beating of the drum. The voice and its breath close to
My cheek said: "Take up your pen and write, Son of the Lion."
And I saw a vision. It was in summer on the Southern mountains
Like Fouta-Djallon, in the mildness of tamarind trees.
And on a hillock was seated the Being who is All Force, glimmering
Like a black diamond. His beard let roll the splendor of comets,
And at his feet under blue shadows, the streams of white honey
And cool fragrances of peace. Then I recognized
Around his Perfect Goodness the mixed elect, Black and White,
Those for whom Martin Luther had prayed. Mix them so, Lord,
Under your eyes and white beard:
The middle-class with the peaceful peasant, cane cutters
And cotton pickers, laborers with feverish hands, and they will turn
The factories red and in the evening get drunk from bitter
Bitterness. Whites and Blacks, all sons of the same Mother Earth.
And they sing in several voices, singing *Hosanna! Hallelujah!*
As in the long-ago Kingdom of Childhood when I dreamed.
They sang the innocence of the world and they danced the flowery
Dancing, the rhythmic forces, who sounded the Force of forces,
And Justice gained, which is Bountiful Beauty.
And the tapping of their syncopated feet was a black and white
Symphony that pressed the flowers, crushed the grapes
For the marriage of souls: the Only Son with a myriad of stars.
I saw all this, and I saw George Washington and Phillis Wheatley,
Mouth of blue bronze announcing freedom—her song consumed her,
And Benjamin Franklin and the Marquis de Lafayette in his crystal
Flair, Abraham Lincoln, who gave this blood to America
Like a life-giving drink. And I saw Booker T. Washington

The Patient One, and William E. B. Dubois the Untameable
Who left to plant his tomb in Nigritia.
I heard the *blues* voice of Langston Hughes, young as Armstrong's
Trumpet. Turning around I saw near me John F. Kennedy, more
  handsome
Than the people's dream, and his brother Robert, armored
In fine steel. And I saw—let me sing—all the Just and the Good
Which the cyclone of destiny had laid to rest, and they were standing
In the name of the poet's voice like tall slender trees which line
The path, and in the midst of them was Martin Luther King.
I sing of Malcolm X, the red angel of our night.
And through Angela's eyes sing George Jackson, shining like love
Without wings or arrows, but not without torment.
I sing with my brother, *Rise Up Negritude*, a white hand
In his living hand, I sing transparent America where light
Is a polyphony of colors. I sing a paradise of peace.

Léopold Sédar Senghor
Translated from the French by Melvin Dixon

:::::

Black Thursday

I
Night, precursor of fears.
Night of a mysterious silence.
Rapid steps in the streets . . .
Loud voices of black men . . .

Hidden, the venomous serpent.
Racial hate points the far off rifle.
The shot of a cowardly traitor
cuts through the tranquil night air.

A wounded and painful chest
opens with gushes of blood

which escapes blood red,
while a sublime life falls.

It is Martin Luther King who is dying.
The Nobel Prize winner is bleeding.
Martin Luther King the pacifist,
Preacher of love and non violence.

Oh! What a cruel destiny for men
who like Christ are crucified.
The tragic destiny of pacifists
who like Gandhi are sacrificed.

But that blood is not shed in vain.
It fertilizes glorious seeds in their furrows,
so that one day no racial hatred will exist,
that there is no hunger, fear, nor misery.

II
The caisson with the body,
carrying the body.
The dead body, bloodless,
perforated by a bullet on that holy Thursday.

The horse's hooves
echo monotonously over the asphalt.
Hoofprints over the black asphalt,
observed by all persons with sad faces.

A monotonous pace, a bitter pace,
followed by a caudal of weeping,
enough to fill a river.
A river which rises with the world's tears.

It is a prolonged and painful march.
a dead silent march;
the caisson squeaks on its way;
the wheels approach their destiny.

Broken hope is left
with its umbilical cord mutilated,
by the sharp cut of the bullet,
which was fired on Black Thursday.

Yet the black hope is not dead!
It multiplies in a perpetual reincarnation!
It becomes light to its black auroras
Unconcerned about the existence of Black Thursdays.

Victor Manuel Rivera Toledo, 1968
Translated by Luis Rivera

:::::

White Weekend

April 5–8, 1968

They deployed military troops
Surrounded the White House
And on the steps of the Senate building
A soldier behind a machine gun

32,000 in Washington and Chicago
1900 in Baltimore Maryland
76 cities in flames on the landscape
and the bearer of peace
lying still in Atlanta . . .

Lamentations! Lamentations! Lamentations!
Worldwide!
But in New York, on Wall Street
The stock market went up 18 points . . .

Quincy Troupe, 1968

Amos, 1963

Amos is a Shepherd of suffering sheep;
A pastor preaching in the depths of Alabama
Preaching social justice to the Southland
Preaching to the poor a new gospel of love
With the words of a god and the dreams of a man
Amos is our loving Shepherd of the sheep
Crying out to the stricken land
"You have sold the righteous for silver
And the poor for a pair of shoes.
My God is a mighty avenger
And He shall come with His rod in His hand."
Preaching to the persecuted and the disinherited millions
Preaching love and justice to the solid southern land
Amos is a Prophet with a vision of brotherly love
With a vision and a dream of the red hills of Georgia
"When Justice shall roll down like water
And righteousness like a mighty stream."
Amos is our Shepherd standing in the Shadow of our God
Tending his flocks all over the hills of Albany
And the seething streets of Selma and of bitter Birmingham.

Margaret Walker, 1970

:::::

Amos (Postscript, 1968)

From Montgomery to Memphis he marches
He stands on the threshold of tomorrow
He breaks the bars of iron and they remove the signs
He opens the gates of our prisons.
He speaks to the captive hearts of America
He bares raw their conscience

He is a man of peace for the people
Amos is a Prophet of the Lord
Amos speaks through Eternity
The glorious Word of the Lord!

Margaret Walker, 1970

13

"A gun / Struck, as we slept, a caring public man"

THE ASSASSINATION OF ROBERT F. KENNEDY, 5 JUNE 1968

Robert F. Kennedy was shot by Sirhan Sirhan in Los Angeles on 5 June 1968 shortly after winning the California presidential primary. His brief victory speech at the Ambassador Hotel around midnight, the last he would ever deliver, broached the subjects of violence, civil rights, and the Vietnam War, among other topics. "I think we can end the divisions in the United States," Kennedy asserted, "the violence, the disenchantment with our society, the divisions, whether it's between blacks and whites, between the poor and the more affluent, or between age groups, or over the war in Vietnam. . . . We are a great country, an unselfish country, and a compassionate country" (Steel 189). Kennedy died the following day.

The themes of compassion and unity were not new to Kennedy. Just two months earlier he had the unenviable task of informing a largely African American crowd in Indianapolis that

Martin Luther King Jr. had been assassinated. Kennedy was scheduled to speak in Indianapolis on 4 April as part of his presidential campaign, but the news of King's death in Memphis, which Kennedy learned of shortly before his flight landed, forced him to forgo his planned address. The speech he gave in its place would become one of the most significant of his life and an enduring legacy of the era. In addition Kennedy's remarks that evening, combined with previous decisions he made with respect to King, including ordering surveillance measures, would go a long way in helping to define his standing within the civil rights community. Riots erupted across 110 cities in the U.S. following King's death. Thirty-nine people were killed, more than twenty-five hundred were injured, and approximately seventy-five thousand troops were activated to help contain the violence. However, Indianapolis remained calm, in part due to Kennedy's influence (Steel 172).

As attorney general in his brother's administration, Bobby authorized J. Edgar Hoover and the FBI to wiretap King's home telephone in Atlanta and future addresses where King might reside. The wiretaps were active from 8 November 1963 to 30 April 1966 (Hersh 372). Hoover was convinced King had ties to the Communist Party, but the wiretaps produced no evidence to support this. Although Kennedy would later regret his decision, the surveillance of King was by no means an isolated event. Kennedy also approved surveillance of Malcolm X and others, including lobbyists, executive branch officials, a House staff member, a U.S. congressman, and a law firm (Church Committee 49, 142–43). In an attempt to place the covert activity of the Kennedy administration in perspective, Joe Allen claims, "The Eisenhower administration had authorized the CIA to carry out 170 major covert operations in eight years, while the Kennedy brothers authorized 163 in less than three years." However, most Americans were unaware of these activities and viewed the Kennedys as a source of hope for improving conditions at home and abroad. Bobby's assassination brought an abrupt end to those hopes for many, especially in light of King's assassination two months earlier and the assassinations of Medgar Evers and John Kennedy in 1963.

The hope that Robert Kennedy's life inspired was not restricted to American shores. The Russian poet Yevgeny Yevtushenko, the St. Lucian poet Derek Walcott, and the Canadian poet Al Purdy, for example, wrote poems in Bobby's honor. Yevtushenko and Walcott place Kennedy's death in a political context, while Purdy approaches the assassination from a personal perspective.

Yevtushenko excoriates America for its culture of violence, the same brand of violence Bobby Kennedy spoke of in his final public address at the Ambassador Hotel. "You shoot at yourself, America," the poet states in line 5 of "Freedom to Kill," clearly establishing a critical voice that accuses the U.S. of not living up to its professed ideals. Phrases such as "false fairy tales," "a façade of noble ideas," "bottomless shame," and "the shame of the nation" serve to reinforce the poem's central theme of America's self-inflicted social and moral crises (lines 15, 16, 38, 51). These crises, Yevtushenko asserts, were also responsible for the assassinations of JFK (12, 21–23, 28) and King (39).

Likewise Bobby's death serves as the impetus for a wide-ranging critique of American culture in Walcott's "Elegy." "We miss you, Liberty," he writes in line 2, acknowledging the death of hope that seemed to accompany Kennedy's assassination, particularly within the civil rights community. Walcott then proceeds to bemoan the death of Che Guevera (who was murdered in October of the previous year), linking America's desire for change, especially with respect to the black power struggle, to Third World revolutions. As a whole, "Elegy" reminds readers that the type of violence that downed Kennedy can be traced to the founding of America. The poem, dated 6 June, the day Kennedy died, is an unrepentant criticism of America's past and present culture of violence and injustice.

Purdy forgoes politics and connects to Kennedy on a personal and familial level in his poem "For Robert Kennedy." He offers "men newspapers never heard of," like his grandfather, who was a "scarred lumberjack / hellraiser and backwoods farmer" (12, 15–16).

The concluding line of Robert Lowell's "For Robert Kennedy 1925–68"—"forever approaching your maturity"—best sums up the sense of loss and unfulfilled potential that permeates most poems in this chapter.

Carolyn Kizer's "Season of Lovers and Assassins" echoes Lowell's sentiments when she writes, "The other ocean wakes us, where a gun / Struck, as we slept, a caring public man" (7–8). Kizer's poem, which intertwines sensuality and grief, implies that death, especially the death of a public figure like Kennedy, often leaves the living feeling vulnerable and apprehensive.

"The Assassination" by Donald Justice also speaks to Bobby's life as a public figure and his impact on ordinary Americans. In the second stanza his death is announced, becomes headline news, and affects street vendors, "the woman selling carnations / And the man in the straw hat stand" (9–10).

Lawrence Ferlinghetti's "Assassination Raga" recalls the transportation of Kennedy's body and his funeral procession, while Edward Sanders's "A Flower from Robert Kennedy's Grave" proceeds from President Nixon's inauguration in 1973 to Kennedy's burial site at Arlington Cemetery. Taken together, the poems construct an emotional and political frame that contains vivid images of reactions to the assassination as well as images that depict the lingering effects of Kennedy's death almost four years later.

:::::

Assassination Raga

Tune in to a raga
on the stereo
and turn on Death TV
without its sound
Outside the plums are growing in a tree
"The force that through the green fuse
drives the flower"
drives Death TV
"A grief ago"
They lower the body soundlessly
into a huge plane in Los Angeles
marked "United States of America"
and soundlessly
the "United State of America"
takes off
& wings away with that Body
Tune out the TV sound

& listen soundlessly
to the blind mouths of its motors
& a sitar speaking on the stereo
a raga in a rage
at all that black death
and all that bad karma
La illaha el lill Allah
There is no god but God
The force that through the red fuze
drives the bullet
drives the needle in its dharma groove
and man the needle
drives that plane
of the "United States of America"
through its sky full of shit and death
and the sky never ends
as it wings soundlessly
from those fucked-up cities
whose names we'd rather not remember
Inside the plane
inside the plane a wife
lies soundlessly
against the coffin
Engine whines as sitar sings outrageously
La illaha el lill Allah
There is no god but God?
There is no god but Death
The plums are falling through the tree
The force that drives the bullet
through the gun
drives everyone
as the "United States of America"
flies on sightlessly
through the swift fierce years
with the dead weight of its Body
which they keep flying from Dallas
which they keep flying from Los Angeles

And the plane lands
Without folding its wings
its shadow in mourning for itself
withdraws into itself
in death's draggy dominion
La illaha el lill Allah
There is no god but Death
The force that through the green fuze
drove his life
drives everyone
La illaha el lill Allah
And they are driving the Body
they are driving the Body
up Fifth Avenue
past a million people in line
"We are going to be here a long time"
says Death TV's spielman
The cortège passes soundlessly
"Goodbye! Goodbye!" some people cry
The traffic flows around & on
The force that drives the cars
combusts our karma
La illaha el lill Allah
There is no god but Death
The force that drives our life to death
Drives sitar too
so soundlessly
La illaha el lill Allah
And they lift the Body
They lift the Body
of the United States of America
and carry it into a cathedral
singing Hallelujah He Shall Live
For ever & ever
And then the Body moves again
down fifth Avenue
Fifty-seven black sedans after it

There are people with roses
behind the barricades
in bargain-basement dresses
And sitar sings & sings nonviolence
sitar sounds in us its images of ecstasy
its depth of ecstasy
against old dung & death
La illaha el lill Allah
La illaha el lill Allah
The force that strikes its strings
strikes us
And the funeral train
the silver train
starts up soundlessly
at a dead speed
over the hot land
an armed helicopter over it
They are clearing the tracks ahead of assassins
The tracks are lined with bare faces
A highschool band in New Brunswick plays
"The Battle Hymn of the Republic"
They have shot it down again
They have shot him down again
& will shoot him down again
& take him on a train
& lower him again
into a grave in Washington
La illaha el lill Allah
Day & night journeys the coffin
through the dark land
too dark now to see the dark faces
La illaha el lill Allah
Plums & planes are falling through the air
La illaha el lill Allah
as sitar sings the only answer
sitar sings its only sound
that still can still all violence

La illaha el lill Allah
There is no god but Life
Sitar says it Sitar sounds it
Sitar sounds on us to love love & hate hate
Sitar breathes its Atman breath in us
sounds & sounds in us its lovely *om om*
La illaha el lill Allah
At every step the pure wind rises
La illaha el lill Allah
People with roses
behind the barricades!

Lawrence Ferlinghetti, 1968

Poet's notes

First read, to a loud evening raga, at "The Incredible Poetry Reading," Nourse Auditorium, San Francisco, June 8, 1968, the day Robert Kennedy was buried.

line 8: "Death TV": The phrase comes from "So Who Owns Death TV" by William Burroughs, Claude Pélieu & Carl Weissner.

lines 6–7, 9: "The force that through the green fuse drives the flower" & "A grief ago": From Dylan Thomas.

line 24 et al.: "*La illaha el lill Allah*": variation of a Sufi ecstatic chant. A corruption of the Koran. Sirhan Sirhan also corrupted the Koran.

line 51: "the swift fierce years": From a phrase in Eldridge Cleaver's "Soul on Ice."

line 133: Atman: Breath, soul, life principle.

line 134: Om: Originally a syllable denoting assent—the "ideal, inaudible sound" of the universe.

:::::

The Assassination

It begins again, the nocturnal pulse.
It courses through the cables laid for it.
It mounts to the chandeliers and beats there, hotly.
We are too close. Too late, we would move back.
We are involved with the surge.

Now it bursts. Now it has been announced.
Now it is being soaked up by newspapers.
Now it is running through the streets.
The crowd has it. The woman selling carnations
And the man in the straw hat stand with it in their shoes.

Here is the red marquee it sheltered under.
Here is the ballroom, here
The sadly various orchestra led
By a single gesture. My arms open.
It enters. Look, we are dancing.

Donald Justice, June 5, 1968

:::::

Season of Lovers and Assassins

Safe from the wild storms off Cape Hatteras,
Hastily stripped, in the warm surf we embrace.

The storm we made has flung us to the sand.
A force not thought has plunged each into each.

Trailing our clothes like seaweed up the beach,
We swim to sleep, and drown, entwined in dreams.

The other ocean wakes us, where a gun
Struck, as we slept, a caring public man.

From early dawn, zoo noises bruise our ears
Played on TV's gray window to the news.

Blood fills the famous brain. The rains descend
(your gentle hands), a continent of tears.

One passionate harsh light has been put out.
Numbly we move to the noontime of our love:

The strip of rain-pocked shore gleams pallidly.
Fragments of broken palm-frond fly like knives

Through tropic wind. Soon we bear star-shaped wounds,
Stigmata of all passion-driven lives.

We leave this island, safety, to our fate,
Wrapt in a caul of vulnerability,

Marked lovers now, the moony night is ours,
Surf-sounds reminding us that good decay

Surrounds us: force which pounds on flesh or stone,
The slow assassination of the years.

Carolyn Kizer, June 5, 1968

:::::

For Robert Kennedy

Here in my workroom, in its listlessness
of Vacancy, like the old town house we shut for summer,
airtight and sheeted from the sun and smog,
far from the hornet yatter of his gang—
is loneliness, a thin smoke of thread of vital
air. But what will anyone teach you now?
Doom was woven in your nerves, your shirt,
woven in the great clan; they too were loyal,
and you too were loyal to them, to death.
For them like a prince, you daily left your tower
to walk through dirt in your best cloth. Untouched,
alone in my Plutarchan bubble, I miss

you, you out of Plutarch, made by hand—
forever approaching your maturity.

Robert Lowell, 1968

:::::

For Robert Kennedy

There are public men
become large as mountains or the endless forests
in the love men bear them
and when they die it is as if a great emptiness became
solid things turn misty and hard to hold onto
and the stunned heart clutches at dear remembrance
retraces its steps back somewhere in the past
when nothing changed and the high sun hangs motionless
friends remain fixed there and dogs bite gently
it is always morning it is always evening
                                        it is always noon

And there are men newspapers never heard of
but loved for no reason or every reason
like my ugly grandfather who was
260 pounds of scarred lumberjack
hellraiser and backwoods farmer
of whom I said and say again
"—death takes him
as it takes more beautiful things
populations of whole countries
museums and works of art
and women with such a glow
                          it makes their background vanish
they vanish too—"

But I'm wrong
one drives a beatup Ford to find them
ten towns away across the belted planets
or waiting in the next apartment
one travels light
years across our heavy sorrow
to find the one man one man
and then another yet another
in the alchemy that changes
men but keeps them changeless
and solves the insoluble enigma
of blackjack death and the day's brief tenure
or fails perhaps
and becomes a genetic awareness
and added detail floating outward
inside the collective mind of humanity

Al Purdy, 1973

:::::

A Flower from Robert Kennedy's Grave

> During demonstrations at Nixon's second inauguration,
> we watched his limo pass, on the way to the White House;
> then I drove over to Arlington Cemetery
>
> January 20, 1973

After
a winding walk
up past the white stones
of snuff,

past the guardhouse
circling circling
around the Catholic henge

to John Kennedy's bright taper
burning on the ground
in windy cold winter after-speech
afternoon

then walk down
to the left-hand

edge of the hill-
ock — there in speechless serenity,

built on the steepness
a small
elegant
perfectly proportioned
white cross 'bove
white flat marble marker

Robert Francis Kennedy

Nearby a fount jets horizontal
over a slab o' stone

water curving down abruptly on the
rock front lip

R.F.K.'s words of race heal
writ upon the rock above
the flat-fount.

Across the walkway
by the grave
a long red rose
with a vial of water
slipped upon the stem end
& wrapped with shiny tape
lay singly
& to the left of it a
basket of yellow chrysanthemums

and this: that
only a whining hour past,
Richard Nixon
oozed down Pennsylvania Avenue
flashing v's from a limousine
behind a stutter-footed wary pack of Marines
Their
bayonets stabbing the January
in a thickery of different directions
like small lance hairs
pricked up on the forehead of a
hallucinated drool fiend
during a bummer

but big enough to stab the
throats of hippie rioters

buddy.

I picked a yellow petal

from thy grave
Mr. Robert Kennedy

& brought it home
from Arlington, where many young mourners
stood crying quietly this inauguration day

Picked a dream
Mr. Robert Kennedy
brought it home in our hearts
burning like a brand in a fennel stalk

Picked a thought-ray
Robert Kennedy

brought it back from this
henge of park-side
eternity

buses of protesters parked
in the lots beneath your hill

Tears splash
in the vessels
of the sun

Picked yellow
molecules bunched
in beauty
from the beauty fount
Mr. Robert Kennedy

The peace-ark
glides in the vastness,
though weirdness clings to your death.

But nothing can touch the ark
sails through the trellis of evil
brazen American wrought of light hate

Nothing can touch it
not even pyramidal battlements of gore-spore
nor tricky's pitiless flood
of dungeonoid luciphobian losers.

Edward Sanders, 1971

:::::

Elegy

Our hammock swung between Americas,
we miss you, Liberty. Che's
bullet-riddled body falls,
and those who cried, the Republic must first die

to be reborn, are dead,
the freeborn citizen's ballot in the head.
Still, everybody wants to go to bed
with Miss America. And, if there's no bread,
let them eat cherry pie.

But the old choice of running, howling, wounded
Wolf-deep in her woods,
While the white papers snow on
genocide is gone;
no face can hide
its public, private pain,
wincing, already statued.

Some splintered arrowhead lodged in her brain
sets the black singer howling in his bear trap,
shines young eyes with the brightness of the mad,
tires the old with her residual sadness;
and yearly lilacs in her dooryards bloom,
and the cherry orchard's surf
blinds Washington and whispers
to the assassin in his furnished room
of an ideal America, whose flickering screens
show, in slow herds, the ghosts of Cheyennes
scuffling across the staked and wired plains
with whispering, rag-bound feet,

while the farm couple framed in their Gothic door
like Calvin's saints, waspish, pragmatic, poor,
gripping the devil's pitchfork
stare rigidly towards the immortal wheat.

Derek Walcott, June 6, 1968

Freedom to Kill

The statue of Liberty's color
Grows ever so deathly pale
As, loving freedom with bullets
And taking liberty with bullets,
You shoot at yourself, America

You can kill yourself like that!
It's dangerous to go out
Into this nightmare world,
But it's still more dangerous
To hide in the woods.

There's a smell on earth
Of a universal Dallas.
It's frightful to live
And this fright is full of shame.

Who's going to believe false fairy tales,
When behind a façade of noble ideas
The price of gun oil rises
And the price of human life falls?

Murderers attend funerals in mourning,
And become stockholders later,
And, once again,
Ears of grain filled with bullets
Wave in Texas fields.

The eyes of murderers peer out
From under hats and caps,
The steps of murderers
Are heard at every door,
And a second Kennedy falls . . .
America, save your children!
Children in other countries turn gray,
And their huts

Bombed at night
Burn in your fire
Just like your
Bill of Rights.

You promised to be
The world's conscience
But, at the brink of bottomless shame,
You're shooting not at King
But at your own conscience.
You're bombing Vietnam
And also your own honor.

When a nation's going dangerously insane
It can't be cured of its troubles
By hastily prescribed peace.
Perhaps the only way is shame.
History can't be cleaned in a laundry.
There are no such washing machines
Blood can't ever be washed away!

O where's it hiding,
The shame of the nation,
As if it were a runaway slave?
There are slaves within slaves.

There are many murderers at large.
They carry out their mob justice
And pogroms,
And Raskolnikov wanders through America,
Insane,
With a bloody axe.
O, Old Abe,
What are people doing,
Sadly understanding only one truth:
That the greatness of a tree
Can be judged only after it's cut down.

Lincoln basks in his marble chair,
Bleeding.

They're shooting at him again!
The beasts!

The stars in your flag,
America,
Are bullet holes.

Arise from the dead,
Bullet-holed Statue of Liberty,
Murdered so often,
And speak out
Like a woman and a mother
And curse the freedom to kill.

And without wiping the blood
From your forehead,
Oh, Statue of Liberty, raise up
Your green, drowned woman's face
Against this death of freedom.

Yevgeny Yevtushenko, 1968
Translated by Lawrence Ferlinghetti with Anthony Kahn

14

"Mighty mountains loom before me and I won't stop now"

STRUGGLE, SURVIVAL, AND SUBVERSION DURING THE CIVIL RIGHTS ERA

Previous chapters have focused on a significant representative event, but many of the poems written about and published during the civil rights era do not lend themselves to event-specific categories. This chapter recognizes poems that capture the cultural and political climate of the period. These poems, with few exceptions, are not written in the elegiac mode that dominates earlier sections. These poems differ in significant ways from poems intended to honor a fallen activist, but are united with those poems in that they were written in opposition to the status quo and in support of advancing the social conscience of America. By critiquing—some more vociferously than others—systems of oppression that tend to keep Americans divided, these poems, like the poems that precede them, are concerned with helping America become what she has long claimed to be. In this sense the poems throughout *Words of Protest, Words of*

Freedom complement each other regardless of their specific thematic concerns. Taken together they provide readers with a sense of the conflicts poets experienced during the period and how they responded to injustices caused by segregation and inequality. This chapter contains representative poems that are primarily concerned with identity (personal and cultural); ideologies of resistance (nonviolent and retaliatory); chronicling civil rights protests, marches, and demonstrations; and offering instruction and wisdom to fellow poets and activists.

As the 1960s progressed, identity in the African American community became an increasingly more significant if not tension-filled issue. Black power and black nationalist sentiments, both offshoots of civil rights ideology, offered alternatives to nonviolent practices. The black arts movement provided a voice for writers grounded in a black identity that did not involve an essential desire for integration. Amiri Baraka's "Black Art" and "Poem for HalfWhite College Students" express a need for the black community to accept blackness in the ubiquitous face of whiteness. In the latter poem, Baraka writes, "Ask / in your black heart who it is you are, and is that image black or white" (lines 21–22). This poem, similar to others from the black arts movement, attempts to raise the level of black consciousness and black beauty in African Americans who for centuries have been inundated with messages of white supremacy.

Nikki Giovanni shares Baraka's consciousness-raising goals. She conveys similar sentiments about the need for blacks to counteract an array of psychological and fiscal detriments. Giovanni states, "Black love is Black wealth" in "Nikki Rosa," a poem concerned with, among other issues, self-determination and self-definition within the African American community (25).

Poets, regardless of race, also wrestled with Dr. King's philosophy of nonviolent protest, including Margaret Danner, Diane di Prima, and James A. Emanuel. Danner's poem, "Passive Resistance," is a testament to the difficulty of following a nonviolent philosophy. The speaker wants to "strike back" at tormentors and "see them quail / in some rat-ridden jail" rather than turn the other cheek (7–9). In the end, however, she adheres to nonviolence. In "Revolutionary Letter #8," di Prima warns, "Don't waver between active and passive resistance" in line 23, but three lines later concedes, "NO ONE WAY WORKS, it will take all of us / Shoving at the thing from all sides / to bring it down" (26–28). Emanuel appears to heed di Prima's "Don't waver" advice. In "Freedom Rider: Washout," a poem about the violence riders faced while testing interstate travel laws in 1961, the speaker eschews nonviolence after "a single freckled fist / Knocked out the memory of His name" (9–10). At the poem's end the speaker strikes back, recalling as inspiration Prosser's slave rebellion of 1800.

Although Emanuel's protagonist retaliates, most poems reflect King's adherence to a nonviolent strategy. In fact several poems speak directly to the practice of holding peaceful marches and demonstrations, even in the face of imminent danger and violence. John Beecher, Bruce Hartford, Galway Kinnell, Carolyn Kizer, and Denise Levertov depict acts of protest in their respective poems.

Beecher's "Free World Notes" and "Georgia Scene: 1964" are delivered in the voices of a white racist Mississippian and an African American from Georgia, respectfully, but both poems offer descriptions of what many racists called "outside agitators." "Free World Notes" is an account in three sections of events that transpired in Mississippi in 1961. The poem is delivered from the point of view of a white racist Mississippian who detests the presence of a "lowdown white sonofabitch" civil rights worker in his community (1). According to Beecher's narrator, the white outsider is intent on invading McComb for the purpose of "stirrin up [local] niggers to vote" (2). The poem then briefly describes the results of two instances of civil protest in Mississippi. Brenda Travis, a student from McComb, was accompanied by Ike Lewis and Robert Talbert Jr., both twenty, when they were arrested on 30 August for conducting a sit-in at the Greyhound bus terminal. Travis's $200 fine, four-month sentence, and expulsion from high school set off rounds of protests, especially from her classmates (Cagin and Dray 149–59). Herbert Lee, fifty-two, had been encouraged to participate in the movement by Bob Moses and other activists. Lee was especially involved with local voter registration efforts. His active involvement in the movement angered many whites, including Mississippi State Representative Eugene H. Hurst, who shot and killed Lee in September following a brief argument. Hurst claimed "self-defense," and the murder, as Beecher's poem indicates in line 20, was ruled a justifiable homicide (Cagin and Dray 152–53).

The "outside agitator" in Beecher's "Georgia Scene: 1964" takes on a more prominent role than the agitator in "Free World Notes." The outsider in this instance is a white woman who endures physical abuse by white state bureau of investigation officials. The seventy-year-old civil rights worker is killed and her body abandoned until an African American drives her body to a local hospital, where it suffers neglect by a racist staff. The black speaker of the poem appears simultaneously impressed and confused by the woman's activism: "Sure ain't like no ofays I ever knowed / coming down here and getting they heads beat for nothing" (29–30). The closing lines of the poem reflect the tension and animosity that existed among many blacks and whites in Georgia in the 1960s. The speaker cannot understand why the murdered woman, a white nonviolent activist intent on improving race relations, would sacrifice her life for the cause by "trying to love these crackers into being Christian / like crackers was human" (31–32). Obviously the speaker considers racists in the state of Georgia beyond help, beyond redemption.

Activists are also depicted in Bruce Hartford's "Mississippi Voter Rally" and "Grenada March #107." Hartford, an activist with CORE, the SCLC, and other civil rights organizations in the 1960s, created the educational Veterans of the Civil Rights Movement website (www.crmvet.org) in 1996 for individuals interested in learning about the movement from those who participated in the struggle. Both poems, composed in Grenada, Mississippi, in 1966, are autobiographical. The first was written in August after a voter registration rally was disrupted by local police and helmeted state troopers who tear-gassed and abused the marchers. The second poem, "Grenada March #107" was written two months later and contains similar imagery. The poem is also notable for its incorporation of the Negro spiritual "Oh, Freedom," which was popularized in the late 1950s and 1960s by the folk singer Odetta and others. Like most songs used during civil rights demonstrations, "Oh, Freedom" was often modified to suit specific events. In this instance, the modification "*No more gassings, no more beatings / no more jailings, over me*" arrives after the third stanza.

The song most affiliated with the civil rights movement, "We Shall Overcome," is invoked by Denise Levertov in "A Note to Olga (1966)." The poem is an homage to Levertov's older sister, a poet and activist who died of cancer in 1964 and who was primarily responsible for awakening Levertov's social consciousness. "A Note to Olga" was written after Levertov was arrested during an anti–Vietnam War demonstration (Pope

109), but the overriding theme of the poem is the memory of Olga's activism and her fondness for singing "We Shall Overcome" during marches. In fact the memory of Olga's rendition of the song overwhelms Levertov. Olga's "presence," which is the impetus for the poem, is signaled and framed by a reference to the civil rights movement. It is interesting to note that "We shall," in Olga's voice, seems to bellow from behind Levertov while "overcome," also in Olga's voice, comes from "somewhere in front" (20, 29). The power of Olga's memory becomes intertwined with the power of the song, creating a potent combination that seems to surround and overtake Levertov. Indeed by poem's end, Levertov is unsure if she or Olga inhabits the body being arrested and carted off in a paddy wagon. The poem manages to achieve three goals: it honors Levertov's sister, it honors the civil rights movement, and it documents the poet's arrest at a demonstration against the Vietnam War.

The arrest of Galway Kinnell in Louisiana in the 1960s figures prominently in "The Last River." Kinnell, a member of CORE in the 1960s, participated in integration and voting rights efforts in various parts of the state. "The Last River," whose structure is largely influenced by Dante's Inferno, appeared in *Body Rags*, Kinnell's collection published in 1968. The poem carries readers on a journey—it runs for more than four hundred lines—where the speaker encounters fellow travelers and witnesses acts of injustice and brutality. Kinnell himself became a victim of violence when he led a group of students from Juniata College in Pennsylvania to Selma, Alabama, in 1965 to participate in a march and the group was attacked by horse-mounted state troopers. A photograph of a bloodied Kinnell, his fellow marcher Harriet Richardson Michel, and others was taken by the civil rights photographer Charles Moore. Moore would later publish the photograph in *Life* magazine.

Carolyn Kizer's "Poem, Small and Delible" captures a protest in motion and provides an etymology lesson on words and practices commonly used in the movement. Words such as "picket," "Woolworth's," "sit-ins," and "boycott" are "decoded" for future generations. Kizer addresses both the need for civil disobedience and the general confusion over or opposition to those forms of social protest. The poem is ultimately optimistic and forward-looking in the sense that it is intended to be read in the future, when the need for such terms and demonstrations will be unnecessary.

Not all protest poems were explicit in their reference to racial conditions or issues pertaining to the movement. Poems by Robert Bly and Robert Lowell exemplify this aesthetic approach. "War and Silence" by Bly and "For the Union Dead" by Lowell address issues of movement-related injustice, but addressing those issues is not the poems' central concern. Both poems are decidedly about wars—the war in Vietnam for Bly, and the Civil War for Lowell. However, the poets intentionally connect those battles to broader—and in the case of Lowell, more contemporary—social problems. Bly's second line, "A Negro's ear sleeping in an automobile tire," is a reference to the practice of lynching and dismemberment. The practice was still in use when "War and Silence" appeared in *The Light around the Body* in 1967, a collection that earned Bly the National Book Award. As for Lowell, his poem addresses school desegregation: "When I crouch to my television set, / the drained faces of Negro school-children rise like balloons" (59–60). Lowell delivered the commissioned poem during the Boston Arts Festival in 1960, six years after the *Brown* decision and a year when sit-ins, demonstrations, and educational disparities received considerable media attention.

Poems intended to advise or inspire others were also evident during the period. Diane di Prima, Alice Walker, Julius Lester, and Naomi Long Madgett, among others, produced works that offered instruction or encouragement during the movement. Di Prima's "Revolutionary Letter #19" is unrelenting in its insistence that activists thoroughly contemplate their demands for changes in public policy before they approach politicians. The repetition of "if what you want" propels the poem through issues such as employment, housing, assimilation through the educational system (where "it's better to be 'American' than black / or Indian, or Jap, or [Puerto Rican]"), heath care, and the American Dream of a life in the suburbs (17–18). All of the above, according to the poem, have their drawbacks and should not be "joined" as much as taken over, remade, improved, or revolutionized. Di Prima's poem warns against compromises, or "selling / yourself short," and instead demands that activists think long term and seek lasting power (44–45). Di Prima wrote the poem with the Poor People's Campaign of 1968 in mind, Dr. King's last campaign before his assassination in April of that year.

Walker's "Be Nobody's Darling" was also written with fellow activists in mind. The poem, which appeared in Walker's *Revolutionary Petunias*

(1970), is dedicated to the civil rights worker and photographer Julius Lester but is intended to inspire others as well. In *Anything We Love Can Be Saved: A Writer's Activism* (1997), Walker asks, "What can I give you to help you stay strong when you feel the world is turned against you and that you are standing, perhaps even naked, absolutely all alone? I give you this poem" (92). "Be Nobody's Darling" encourages individuals, especially African Americans, to gain wisdom and direction from past leaders and to live in a manner that makes them "qualified" (28) or worthy to live among and be respected by those fallen activists.

In a similar spirit, Lester mandates that civil rights workers honor fellow workers and leaders who are still alive, because they "may never have the opportunity again" (22). "Revolutionary Mandate 1" acknowledges the fragile nature of life and the ever-present dangers that face activists in the movement and memorializes those who have died as a result of their activism. Lester also acknowledges that "poets and artists and musicians" are "responsible for / the spirit and soul of the revolution" (15–16).

A revolutionary spirit is in full display in Madgett's poem "Midway," written in 1959. While the poem is delivered in the first person it transcends a personal or individual voice and can easily be read as advice to the collective. The poem is intended to appeal to anyone vaguely familiar with the struggles of African Americans to gain a semblance of equality in America. Furthermore the poem is a testament to and blueprint for perseverance among African American activists. Many of the poetic sentiments expressed throughout *Words of Protest, Words of Freedom* are capsulized in the poem's unyielding quest for freedom and justice. Indeed Madgett's closing stanza captures the fierce determination shared by poets and activists over the course of the American civil rights movement,

> I've seen the daylight breaking high above the bough
> I've found my destination and I've made my vow;
> so whether you abhor me
> Or deride me or ignore me
> Mighty mountains loom before me and I won't stop now. (11–15)

Black Art

Poems are bullshit unless they are
teeth or trees or lemons piled
on a step. Or black ladies dying
of men leaving nickel hearts
beating them down. Fuck poems
and they are useful, wd they shoot
come at you, love what you are,
breathe like wrestlers, or shudder
strangely after pissing. We want live
words of the hip world live flesh &
coursing blood. Hearts Brains
Souls splintering fire. We want poems
like fists beating niggers out of Jocks
or dagger poems in the slimy bellies
of the owner-jews. Black poems to
smear on girdlemamma mulatto bitches
whose brains are red jelly stuck
between 'lizabeth taylor's toes. Stinking
Whores! We want "poems that kill."
Assassin poems, Poems that shoot
guns. Poems that wrestle cops into alleys
and take their weapons leaving them dead
with tongues pulled out and sent to Ireland. Knockoff
poems for dope selling wops or slick halfwhite
politicians Airplane poems, rrrrrrrrrrrrrrr
rrrrrrrrrrrrrr . . . tuhtuh tuhtuh tuhtuhtuhtuhtuh
. . . rrrrrrrrrrrrrrr . . . Setting fire and death to
whities ass. Look at the Liberal
Spokesman for the jews clutch his throat
& puke himself into eternity . . . rrrrrrr
There's a negroleader pinned to
a bar stool in Sardi's eyeballs melting
in hot flame Another negroleader
on the steps of the white house one
kneeling between the sheriff's thighs

negotiating coolly for his people.
Agggh . . . stumbles across the room . . .
Put it on him, poem. Strip him naked
to the world! Another bad poem cracking
steel knuckles in a jewlady's mouth
Poem scream poison gas on beasts in green berets
Clean out the world for virtue and love,
Let there be no love poems written
until love can exist freely and
cleanly. Let Black People understand
that they are the lovers and the sons
of lovers and warriors and sons
of warriors Are poems & poets &
all the loveliness here in the world

We want a black poem. And a
Black World.
Let the world be a Black Poem
And Let All Black People Speak This Poem
Silently
or LOUD.

Amiri Baraka, 1966

:::::

Poem for HalfWhite College Students

Who are you, listening to me, who are you
listening to yourself? Are you white or
black, or does that have anything to do
with it? Can you pop your fingers to no
music, except those wild monkies go on
in your head, can you jerk, to no melody,
except finger poppers get it together
when you turn from starchecking to checking

yourself. How do you sound, your words, are they
yours? The ghost you see in the mirror, is it really
you, can you swear you are not an imitation greyboy,
can you look right next to you in that chair, and swear,
that the sister you have your hand on is not really
so full of Elizabeth Taylor, Richard Burton is
coming out of her ears. You may even have to be Richard
with a white shirt and face, and four million negroes
think you cute, you may have to be Elizabeth Taylor, old lady,
if you want to sit up in your crazy spot dreaming about dresses,
and the sway of certain porters' hips. Check yourself, learn who it is
speaking, when you make some ultrasophisticated point, check
yourself
when you find yourself gesturing like Steve McQueen, check it out, ask
in your black heart who it is you are, and is that image black or white,
you might be surprised right out the window, whistling dixie on the
way in

Amiri Baraka, 1969

:::::

Free World Notes

I
Lowdown white sonofabitch
comin in here and stirrin up our niggers to vote
lemme at him with this here blackjack
the cops done turned their backs

II
I find you guilty Brenda Travis age 16
of an aggravatin breach of the public peace
for sitting down at the counter
of the bus station café
and I therefore sentence you

to one year's imprisonment
in the colored females' reformatory

III
We the coroner's jury bein duly sworn
do find the State Rep'sentative Hurst
did whip Herbert Lee a nigra boy age 52
right smart over the head with the butt of his pistol
and did also fire a 45-caliber projectile
into the nigra's intercranial cavity
such bein the proximate cause of said Herbert's demise
and we do further find and pronounce
this act to have been justifiable homicide
the nigra boy having provoked the Rep'sentative
unwarrantably
by insistin that he be registered on the book
and permitted to vote like a citizen

John Beecher, 1966

:::::

Georgia Scene: 1964

And so this cat
he was from the GBI
that's the cracker FBI
kept feeling up the chicks' legs with the electric cattle prod
and making them wiggle and holler
He couldn't get enough of that stuff
poking that hot thing up under they dresses
and I be dog
if one of them cracker polices
didn't break down and cry like a baby
just watching him

but he didn't try to stop him
no I guess that would be too much to expect of any cracker
I disremember all the meanness they did
treating them Yankees like they was us
dragging that 70-year-old white lady
down the courthouse steps
with her head going bam on every step
Her heart give out
and the ambulance came
but when the driver saw she was
one of them agitators
he just took off again and left her laying in the street
Finally one of us took her to the hospital
propped up in the back seat of a car
but wouldn't no white doctor touch her when she got there
Had to find one of ours
and put her in the Jim Crow section
Sure ain't like no ofays I ever knowed
coming down here and getting they heads beat for nothing
trying to love these crackers into being Christian
like crackers was human

John Beecher, 1964

:::::

War and Silence

The bombers spread out, temperature steady
A Negro's ear sleeping in an automobile tire
Pieces of timber float by, saying nothing

Bishops rush about crying, "There is no war,"
And bombs fall,
Leaving a dust on the beech trees.

One leg walks down the road and leaves
The other behind, the eyes part
And fly off in opposite directions

Filaments of death grow out.
The sheriff cuts off his black legs
And nails them to a tree.

Robert Bly, 1967

:::::

Passive Resistance

And to this Man who turned the other cheek,
this Man who murmured not a word,
or fought at persecutors,
remained meek under it all,
I crawl, in wonder.

For as the evil tongues begin to turn on me
I want to fight, strike back,
and see them quail
in some rat-ridden jail,
or suffering for
the suffering they've caused.
I want no more of this humility.
But I must bow,
bow low before it now,
and love the evil ones,
as You did. Yet, I am sure
it was much easier for
God's son.

Margaret Danner, 1966

Revolutionary Letter #8

Everytime you pick the spot for a be-in
a demonstration, a march, a rally, you are choosing the ground
for a potential battle.
You are still calling the shots.
Pick your terrain with that in mind.
Remember the old gang rules:
stick to your neighborhood, don't let them lure you
to Central Park everytime, I would hate
to stumble bloody out of that park to find help:
Central Park West, or Fifth Avenue, which would you
choose?

go to love-ins
with incense, flowers, food, and a plastic bag
with a damp cloth in it, for tear gas, wear no jewelry
wear clothes you can move in easily, wear no glasses
contact lenses
earrings for pierced ears are especially hazardous

try to be clear
in front, what you will do if it comes
to trouble
if you're going to try to split stay out of the center
don't stampede or panic others
don't waver between active and passive resistance
know your limitations, bear contempt
neither for yourself, nor any of your brothers
NO ONE WAY WORKS, it will take all of us
Shoving at the thing from all sides
to bring it down.

Diane di Prima, 1968

Revolutionary Letter #19

(for The Poor People's Campaign)

if what you want is jobs
for everyone, you are still the enemy,
you have not thought thru, clearly
what that means

if what you want is housing,
industry
        (G.E. on the Navaho
        reservation)
a car for everyone, garage, refrigerator,
TV, more plumbing, scientific
freeways, you are still
the enemy, you have chosen
to sacrifice the planet for a few years of some
science fiction utopia, if what you want

still is, or can be, schools
where all our kids are pushed into one shape, are taught
it's better to be "American" than black
or Indian, or Jap, or PR, where Dick
and Jane become and are the dream, do you
look like Dick's father, don't you think your kid
secretly wishes you did

if what you want
is clinics where the AMA
can feed you pills to keep you weak, or sterile
shoot germs into your kids, while Merke & Co
grows richer

if you want
free psychiatric help for everyone
so that the shrinks
pimps for this decadence, can make

it flower for us, if you want
if you still want a piece
a small piece of suburbia, green lawn
laid down by the square foot
color TV, whose radiant energy
kills brain cells, whose subliminal ads
brainwash your children, have taken over
your dreams

degrees from universities which are nothing
more than slum landlords, festering sinks
of lies, so you too can go forth
and lie to others on some greeny campus

THEN YOU ARE STILL
THE ENEMY, you are selling
yourself short, remember
you can have what you ask for, ask for
everything

Diane di Prima, 1968

:::::

Freedom Rider: Washout

The first blow hurt.
(God is love, is love.)
My blood spit into the dirt.
(Sustain my love, oh, Lord above!)
Curses circled one another.
(They were angry with their brother.)

I was too weak
For this holy game.
A single freckled fist

Knocked out the memory of His name.
Bloody, I heard a long, black moan,
Like waves from slave ships long ago.
With Gabriel Prosser's dogged knuckles
I struck an ancient blow.

James A. Emanuel, 1964

:::::

Adulthood

(for Claudia)

i usta wonder who i'd be
when i was a little girl in idianapolis
sitting on doctors porches with post-dawn pre-debs
(wondering would my aunt drag me to church sunday)
i was meaningless
and i wondered if life
would give me a chance to mean

i found a new life in the withdrawal from all things
not like my image

when i was a teen-ager i usta sit
on front steps conversing
the gym teachers son with embryonic eyes
about the essential essence of the universe
(and other bullshit stuff)
recognizing the basic powerlessness of me

but then i went to college where i learned
that just because everything i was was unreal
i could be real and not just real through withdrawal
into emotional crosshairs or colored bourgeoisie intellectual
pretensions

but from involvement with things approaching reality
i could possibly have a life

so catatonic emotions and time wasting sex games
were replaced with functioning commitments to logic and
necessity and the gray area was slowly darkened into
a black thing
for a while progress was being made along with a certain degree
of happiness cause i wrote a book and found a love
and organized a theatre and even gave some lectures on
Black history
and began to believe all good people could get
together and win without bloodshed
then
hammarskjold was killed
and lumumba was killed
and diem was killed
and kennedy was killed
and evers was killed
and schwerner, cheney and Goodman were killed
and liuzzo was killed
and stokely fled the country
and le roi was arrested
and rap was arrested
and pollard, thompson and cooper were killed
and king was killed
and kennedy was killed
and i sometimes wonder why i didn't become a debutante
sitting on porches, going to church all the time, wondering
is my eye make-up on straight
or a withdrawn discoursing on the stars and moon
instead of a for real Black person who must now feel
and inflict
pain

Nikki Giovanni, 1968

Nikki-Rosa

childhood remembrances are always a drag
if you're Black
you always remember things like living in Woodlawn
with no inside toilet
and if you become famous or something
they never talk about how happy you were to have your mother
all to your self and
how good the water felt when you got your bath from one of those
big tubs that folk in chicago barbecue in
and somehow when you talk about home
it never gets across how much you
understood their feelings
as the whole family attended meetings about Hollydale
and even though you remember
your biographers never understand
your father's pain as he sells his stock
and another dream goes
and though you're poor it isn't poverty that
concerns you
and though they fought a lot
it isn't your father's drinking that makes any difference
but only that everybody is together and you
and your sister have happy birthdays and very good christmasses
and I really hope no white person ever has cause to write about me
because they never understand Black love is Black wealth and they'll
probably talk about my hard childhood and never understand that
all the while I was quite happy.

Nikki Giovanni, 1968

Mississippi Voter Rally

Hot, drippy evening,
    red & yellow bars of neon light.
A crowd of dark shadows
    defiantly stand in the Mississippi night.
Car roof buckles under the weight
    of silhouetted shadows against the neon.
Courage and song rise up from
    the surrounding sea of unseen folk
    engulfing us like a warm friendly ocean.
Helmets advance out of the dark
    fearsome, their long false faces
    hideous masks of death.
A shouted command, choking fumes,
    explosions,
            screams,
                terror.
Can't breathe, can't see.
The warm ocean scatters like
    spilled quicksilver.
Blindly running, blindly escaping.
Clubs thud against fragile flesh
    as helmets leap out of the night,
out of the agonizing blinding fog
    to fall on helpless innocence.
Quiet, echoing quiet,
    the damp Mississippi night closes in
on homes strangely dark.
Black shadows peer from dark windows
    as the Mars-men patrol their temporarily conquered territory,
      boots echoing off stony-faced homes.
Inside, in the dark, human blast furnaces
    forge inner resolve.
Hammers of anger pounding out determination,
    tomorrow . . . tomorrow. . tomorrow . . .

Bruce Hartford, 1966

Grenada March #107

Echoing songs on the square
White breath in cold night air
Black shadows, two by two
Marching strong, me and you.

> *"Ohhh freedom, ohhhh freedom*
> *ohhhh freedom over me. . . ."*

Beneath a lonely street light
Children singing out at night.
The mobs are gone, for this time
And tension eases down the line.

> *". . . and before I'll be a slave*
> *I'll be buried in my grave*
> *and go home to my Lord*
> *and be free-oh and be free . . ."*

Standing silent round the square
Troopers watch with hard, cold stare.
"Niggers on the march again.
Damn! Will they never end?"

> *". . . No more gassings, no more beatings*
> no more jailings, over me . . ."

Around, around, the square we stride
Cold air filled with freedom's pride.
We'll keep marching side by side
'till freedom gates are opened wide.

> *". . . and before I'll be a slave*
> *I'll be buried in my grave*
> *and go home to my Lord*
> *and be free-oh and be free."*

It's quiet on the square again
As one-oh-seven comes to end.
Proud, we march down Pearl Street
Back to church where we meet.

Bruce Hartford, 1966

:::::

The Last River

1

When I cross
on the high, back-reared ferry boat
all burnished and laboring pistons
and look at the little tugs and sticklighters
and the great ships from foreign lands
and wave to a deckhand gawking at the new world
of sugar cane and shanties and junked cars
and see a girl by the ferry rail,
the curve the breeze makes down her thigh,
and the green waves lighting up . . .
the cell-block
door crawls open and they fling us a pimp.

2

The lights dim,
the dirty jokes die out.

Rumble of trailertrucks
on Louisiana 1 . . . I think
of the rides
back from the courthouse in Amite,
down the canyon between
faces smiling from the billboards,
the car filled

with black men who tried to register to vote . . .
Tickfaw . . . Independence . . . Albany . . .

Moan of
a riverboat creeping
upstream . . . yap and screech
of police dogs
attacking the police in their dreams.

3

Under the blue flasher
and the siren's wail, I gazed out,
I remember, at anything,
anything at all of the world . . .
surreal spittoon . . .
glow of EAT . . .
fresh-hit carcass . . . cat . . . coon . . .
polecat . . .

and then lightning flashed,
path strung out a moment across the storm,
bolt of love even made of hellfire
between any strange life and any strange life,
blazed
for those who shudder in their beds
hearing a siren's wail
fading down a dead-ridden highway at night . . .
thump . . . armadillo . . . thump . . . dog . . .

4

Somebody wakes,
he's got himself a "nightcrawler"—one of those
jokes that come to you in your sleep—
about girls who have "cross-bones"
and can't, consequently,
be entered . . . An argument flares up
on whether there is, or is not,
a way to circumvent the cross-bone . . .

"Sheee-it! Sheee-it!" the copbeater cries,
and the carthief says, "Jeee-ziz! Jeee-ziz!"
"All right boys," the pimp puts in from time to time,
"What say? Let's get a little fucking sleep."

5
I turn on the iron bunk . . .
One day in Ponchatoula
when the IC from Chicago crept
into the weeds of the Deep South, and stopped,
I thought I saw three
of my kinsmen from the North
in the drinking car, boozing their way
down to New Orleans,
putting themselves across,
selling themselves,
dishing up soft soap,
plump, manicured, shit-eating, opulent, razor-sharp . . .

Then the train
lurched and pushed on, carrying them off,
Yankee . . . equalitarian . . .
grease in the palm of their golden aspirations.

6
When I think America consists
only of billboards that smile,
I think of my friends
out there,
from Plaquemine or Point Coupee,
who go from shanty to shanty
in the dust,
fighting to keep empty
the space in their breast, to trudge
through the dust for nothing,
nothing at all,

the dust
suddenly changed
into pollen or sunflowers, giving light to their feet.

7
The carthief's face,
Oddly childish as he sleeps,
Reminds me now of Jesus—a Jesus
I saw on a Negro funeral parlor calendar,
blue-eyed, rosy-cheeked, milky and soft . . .

I remember his beautiful speech of the old days . . .
those prayers, funeral orations, anthems,
war songs, and—actual poems! some of them
as beautiful as,
for example, "Wall Kill," "Terre Haute,"
"Stillwater," "Alcatraz" . . . under its name
each more escapeproof,
more supersecure,
more insane than the last,
liberty, said Shelley, being
"brightest in dungeons."

The carthief moans in his sleep, his face
now like a cat's.

8
Through the crisscross
of bars at the tiny window
I could see the swallows
that were darting in the last light,
late-flying creatures that surpass us in plain view . . .
bits of blurred flesh . . .
wavy lines . . .

Nothing's there now but a few stars
Brightening
under the ice-winds of the emptiness . . .

Isn't it strange
that all love, all granting of respect,
has no face for its passing expressions but yours,
Death?

9
I hear now
the saddest of songs, the humming
the dew makes
as it dries from the garlic leaf.

A new night
and the dew will come back again,
for so many men
the chance to live as men
does not ever come.

10
I remember
The ancient ex-convict
who teaches voter-registration
in his shanty under the levee, standing
in the sun on the dirt road . . .
a crepe myrtle tree,
a passion flower,
a butterfly . . .

In the green, blistered sewer,
Among beer cans, weeds, plastic flowers,
a few lumps of excrement, winged
with green flies.

The dust on the road
Swirls up into little wing-shapes, that blow off,
the road made of dust goes down . . .

He smiles,
the air brightens as though ashes
of lightning bolts had been scattered through it.

What is it that makes the human face,
bit of secret,
lighted flesh, open up the earth?

11

A girl and I are lying
on the grass of the levee. Two
birds whir overhead. We lie close,
as if having waked
in bodies of glory.

And putting on again
its skin of light, the river
bends into view. We watch it, rising
between the levees, flooding for the sky,
and hear it,
a hundred feet down, pressing its long weight
deeper into the world.

The birds have gone,
we wander slowly homeward, lost
in the history of every step . . .

12

I am a child
and I am lying face-down
by the Ten Mile River, one half mud
and one half piss, that runs
between the Seekonk Woods
and the red mills of Pawtucket
with their thousand windows and one smokestack,
breathing the burnt odor
of old rocks,
watching a bug breaking itself up,
holding
to my eye a bleached catfish
skull I turned up in the grass,
inside it, in the pit of light, a cross,

hearing the hornpout sounding
their horns mournfully deep inside the river.

13
Across
the dreamlit water pushes
the flag-topped Plaquemine ferry,
and midway between shore and shore
it sounds its horn, and catfishes
of the Mississippi caterwaul and nose over,
heavy-skilled,
into the flinty, night-smelling depths.

14
All my life, of rivers
I hear
the longing cries, rut-roar
of shifted wind
on the gongs of beaten water . . .

the Ten Mile of Hornpout,
the Drac hissing in its bed of sand,
the Ruknabad crossed by ghosts of nightingales,
the Passumpsic bursting down its length in spring,
the East River of Fishes, the more haunting for not
        having had a past either,
and this Mississippi coursing down now through the silt of
        all its days,
and the Tangipahoa, snake-cracked, lifting with a little
        rush from the hills and going out in thick, under-
            nourished greenery.

15
Was there some last
fling at grace in those eddies, some swirl
back toward sweet scraping, out there
where an Illinois cornstalk
drifts, turning the hours,
and the grinned skull of a boy?

The burning fodder dowses down,
seeking the snagged
bodies of the water-buried,
bits
of sainfoin sopped in fire, snuffed from below

down the flesh-dark Tallahatchie,
the bone-colored Pearl.

16
I wrench
a tassel of moss from a limb
to be my lightning-besom and sweep
the mists from the way.

Ahead of me a boy is singing,

> didn't I ramble
> I rambled
> I rambled all around
> in and out of town
> I rambled
> I rambled till the butcher cut me down . . .

He comes out of the mist,
he tells me his name is Henry David,
he takes my hand and leads me over the plain of crushed
asphodels.

17
Who's this
at water's edge,
oar in hand, kneeling beside
his pirogue of blue stern . . .
no nose left,
no hair,
no teeth,
little points of flame for eyes,
limbs tied on with knots and rags?

"Let's go," I say, a big
salty wafer of spit in my mouth.

We step in
to the threshold groan, the pressurized
bayou water squirts in
at the seams, we oar out
on water brown-green
in the patches free of scum, nothing on all sides
but the old, quiet, curious diet of green,
alligatorwood,
swamp gum, tupelo, liquid amber,
live oak chrisomed in air-eating moss,
cypress grief-shaped among her failed roots . . .

18

Down here the air's
so thick with American radio-waves,
with our bare ears we can pick up
the groggy, backcountry announcers
drawling their pitch and hardsell:
to old men forgotten under armies of roaches,
to babies with houseflies for lips and eyelashes,
to young men without future puking up present and past,
to recidivists sentenced deep into the hereafter,
to wineheads only a rusty penknife and self-loathing for
        arms,
to hillbilly boys breaking out in sweat at the ant-sweat
        ads,
to . . .
        "Listen!" says Henry David.
Sheee-it! Sheee-it!" a cupreous-
throated copbeater's chattering far-off in the trees.

19

On the shore four souls
cry out in pain, one lashed

by red suspenders to an
ever-revolving wheel, one with
red patches on the seat of his pants
shrieking while paunchy vultures
stab and gobble at his bourbon-squirting liver,
one pushing uphill
his own belly puffed up with the blood-money
he extorted on earth, that crashes back
and crushes him, one
standing up to his neck
in the vomit he caused the living to puke . . .

"Southern politicians," Henry David says,
"Yonder, in Junkie's Hollow,
you'll find Northern ones . . ." I see one,
formerly mayor of a great city, as he draws
a needle from his arm, black
blood, bits
of black testicle dribble from the puncture.

20

A man comes lurching
toward me with big mirrors for eyes,
"Sammich!" he cries and doubles up in laughter.
I remember him at once, from ten years ago,
in Chicago, on a Sunday
in a park on the death-scented South Side,
in the days before my own life had even begun,
when full of strut and happiness
this person came up and cried, "Sammich!'
and now he says, "A fight,
I was makin' the scene and the fuzz
did blast my fuckin' ass off." He laughs.
He is also crying. He shrinks back. "Hey,"
he calls, "thanks for that sammich that day . . .
fat white bastard . . ."

21
We come to a crowd, hornets
in their hair, worms in their feet.
"They weren't for anything or against anything."
Henry David says, "they looked out
for themselves."

Three men trot beside us,
peddling bits of their flesh,
dishing up soft screams,
plump, manicured, shit-eating, opulent . . .

Underfoot a man
with stars on his shoulders
grapples in the slime with his Secretary of Profit.
I kick it off him and he gets up.
"I stood above all partisan squabbles,"
he howls,
flashes the grin
that so loved itself it sold itself to the whole world,
and plunges into the slime, throttling his Secretary of
Sanctimony.

22
We come to robed
figures bunched on their knees,
meek eyes rolled up. By twitches
in their throats we gather they're alive.
"Rafel mai ameck zabi almi," they intone together.

Down on all fours, like a cat
at his saucer of fresh cream, their leader,
blue-eyed, rosy-cheeked, milky and soft, laps
with big tongue at a mirror.

23
Off to one side there's a man
signing restrictive covenants with his fingernails
on a blackboard. "That one,"

says my guide, "was
well-meaning; he believed
in equality and supported the good causes;
he got a shock, when he found out
this place is run by logicians . . ."
Hearing us talk, the man half-turns . . .
"Come on," I say, sweating, for I know him.

24
We pass
Victims of the taste for blood
who were hanged by the mob
just as the law was about to hang them,
we pass victims of justice
who were hanged by the mob for having got
stays of execution, executive pardons, or fair trials,
we pass victims of sexual dread
who cover, as we approach, the scabs at their crotches.

Here and there we see
"unknown persons"
killed for "unknown reasons"
at the hands of "persons unknown" . . .

25
We come to a river
where many thousands kneel, sucking up
its cloudy water
in a kind of frenzy . . .

"What river is it?" I ask.
"The Mystic River," Henry David says,
"the Healing Stream free to all
that flows from Calvary's Mountain . . . the liquor
that makes you forget . . ."

"And what's over there,
on the far shore?" "That?"
he says, "that's Camp Ground . . ."

I turn to see the police whipping
a child who refuses to be born,
she shrieks
and scrambles for the riverbank
and stands
singing in a floating, gospel wail,
"Oh Death, he is a little man . . ."

"What's it like in Camp Ground?" I ask

But in the mist I only hear,

> I rambled
> in and out the town
> didn't I ramble
> I rambled . . .

26

My brain rids itself of light,
at last it goes out completely,
slowly
slowly
a tiny cell far within it
lights up:

a man of noble face
sits on the iron bunk, wiping
a pile of knifeblades clean
in the rags of his body.
My old hero. Should I be surprised?

"Hard to wash off . . .
buffalo blood . . . Indian blood . . ." he mutters,
at each swipe singing, "*mein herz! mein herz!*"

"Why you," I ask him,
"You who, in your life, loathed our crimes?"

"Seeking love . . . love
without human blood in it,
that leaps above
men and women, flesh and erections,
which I thought I had found
in a Massachusetts gravel bank one spring . . .
seeking love . . .
failing to know I only loved
my purity . . . *mein herz! mein fucking herz!*"

"Hey," somebody
from another cellblock shouts, "What say?
Sleep . . . sleep . . ."

The light goes out. In the darkness
a letter for the blind
arrives in my stunned hands.
Did I come all this way only for this, only
to feel out the world-braille of my complicity,
only to choke down these last poison wafers?

For Galway alone.
I send you my mortality.
Which leans out from itself, to spit on itself,
Which you would not touch.
All you have known.

27
On one bank
of the last river stands
a black man, on the other
a white man, on the water between
a man of no color,
body of beryl,
face of lightning,
eyes lamps of wildfire,
arms and feet of polished brass.

There will come an agony upon you
beyond any
this nation has known;
and at that time thy people,
given intelligence, given imagination, given love,
given . . .

Here his voice falters, he drops
to his knees, he is
falling to pieces,
no nose left,
no hair,
no teeth,
limbs dangling from prayer-knots and rags,

waiting by the grief-tree
of the last river.

Galway Kinnell, 1965

:::::

Poem, Small and Delible

We have been picketing Woolworth's.

This page, some day, under the Poetry Decoder
Set for 20, Midcentury, Western, White, Decline,
A brown tatter pinned beneath a lens
Will stall here: What is the verb "to picket"?
And what, a Woolworth? A form of primitive market?
Perhaps they weighed and sorted fleece, then sold it.

We have been picketing Woolworth's

It is mysterious to many, even now:
Thirty-six people sweating and circling

Woolworth's on a summer's day, in a Northern town.
Three spectators ask: What *Is* Segregation?
You Should Be Ashamed!!! SIT-INS. What's them?
Laboriously picking out syllables

From our home-made posters, picketing Woolworth's

Notes for the student: Woolworth's, one of a series
Of regional emporia, privately owned, and under
A centralized management, designed to cater
To mass taste and income . . . Picket: See *Pike,* a weapon.
(2) A pointed or sharpened stake, a peg or pale.
Or, (3) A sentry, set to guard an army.

And so we walked with words impaled on stakes:

SUPPORT OUR SOUTHERN BRETHREN.

BOYCOTT WOOLWORTH'S.

(From *Boycott,* a notorious Irish captain.)
Sit-ins? But the words are baffling, as arcane
As poems. Who cares, lady? I'd picket Woolworth's
Any day, on general principles. Indignation:
Why don't you people leave poor old Woolworth's alone?

We, paying our homage to Mohandas Gandhi,

Cast our handwritten signs, our unwritten poems
On his pyre. Here the decoder won't stutter
Nor the lens hesitate. They will know who *he* was,
And that Art and Action, mostly incompatible,
Could support each other now and then. *Voici*
Que j'ai dessein encore d'un petit poème délébile
Picketing Woolworth's.

Carolyn Kizer, 1961

Revolutionary Mandate 1

These are not the times to take your friends for granted—to assume
that they will always be there. They may not be.
And if you wait until the next time to tell them that they are very
special to you
You may wait until
someone calls you and says that
so and so's body was found
beneath the bricks
of a dynamited building or
so and so was blown like water from a fountain over a midnight
highway
or
so and so was shot while he slept.
Therefore
it is hereby mandated
(by the poets and artists and musicians who are responsible for
the spirit and soul of the revolution) that when you finish this poem
you are to call your brothers and sisters, and in your own way
make them know that you love them
that because of their love you have become more you
Let them know
Five minutes from now
You may never have the opportunity again.

Julius Lester, 1970

A Note to Olga (1966)

I

Of lead and emerald
the reliquary
that knocks my breastbone,

slung round my neck
on a rough invisible rope
that rubs the knob of my spine.

Though I forget you
a red coal from your fire
burns in that box.

II

On the Times Square sidewalk
we shuffle along, cardboard signs
—Stop the War—
slung round our necks.

The cops
hurry about,
shoulder to shoulder,
comic.

Your high soprano
sings out from just
in back of me—

We shall—I turn,
you're, I very well know,
not there,

and your voice, they say,
grew hoarse
from shouting at crowds. . . .

yet *overcome*
sounds then hoarsely
from somewhere in front,

the paddywagon
gapes.—It seems
you that is lifted

limp and ardent
off the dark snow
and shoved in, and driven away.

Denise Levertov, 1966

:::::

For the Union Dead

"Relinquunt Omnia Servare Rem Publicam."

The old South Boston Aquarium stands
in a Sahara of snow now. Its broken windows are boarded.
The bronze weathervane cod has lost half its scales.
The airy tanks are dry.

Once my nose crawled like a snail on the glass;
my hand tingled
to burst the bubbles
drifting from the noses of the cowed, compliant fish.

My hand draws back. I often sigh still
for the dark downward and vegetating kingdom
of the fish and reptile. One morning last March,
I pressed against the new barbed and galvanized

fence on the Boston Common. Behind their cage,
yellow dinosaur steamshovels were grunting

as they cropped up tons of mush and grass
to gouge their underworld garage.

Parking spaces luxuriate like civic
sandpiles in the heart of Boston.
A girdle of orange, Puritan-pumpkin colored girders
Braces the tingling Statehouse,

shaking over the excavations, as it faces Colonel Shaw
and his bell-cheeked Negro infantry
on St. Gaudens shaking Civil War relief,
propped by a plank splint against the garage's earthquake.

Two months after marching through Boston,
half the regiment was dead;
at the dedication,
William James could almost hear the bronze Negroes breathe.

Their monument sticks like a fishbone
in the city's throat.
Its Colonel is as lean
as a compass-needle.

He has an angry wrenlike vigilance,
a greyhound's gentle tautness;
he seems to wince at pleasure,
and suffocate for privacy.

He is out of bounds now. He rejoices in man's lovely,
peculiar power to choose life and die—
when he leads his black soldiers to death,
he cannot bend his back.

On a thousand small town New England greens,
the old white churches hold their air
of sparse, sincere rebellion; frayed flags
quilt the graveyards of the Grand Army of the Republic.

The stone statues of the abstract Union Soldier
grow slimmer and younger each year—
wasp-waisted, they doze over muskets
and muse through their sideburns . . .

Shaw's father wanted no monument
except the ditch,
where his son's body was thrown
and lost with his "niggers."

The ditch is nearer.
There are no statues for the last war here;
on Boylston Street, a commercial photograph
shows Hiroshima boiling

over a Mosler Safe, the "Rock of Ages"
that survived the blast. Space is nearer.
When I crouch to my television set,
the drained faces of Negro school-children rise like balloons.

Colonel Shaw
is riding on his bubble,
he waits
for the blessed break.

The Aquarium is gone. Everywhere,
giant finned cars nose forward like fish;
a savage servility
slides by on grease.

Robert Lowell, 1964

Midway

I've come this far to freedom and I won't turn back
I'm climbing to the highway from my old dirt track
  I'm coming and I'm going
  And I'm stretching and I'm growing
And I'll reap what I've been sowing or my skin's not black

I've prayed and slaved and waited and I've sung my song
You've bled me and you've starved me but I've still grown strong
  You've lashed me and you've treed me
  And you've everything but freed me
But in time you'll know you need me and it won't be long.

I've seen the daylight breaking high above the bough
I've found my destination and I've made my vow;
  so whether you abhor me
  Or deride me or ignore me
Mighty mountains loom before me and I won't stop now.

Naomi Long Madgett, 1959

Be Nobody's Darling

for Julius Lester

Be nobody's darling;
Be an outcast.
Take the contradictions
Of your life
And wrap around
You like a shawl,
To parry stones
To keep you warm.

Watch the people succumb
To madness
With ample cheer;
Let them look askance at you
And you askance reply.

Be an outcast;
Be pleased to walk alone
(Uncool)
Or line the crowded
River beds
With other impetuous
Fools.

Make a merry gathering
On the bank
Where thousands perished
For brave hurt words
They said.

Be nobody's darling;
Be an outcast.
Qualified to live
Among your dead.

Alice Walker, 1973

SELECTED BIBLIOGRAPHY

Adoff, Arnold, ed. *The Poetry of Black America: Anthology of the 20th Century*. New York: Harper Collins, 1973.

Alexander, Elizabeth, ed. *The Essential Gwendolyn Brooks*. New York: Library of America, 2005.

Allen, Joe. "The Bobby Kennedy Myth." SocialistWorker.org, 6 June 2008. Accessed 12 June 2008.

Ammons, A. R. "Belief." Glikes and Schwaber 37–38.

Angelou, Maya. "Riot: 60's." *The Complete Collected Poems of Maya Angelou*. New York: Random House, 1994.

Ascher, Rhoda Gaye. "Remembrance." *Freedomways* 9, no. 2 (1969), 138.

Auden, W. H. *Collected Poems: Auden*. New York: Modern Library, 2007.

Baird, Keith. "Poplarville II." *Freedomways* 2, no. 2 (1962), 172.

Baraka, Amiri "Black Art." *Selected Poetry of Amiri Baraka / LeRoi Jones*. New York: William Morrow, 1979.

———. "A Poem for Black Hearts." *Selected Poetry of Amiri Baraka / LeRoi Jones*. New York: William Morrow, 1979.

———. "Poem for Half White College Students." *Selected Poetry of Amiri Baraka / LeRoi Jones*. New York: William Morrow, 1979.

Baraka, Amiri, and Larry Neal, eds. *Black Fire: An Anthology of Afro-American Writing*. New York: William Morrow, 1968.

Barrax, Gerald W. "For Malcolm: After Mecca." Adoff 224.

Bass, Jack, and Jack Nelson. *The Orangeburg Massacre*. Macon, Ga.: Mercer University Press, 1996.

Bass, Paul, and Douglass W. Rae. *Murder in the Model City: The Black Panthers, Yale, and the Redemption of a Killer*. New York: Basic Books, 2006.

Bass, Paul, and Douglass W. Rae. "The Panther and the Bulldog: The Story of May Day 1970." *Yale Alumni Magazine*, July–August 2006.

Bates, Daisy. *The Long Shadow of Little Rock*. Fayetteville: University of Arkansas Press, 1987.

Beecher, John. "The Better Sort of People." S. F. Brown 197–98.
———. "A Commemorative Ode." S. F. Brown 229–32.
———. "Escort for a President." S. F. Brown 228–29.
———. "Free World Notes." S. F. Brown 212.
———. "Georgia Scene: 1964." S. F. Brown 236–37.
Berry, Mary Frances. *Black Resistance / White Law: A History of Constitutional Racism in America*. New York: Penguin Books, 1994.
Berryman, John. "Formal Elegy." Glikes and Schwaber 44–47.
Bly, Robert. "War and Silence." *The Light around the Body*. London: Harper and Row, 1967.
———. "A Wrong Turning in American Poetry." *Claims for Poetry*, ed. Donald Hall. Ann Arbor: University of Michigan Press, 1986.
Branch, Taylor. *At Canaan's Edge: America in the King Years, 1965–68*. New York: Simon and Schuster, 2006.
———. *Parting the Waters: America in the King Years, 1954–63*. New York: Touchstone, 1988.
Brodsky, Louis Daniel. "Selma, Alabama, 3/6/65." *"A Hard Coming of It" and Other Poems*. St. Louis: Time Being Books, 1995.
Brooks, Gwendolyn. "The Assassination of John F. Kennedy." Glikes and Schwaber 22.
———. *The World of Gwendolyn Brooks*. New York: Harper and Row, 1971.
———. "The *Chicago Defender* Sends a Man to Little Rock." Alexander 68–70.
———. "The Last Quatrain of the Ballad of Emmett Till." Alexander 68.
———. "Malcolm X." Alexander 90.
———. "Martin Luther King, Jr." *A Broadside Treasury*. Detroit: Broadside Press, 1971.
———. "Medgar Evers." Alexander 89–90.
———. "Riot." Alexander 100–105.
Brown, Linda Megget. "Remembering the Orangeburg Massacre." *Black Issues in Higher Education* 18, no. 1 (2001), 22–23.
Brown, Stephen Ford, ed. *One More River to Cross: The Selected Poetry of John Beecher*. Montgomery, Ala.: New South Books, 2003.
Bukowski, Charles. *The Days Run Away Like Wild Horses over the Hills*. Los Angeles: Black Sparrow Press, 1969.
Bullard, Sara. *Free at Last: A History of the Civil Rights Movement and Those Who Died in the Struggle*. New York: Oxford University Press, 1993.
Cagin, Seth, and Philip Dray. *We Are Not Afraid: The Story of Goodman, Schwerner, and Chaney, and the Civil Rights Campaign for Mississippi*. New York: Nation Books, 2006.
Carson, Clayborne. *The Autobiography of Martin Luther King, Jr*. New York: Time Warner, 1998.
Carter, Karl. "Heroes." S. Henderson 311.
Césaire, Aimé. *Aimé Césaire, the Collected Poetry*. Translated with an introduction and notes by Clayton Eshelman and Annette Smith. Berkeley: University of California Press, 1983.

Church Committee. U.S. Senate Select Committee on Intelligence Activities within the United States. *Intelligence Activity and the Rights of Americans: 1976 U.S. Senate Report on Illegal Wiretaps and Domestic Spying by the FBI, CIA, and NSA*. St. Petersburg, Fla.: Red and Black Publishers, 2008.

Churchill, Ward, and Jim Vander Wall. *Agents of Repression: The FBI's Secret Wars against the Black Panther Party and the American Indian Movement*. Cambridge, Mass.: South End Press, 2002.

Cleaver, Kathleen. "The Black Mass Needs but One Crucifixion." *Black Panther* 16 March 1968.

Clifton, Lucille. "apology (to the panthers)." *Good Woman: Poems and a Memoir, 1969–1980*. American Poets Continuum series, vol. 14. Brockport, N.Y.: BOA Editions, 1987.

———. "malcolm." *Good Woman: Poems and a Memoir, 1969–1980*. American Poets Continuum series, vol. 14. Brockport, N.Y.: BOA Editions, 1987.

———. "meeting after the savior gone." *Good Woman: Poems and a Memoir, 1969–1980*. American Poets Continuum series, vol. 14. Brockport, N.Y.: BOA Editions, 1987.

Cohen, Richard. "Testimony before the Subcommittees on Crime, Terrorism, and Homeland Security and on the Constitution, Civil Rights, and Civil Liberties." Committee on the Judiciary, U.S. House of Representatives, 12 June 2007.

Coleman, R. D. "American (In Memory of Medgar Evers)." *Freedomways*, second quarter (1964), 202.

Collins, Durward, Jr. "Temperate Belt: Reflections on the Mother of Emmett Till." *Beyond the Blues: New Poems by American Negroes*, ed. Rosey E. Pool. Kent: Hand and Flower Press, 1962.

Danner, Margaret. "Passive Resistance." *Poem Counterpoem: By Margaret Danner and Dudley Randall*. Detroit: Broadside Press, 1966.

di Prima, Diane. *Revolutionary Letters, etc., 1966–1978*. San Francisco: City Lights Books, 1971.

Dooley, Ebon. "A Poem to My Brothers Killed in Combat or Something about a Conversation with My Father after Rev. King Was Killed." *Negro Digest*, February 1969, 90–91.

Edwards, Harry. "How to Change the U.S.A." *The Struggle That Must Be: An Autobiography*. New York: Macmillan, 1980.

Emanuel, James. *The Treehouse and Other Poems*. Detroit: Broadside Press, 1968.

Evans, Mari. "Litany." *Continuum: New and Selected Poems*. Baltimore: Black Classic Press, 2007.

———. "Speak the Truth to the People." *Continuum: New and Selected Poems*. Baltimore: Black Classic Press, 2007.

Evers-Williams, Myrlie, and Manning Marable. *The Autobiography of Medgar Evers: A Hero's Life and Legacy Revealed through His Writings, Letters, and Speeches*. New York: Basic Civitas Books, 2005.

Farmer, James. *Lay Bare the Heart: An Autobiography of the Civil Rights Movement*. New York: Plume, 1985.

Ferlinghetti, Lawrence. "Assassination Raga." *The Secret Meaning of Things*. New York: New Directions, 1968.

Fleming, John. "The Death of Jimmy Lee Jackson." *Anniston (Ala.) Star*, 6 March 2005.

Frost, Richard. "On Not Writing an Elegy." Glikes and Schwaber 84.

Gilbert, Dorothy. "At the Brooklyn Docks (November 23, 1963)." Glikes and Schwaber 27.

Gilbert, Zack. "For Angela." Adoff 196–97.

Ginsberg, Allen. "May King's Prophecy." P. Bass and Rae 156.

Giovanni, Nikki. "Adulthood (for Claudia)." *Black Feeling, Black Talk, Black Judgement*. New York: William Morrow, 1970.

———. "Black Power (for all the beautiful panthers east)." *Black Feeling, Black Talk, Black Judgement*. New York: William Morrow, 1970.

———. "Nikki-Rosa." *Black Feeling, Black Talk, Black Judgement*. New York: William Morrow, 1970.

———. "Reflections on April 4, 1968." *Black Feeling, Black Talk, Black Judgement*. New York: William Morrow, 1970.

Gitlin, Todd, ed. *Campfires of the Resistance: Poetry from the Movement*. Indianapolis: Bobbs-Merrill, 1971.

Glikes, Erwin A., and Paul Schwaber, eds. *Of Poetry and Power: Poems Occasioned by the Presidency and by the Death of John F. Kennedy*. New York: Basic Books, 1964.

Graham, Donald L. "April 5th." *Understanding the New Black Poetry: Black Speech and Black Music as Poetic References*, ed. Stephen Henderson. New York: William Morrow, 1973.

Guest, Barbara. "Verba in Memoriam." Glikes and Schwaber 105.

Guillén, Nicolás. "Elegy for Emmett Till." Márquez and McMurray 87–91.

———. "Little Rock (for Enrique Amorim)." Márquez and McMurray 59.

———. "What Color?" Márquez and McMurray 55–57.

Hampton, Henry, and Steve Fayer. *Voices of Freedom: An Oral History of the Civil Rights Movement from the 1950s through the 1980s*. New York: Bantam Books, 1990.

Harper, Michael S. "American History." *Images of Kin: New and Selected Poems*. Urbana: University of Illinois Press, 1977.

———. "Here Where Coltrane Is." *Images of Kin: New and Selected Poems*. Urbana: University of Illinois Press, 1977.

———. "A Mother Speaks: The Algiers Motel Incident, Detroit." *Images of Kin: New and Selected Poems*. Urbana: University of Illinois Press, 1977.

———. "Newsletter from My Mother." *Songlines in Michaeltree: New and Collected Poems*. Urbana: University of Illinois Press, 2002.

Harris, W. Edward. *Miracle in Birmingham: A Civil Rights Memoir, 1954–1965*. Indianapolis: Stonework Press, 2004.

Hayden, Robert. "El-Hajj Malik El-Shabazz (Malcolm X)." *Words in the Mourning Time*. London: October House, 1970.

———. "School Integration Riot." *Beyond the Blues: New Poems by American Negroes*, ed. Rosey E. Pool. Kent: Hand and Flower Press, 1962.

———. "Words in the Mourning Time." *Words in the Mourning Time.* London: October House, 1970.

Henderson, David. *De Mayor of Harlem: The Poetry of David Henderson.* New York: E. P. Dutton, 1970.

Henderson, Stephen. *Understanding the New Black Poetry: Black Speech and Black Music as Poetic References.* New York: William Morrow, 1973.

Hersey, John. *The Algiers Motel Incident.* Baltimore: Johns Hopkins University Press, 1997.

Hersh, Burton. *Bobby and J. Edgar: The Historic Face-off between the Kennedys and J. Edgar Hoover that Transformed America.* New York: Carroll and Graf, 2007.

Hollo, Anselm. "Until Death Do Us Part." Glikes and Schwaber 41–42.

Horne, Gerald. *Fire This Time: The Watts Uprising and the 1960s.* New York: Da Capo Press, 1997.

Howes, Barbara. "A Night Picture of Pownal." Glikes and Schwaber 60–61.

Huggins, Ericka. ["let the fault be with the man"]. *Insights and Poems.* San Francisco: City Lights Books, 1975.

Hughes, Langston. "Birmingham Sunday." *The Collected Poems of Langston Hughes,* ed. Arnold Rampersad and David Roessel. New York: Alfred A. Knopf, 1995.

———. "Mississippi—1955." *Daily Worker,* 26 September 1955.

Ignatow, David. "Before the Sabbath." Glikes and Schwaber 23.

———. "For Medgar Evers." *Rescue the Dead: Poems.* Middletown, Conn.: Wesleyan University Press, 1968.

Iman, Yusef. "Love Your Enemy." Baraka and Neal 387.

Inman, Will. "Jacqueline." Glikes and Schwaber 39.

Isoardi, Steven L. *The Dark Tree: Jazz and the Community Arts in Los Angeles.* Berkeley: University of California Press, 2006.

James, Joy. *The New Abolitionists: (Neo)slave Narratives and Contemporary Prison Writings.* Albany: State University of New York Press, 2005.

Jeffers, Lance. *My Blackness Is the Beauty of This Land.* Detroit: Broadside Press, 1970.

Jennings, Regina. "Poetry of the Black Panther Party: Metaphors of Militancy." *Journal of Black Studies* 29, no. 1 (1998), 106–29.

Jordan, June. "Poem against the State of Things." *Directed by Desire: The Collected Poems of June Jordan,* ed. Jan Heller Levi and Sara Miles. Port Townsend, Wash.: Copper Canyon Press, 2005.

Justice, Donald. "The Assassination." *Collected Poems.* New York: Alfred A. Knopf, 2004.

Kennedy, Matthew Maxwell Taylor. *Make Gentle the Life of This World: The Vision of Robert F. Kennedy.* New York: Harcourt Brace, 1998.

Kennedy, X. J. "Down in Dallas." Glikes and Schwaber 127.

King, Martin Luther, Jr. "John F. Kennedy." *Transition* 15 (1964), 27–28.

Kinnell, Galway. "The Last River." *Three Books: Body Rags. Mortal Acts, Mortal Words. The Past.* Boston: Houghton Mifflin, 1993.

Kizer, Carolyn. "Poem, Small and Delible." *Cool, Calm, and Collected: Poems 1960–2000.* Port Townsend, Wash.: Copper Canyon Press, 2001.

———. "Race Relations." *Cool, Calm, and Collected: Poems 1960–2000*. Port Townsend, Wash.: Copper Canyon Press, 2001.

———. "Season for Lovers and Assassins." *Cool, Calm, and Collected: Poems 1960–2000*. Port Townsend, Wash.: Copper Canyon Press, 2001.

Knight, Etheridge. "Portrait of Malcolm X." *Poems from Prison*. Detroit: Broadside Press, 1968.

Koehler, Stanley. "In Arlington Cemetery." Glikes and Schwaber 50–51.

Kotz, Nick. *Judgment Days: Lyndon Baines Johnson, Martin Luther King, Jr., and the Laws that Changed America*. New York: Houghton Mifflin, 2005.

Kramer, Aaron. "Blues for Medgar Evers." *Freedomways*, fourth quarter (1964), 487.

Kuettner, Al. *March to a Promised Land: The Civil Rights Files of a White Reporter, 1952–1968*. Herndon, Va.: Capital Books, 2006.

Lawson, William H. "A Righteous Anger in Mississippi: Genre Constraints and Breaking Precedence." M.A. thesis, Florida State University, 2005.

Lester, Julius. "On the Birth of My Son, Malcolm Coltrane." *Soulscript: A Collection of Classic African American Poetry*, ed. June Jordan. New York: Random House, 1970.

Levertov, Denise. "The Day the Audience Walked Out on Me, and Why." *Poems 1968–1972*. New York: New Directions, 1987.

———. "The Gulf." *Poems 1968–1972*. New York: New Directions, 1987.

———. "A Note to Olga (1966)." *Poems: 1960–1967*. New York: New Directions, 1983.

Levine, Philip. "Coming Home, Detroit, 1968." *They Feed The Lion: Poems*. New York: Atheneum, 1972.

Lewis, John. *Walking with the Wind: A Memoir of the Movement*. New York: Simon and Schuster, 1998.

Lorde, Audre. "Rites of Passage." *The Collected Poems of Audre Lorde*. New York: Norton, 1997.

———. "Suffer the Children." *Negro Digest* 10, no. 3 (1964), 15.

Lowell, Robert. "For Robert Kennedy 1925–68." *Robert Lowell: Selected Poems*. Revised ed. New York: Noonday Press, 1977.

———. "For the Union Dead." *Robert Lowell: Selected Poems*. Revised ed. New York: Noonday Press, 1977.

———. "Two Walls." *Robert Lowell: Selected Poems*. Revised ed. New York: Noonday Press, 1977.

Luce, Phillip Abbott. "Mack C. Parker." *Freedomways* 2, no. 1 (1962), 95–96.

Lynch, Charles. "If We Cannot Live As People." Adoff 461.

Madgett, Naomi Long. "Alabama Centennial." *Star by Star*. Detroit: Lotus Press, 1970.

———. "Midway." *Star by Star*. Detroit: Lotus Press, 1970.

Madhubuti, Haki R (Don L. Lee). "Assassination." *Don't Cry, Scream*. Detroit: Broadside Press, 1969.

———. "One Sided Shoot-Out." *GroundWork: New and Selected Poems of Don L. Lee / Haki R. Madhubuti from 1966–1996*. Chicago: Third World Press, 1996.

Major, Clarence, ed. *The New Black Poetry*. New York: International Publishing, 1969.

Malcolm X. *Malcolm X Speaks: Selected Speeches and Statements*, ed. George Breitman. New York: Grove Weidenfeld, 1990.

Mariani, Paul. *Lost Puritan: A Life of Robert Lowell.* New York: W. W. Norton, 1994.

Márquez, Roberto, and David Arthur McMurray, trans. and eds. *Man-Making Words: Selected Poems of Nicolás Guillén.* Amherst: University of Massachusetts Press, 2003.

Marvin X (Marvin E. Jackmon). "That Old Time Religion." Baraka and Neal 268.

Merriam, Eve. "Money, Mississippi." *Montgomery, Alabama, Money, Mississippi, and Other Places.* New York: Cameron Associates, 1956.

Mezey, Robert. "April Fourth." *Collected Poems, 1952–1999.* Fayetteville: University of Arkansas Press, 2000.

Mir, Marjorie. "Four Days in November." Glikes and Schwaber 85.

———. "Mississippi, 1964." Unpublished manuscript.

Morris, Willie. *The Courting of Marcus Dupree.* Jackson: University Press of Mississippi, 1992.

Morsberger, Robert E. "Segregated Surveys: American Literature." *Negro American Literature Forum* 4, no. 1 (1970), 3–8.

Murray, Pauli. "Collect for Poplarville." *Dark Testament and Other Poems.* Norwalk, Conn.: Silvermine, 1970.

———. "For Mack C. Parker." *Dark Testament and Other Poems.* Norwalk, Conn.: Silvermine, 1970.

Neal, Larry. "Kuntu." *Visions of a Liberated Future: Black Arts Movement Writings.* New York: Thunder's Mouth Press, 1989.

———. "Malcolm X—An Autobiography." *Visions of a Liberated Future: Black Arts Movement Writings.* New York: Thunder's Mouth Press, 1989.

Newton, Huey P. *The Huey P. Newton Reader*, ed. David Hilliard and Donald Weise. New York: Seven Stories Press, 2002.

Newton, Huey P., and Ericka Huggins. *Insights and Poems.* San Francisco: City Lights Books, 1975.

Newton, Melvin. "We Called Him the General." *The Huey P. Newton Reader*, ed. David Hilliard and Donald Weise. New York: Seven Stories Press, 2002.

Nhat Hanh, Thich. "The Sun of the Future." *Call Me by My True Names: The Collected Poems of Thich Nhat Hanh.* Berkeley: Parallax Press, 1999.

Ojenke (Alvin Saxon). "Watts." *From the Ashes: Voices of Watts*, ed. Budd Schulberg. New York: New American Library, 1967.

Orr, Gregory. *The Blessing: A Memoir.* San Francisco: Council Oaks Books, 2002.

———. *The Caged Owl: New and Selected Poems.* Port Townsend, Wash.: Copper Canyon Press, 2002.

Patterson, Raymond. *26 Ways of Looking at a Black Man.* New York: Award Books, 1969.

Pleasants, Ben. *Visceral Bukowski: Inside the Sniper Landscape of L.A. Writers.* Northville, Mich.: Sun Dog Press, 2004.

Pope, Deborah. *A Separate Vision: Isolation in Contemporary Women's Poetry.* Baton Rouge: Louisiana State University Press, 1999.

Purdy, Al. "For Robert Kennedy." *Beyond Remembering: The Collected Poems of Al Purdy.* Madeira Park, British Columbia: Harbour Publishing, 2000.

Pyes, Craig Randolph. "The Panther / After Rilke." Gitlin 240–41.

Raines, Howell. *My Soul Is Rested: The Story of the Civil Rights Movement in the Deep South*. New York: Penguin, 1983.

Randall, Dudley, and Margaret G. Burroughs, eds. *For Malcolm: Poems on the Life and the Death of Malcolm X*. Detroit: Broadside Press, 1969.

Reeves, Thomas. *A Question of Character: A Life of John F. Kennedy*. Roseville, Calif.: Prima Publishing, 1997.

Rich, Adrienne. "Ghazals: Homage to Ghalib, 7/26/68 ii." *The Fact of a Doorframe: Poems Selected and New, 1950–1984*. New York: W. W. Norton, 1984.

River, Conrad Kent. "If Blood Is Black Then Spirit Neglects My Unborn Son." Adoff 236.

Rukeyser, Muriel. "Martin Luther King, Malcolm X." *The Collected Poems of Muriel Rukeyser*, ed. Janet E. Kaufman and Anne F. Herzog. Pittsburgh: University of Pittsburgh Press, 2005.

Sanchez, Sonia. "malcolm." Randall and Burroughs 38–39.

Sanders, Edward. "A Flower from Robert Kennedy's Grave." *Thirsting for Peace in a Raging Century: Selected Poems, 1961–1985*. Minneapolis: Coffee House Press, 1987.

Schwerner, Armand. "Speech for LeRoi." *Seaweed*. Los Angeles: Black Sparrow Press, 1969.

Seale, Bobby. *Seize the Time: The Story of the Black Panther Party and Huey P. Newton*. New York: Vintage, 1970.

Segal, Edith. "Ballad for Four Children and a President." *Take My Hand: Poems and Songs for Lovers and Rebels*. New York: Dialog, 1970.

Senghor, Léopold Sédar. "Elegy for Martin Luther King." *The Collected Poetry*, trans. Melvin Dixon. Charlottesville: University of Virginia Press, 1991.

Smead, Howard. *Blood Justice: The Lynching of Mack Charles Parker*. Oxford: Oxford University Press, 1986.

Solomon, Marvin. "Sonnet for John-John." Glikes and Schwaber 89.

Sorensen, Theodore, comp. *"Let the Word Go Forth": The Speeches, Statements, and Writings of John F. Kennedy 1947 to 1963*. New York: Dell, 1998.

Spellman, A. B. "In Orangeburg My Brothers Did." Adoff 285.

———. "When Black People Are." Adoff 284–85.

Steel, Ronald. *In Love with the Night: The American Romance with Robert Kennedy*. New York: Simon and Schuster, 2001.

Thomas, Lorenzo. "Not That Hurried Grief." Glikes and Schwaber 58–59.

"Those Kennedy Judges." *Time*, 6 November 1964, 44.

Troupe, Quincy. "For Malcolm Who Walks in the Eyes of Our Children." Adoff 444–45.

———. "White Weekend." Major 128.

Turco, Lewis. "November 22, 1963." Glikes and Schwaber 21.

Tyson, Timothy B. "Robert F. Williams, 'Black Power,' and the Roots of the African American Freedom Struggle." *Journal of American History* 85, no. 2 (1998), 540–70.

U.S. Department of Justice. Federal Bureau of Investigation. *Summary of Investigation of the Abduction of Mack Charles Parker from the Pearl River County Jail, Poplarville, Mississippi, April 24–25, 1959*. vault.fbi.gov. Accessed 12 June 2010.

Valentine, Jean. "September 1963." *Door in the Mountain: New and Collected Poems, 1965–2003*. Middletown, Conn.: Wesleyan University Press, 2004.

Varela, Maria. "Crumpled Notes (found in a raincoat) on Selma." Gitlin 36–39.

Vollers, Maryanne. *Ghosts of Mississippi: The Murder of Medgar Evers, the Trials of Byron De La Beckwith, and the Haunting of the New South*. Boston: Little, Brown, 1995.

Walcott, Derek. "Elegy." *Derek Walcott: Collected Poems, 1948–1984*. New York: Farrar, Straus and Giroux, 1986.

———. "The Gulf." *Derek Walcott: Collected Poems, 1948–1984*. New York: Farrar, Straus and Giroux, 1986.

Walker, Alice. *Anything We Love Can Be Saved: A Writer's Activism*. New York: Ballantine, 1997.

———. "Be Nobody's Darling." *Revolutionary Petunias and Other Poems*. New York: Harcourt Brace Jovanovich, 1973.

Walker, Margaret. "Amos, 1963." *This Is My Century: New and Collected Poems*. Athens: University of Georgia Press, 1989.

———. "Amos (Postscript, 1968)." *This Is My Century: New and Collected Poems*. Athens: University of Georgia Press, 1989.

———. "For Andy Goodman, Michael Schwerner, and James Chaney." *This Is My Century: New and Collected Poems*. Athens: University of Georgia Press, 1989.

———. "For Malcolm X." *This Is My Century: New and Collected Poems*. Athens: University of Georgia Press, 1989.

———. "Micah (In Memory of Medgar Evers of Mississippi)." *This Is My Century: New and Collected Poems*. Athens: University of Georgia Press, 1989.

"War at Attica: Was There No Other Way?" *Time*, 27 September 1971.

"When Night Falls." *Time*, 31 July 1964.

Williams, Juan. *Eyes on the Prize: America's Civil Rights Years, 1954–1965*. New York: Penguin, 1987.

Wright, Jay. "The Solitude of Change." Randall and Burroughs 28–29.

Yevtushenko, Yevgeny. "Freedom to Kill," trans. Lawrence Ferlinghetti and Anthony Kahn. *Stolen Apples: Poetry by Yevgeny Yevtushenko*, trans. James Dickey et al. New York: Doubleday, 1972.

Young, Andrew. *An Easy Burden: The Civil Rights Movement and the Transformation of America*. New York: Harper Collins, 1996.

Zinn, Howard. *A People's History of the United States: 1492–Present*. New York: Harper Collins, 2003.

CONTRIBUTORS

A. R. Ammons (1926–2001) published his first book of poems, *Ommateum: With Doxology,* in 1955. He went on to publish nearly thirty collections, including *Bosh and Flapdoodle*; *Glare*; *Garbage* (which won the National Book Award and the Library of Congress's Rebekah Johnson Bobbitt National Prize for Poetry); *A Coast of Trees,* which received the National Book Critics Circle Award for Poetry; *Sphere* (which received the Bollingen Prize); and *Collected Poems 1951–1971* (which won the National Book Award). Other honors included the Wallace Stevens Award of the American Academy of Arts and Letters, the Robert Frost Medal of the Poetry Society of America, the Ruth Lilly Prize, and fellowships from the Guggenheim Foundation, the MacArthur Foundation, and the American Academy of Arts and Letters.

Maya Angelou (1928–) is best known for her autobiographical books: *All God's Children Need Traveling Shoes*; *The Heart of a Woman*; *Singin' and Swingin' and Gettin' Merry Like Christmas*; *Gather Together in My Name*; and *I Know Why the Caged Bird Sings,* which was nominated for the National Book Award. Among her books of poetry are *A Brave and Startling Truth*; *The Complete Collected Poems of Maya Angelou*; *Wouldn't Take Nothing for My Journey Now*; *Now Sheba Sings the Song*; *I Shall Not Be Moved*; *Shaker, Why Don't You Sing?*; *Oh Pray My Wings Are Gonna Fit Me Well*; and *Just Give Me a Cool Drink of Water 'fore I Diiie,* which was nominated for a Pulitzer prize. In 1959, at the request of Dr. Martin Luther King Jr., Maya Angelou became the northern coordinator for the Southern Christian Leadership Conference.

Rhoda Gaye Ascher

W. H. Auden (1907–73) was born in York, England, but moved to the United States in his late thirties and became an American citizen. A prolific writer, Auden was also a noted playwright, librettist, editor, and essayist. Many critics consider him the greatest English poet of the twentieth century. His books of poetry include *Poems*; *Look, Stranger!*; *The Double Man*; and *City Without Walls and Other Poems.* He won the National Book Award in 1956 for *The Shield of Achilles.*

Keith E. Baird (1923–) earned degrees from Columbia University and Union Graduate School and has taught at several colleges, including Hunter College, Hofstra University, and the State University of New York, Buffalo. He was an editor of *Freedomways* and the *Journal of Black Studies* and the author of *Sea Island Roots: African Presence in the Carolinas and Georgia; A Critical Annotated Bibliography of African Linguistic Continuities in the Spanish-Speaking Americas*; and *Names from Africa: Their Origin, Meaning, and Pronunciation*. His poetry has appeared in *Freedomways*. He lives in Atlanta, Georgia.

Amiri Baraka (1934–) was born in Newark, New Jersey, and is Professor Emeritus at the State University of New York, Stony Brook. He published his first book of poetry, *Preface to a Twenty-Volume Suicide Note*, in 1961. His *Blues People: Negro Music in White America* (1963) is still regarded as the seminal work on African American music and culture. His reputation as a playwright was established with the production of the controversial *Dutchman* in 1964, which subsequently won an Obie Award for Best Off-Broadway Play and was made into a film. He has written numerous collections of poetry, including *Selected Poetry of Amiri Baraka/LeRoi Jones* and *Somebody Blew Up America & Other Poems*. He has also published essays and jazz operas. His numerous literary honors include fellowships from the Guggenheim Foundation and the National Endowment for the Arts, the PEN/Faulkner Award, the Rockefeller Foundation Award for Drama, the Langston Hughes Award from City College of New York, and a lifetime achievement award from the Before Columbus Foundation. He was inducted into the American Academy of Arts and Letters in 1995. In 2002 he was named Poet Laureate of New Jersey and Newark Public Schools. His most recent book, *Digging: The Afro American Soul of American Classical Music*, won an American Book Award.

Gerald Barrax (1933–) was born in Attalla, Alabama, grew up in Pittsburgh, and earned degrees from Duquesne University and the University of Pittsburgh. He is the author of five books of poetry: *Another Kind of Rain*; *An Audience of One*; *The Death of Animals and Lesser Gods*; *Leaning Against the Sun*; and *From a Person Sitting in Darkness: New and Selected Poems*. Barrax has been inducted into the North Carolina Literary Hall of Fame, and has won the *Callaloo* Creative Writing Award for Nonfiction Prose, the North Carolina Award for Literature, the Raleigh Medal of Arts for "Extraordinary Achievement in the Arts," the Sam Ragan Award for contribution to the fine arts in North Carolina, and the Donald Justice Award for Poetry. He was a professor of English and creative writing at North Carolina State University from 1969 until his retirement in 1997. There, he also edited the journal *Obsidian II: Black Literature in Review*. He lives in Raleigh with his wife, Joan.

John Beecher (1904–80) was born in New York City and grew up in Birmingham, Alabama. He taught at various colleges from the late 1940s through the 1970s, and covered the civil rights movement as a reporter for the *San Francisco Chronicle* and *Ramparts* magazine. He devoted most of his poetic output to issues of race and class. Among his more celebrated books are, *Report to the Stockholders & Other Poems: 1932–1962*; *To Live and Die in Dixie*; and *Collected Poems: 1924–1973*.

Jim "Arkansas" Benston was born in Tennessee, grew up in Arkansas, and earned B.A. and M.A. degrees from the University of Colorado. He decided to devote his life to social justice after hearing a speech by Fannie Lou Hamer. He was arrested in 1965 for not obeying segregation laws in a Dallas County courtroom and suffered head injuries during the "Bloody Sunday" march in Selma, Alabama. He became a volunteer organizer for SNCC and SCLC in the voting rights movement in Alabama in 1965 and 1966. He loaded trucks and was a steward in the Teamsters and Mailhandlers unions in Chicago from 1968–87. Benston was the founding president of Concerned Truckers for a Democratic Union in Chicago in 1975.

John Berryman (1914–72) was born John Smith in MacAlester, Oklahoma. He received an undergraduate degree from Columbia College in 1936 and attended Cambridge University on a fellowship. He taught at Wayne State University in Detroit and went on to occupy posts at Harvard and Princeton universities. From 1955 until his death, he was a professor at the University of Minnesota. He published fifteen collections of poems, including *77 Dream Songs*, which won a Pulitzer Prize in 1965.

Robert Bly (1926–) was born in Madison, Minnesota. He attended Harvard University and received his M.A. from the University of Iowa in 1956. He is the author of more than thirty books of poetry, including *The Night Abraham Called to the Stars*; *Snowbanks North of the House*; *What Have I Ever Lost by Dying?: Collected Prose Poems*; *Loving a Woman in Two Worlds*; *Mirabai Versions*; *This Body is Made of Camphor and Gopherwood*; and *The Light Around the Body*, which won the National Book Award. He lives on a farm in the western part of Minnesota with his wife and three children.

June Brindel (1919–) was born on a farm in Little Rock, Iowa, and earned her B.A. and M.A. degrees from the University of Chicago. She became actively involved with the civil rights movement in the 1960s. Her short stories and poems have been published in *Beloit Poetry Journal*, *Carolina Quarterly*, *Rhino*, *Primavera*, *MSS*, *Spoon River Poetry Review*, *Story Quarterly*, *Kansas Quarterly*, and *Other Voices*. She is the author of the short story collection *Nobody Is Ever Missing* and the novels *Phaedra* and *Ariadne*. She is currently working on a new novel, *Clytemnestra*, and a volume of her collected poems.

Louis Daniel Brodsky (1941–) was born in St. Louis and earned degrees from Yale, Washington, and San Francisco universities. He is the author of seventy-one books of poetry (five of which have been published in French by Éditions Gallimard) and twenty-five books of prose, including nine scholarly works on William Faulkner and nine books of short fiction. His poems and essays have appeared in *Harper's*, *Faulkner Journal*, *Southern Review*, *Texas Quarterly*, *National Forum*, *American Scholar*, *Studies in Bibliography*, *Kansas Quarterly*, *Forum*, *Cimarron Review*, and *Literary Review*. His work has also been printed in five editions of the *Anthology of Magazine Verse and Yearbook of American Poetry*. In 2004, Brodsky's *You Can't Go Back Exactly* won the award for the best book of poetry, presented by the Center for Great Lakes Culture, at Michigan State University.

Gwendolyn Brooks (1917–2000) was born in Topeka, Kansas, and raised in Chicago. She is the author of more than twenty books of poetry, including *Children Coming Home*; *Blacks*; *To Disembark*; *The Near-Johannesburg Boy and Other Poems*; *Riot*; *In the Mecca*; *The Bean Eaters*; *Annie Allen* (for which she received a Pulitzer Prize); and *A Street in Bronzeville*. She also wrote numerous other books, including a novel, *Maud Martha*, and *Report from Part One: An Autobiography*, and she edited *Jump Bad: A New Chicago Anthology*. In 1968 she was named Poet Laureate for the state of Illinois, and from 1985 to 1986 she was Consultant in Poetry to the Library of Congress. She received an American Academy of Arts and Letters award, the Frost Medal, a National Endowment for the Arts award, the Shelley Memorial Award, and fellowships from the Academy of American Poets and the Guggenheim Foundation.

Charles Bukowski (1920–94) was born in Andernach, Germany, moved to the United States with his family at the age of three, and grew up in Los Angeles. Bukowski published his first story when he was twenty-four and began writing poetry at the age of thirty-five. His writing often featured a depraved metropolitan environment, downtrodden members of American society, direct language, violence, and sexual imagery, and many of his works center around a roughly autobiographical figure named Henry Chinaski. His first book of poetry was published in 1959; he went on to publish more than forty-five books of poetry and prose, including *Pulp*; *Screams from the Balcony: Selected Letters 1960–1970*; and *The Last Night of the Earth Poems*.

Karl Carter (1944–) was born in New Orleans and attended Tennessee State University where he began writing poetry and was awarded a B.S. degree in sociology. Carter then obtained his law degree from Howard University. He practices law in Washington, D.C., and resides in Alexandria, Virginia. Carter wrote two chapbooks in the early 1970s: *A Season in Sorrow* and *Three Poems*, both published by Broadside Press in Detroit. His poems have appeared in numerous books and journals, including *Presence African*; *Black World* (in a special edition dedicated to Sterling Brown); *Understanding the New Black Poetry*; *Off the Record: An Anthology of Poetry by Lawyers*; and *The Legal Studies Forum*. He published *Sojourner and Other Poems* in 2010.

Aimé Césaire (1913–2008) was born in Basse-Pointe on Martinique. He attended the Lycée Schoelcher on the island and the Ecole Normale Supérieure and the Lycée Louis-le-Grand in Paris. His books of poetry include *Aimé Césaire: The Collected Poetry*; *Putting in Fetters*; *Lost Bodies* (with illustrations by Pablo Picasso); *Decapitated Sun*; *Miraculous Arms*; and *Notebook of a Return to the Homeland*. His plays include *Laminaire*; *The Tempest*; *A Season at Congo*; and *The Tragedy of King Cristophe*. Césaire received the International Nâzim Hikmet Poetry Award. He served as the mayor of Fort-de-France on Martinique as a member of the Communist Party before quitting the party to establish his Martinique Independent Revolution Party. He was deeply involved in the struggle for French West Indian rights and served as the deputy to the French National Assembly.

Kathleen Cleaver (1945–) has spent most of her life participating in the human rights struggle and left college in 1966 to work with SNCC. From 1967 to 1971, she was the communications secretary of the Black Panther Party. She lived in exile with her former husband, Eldridge Cleaver, before returning to the United States in 1975. She has won fellowships at the Bunting Institute of Radcliffe College, the W. E. B. Du Bois Institute of Harvard University, the Center for Historical Analysis at Rutgers, and the Schomburg Center for Research in Black Culture. Cleaver was a fellow at the Center for Scholars and Writers of the New York Public Library, where she continued work on her memoirs, *Memories of Love and War*. Her writing has appeared in many magazines and newspapers, and she has contributed scholarly essays to several books, including *Critical Race Feminism*; *Critical White Studies*; *The Promise of Multiculturalism*; and *The Black Panther Party Reconsidered*. She is currently a senior lecturer at Emory University School of Law.

Lucille Clifton (1936–2010) was born in Depew, New York. Her first book of poems, *Good Times* (1969), was rated by the *New York Times* as one of the best books published that year. She became a writer in residence at Coppin State College in Baltimore, where she completed two collections: *Good News About the Earth* and *An Ordinary Woman*. Other collections include *Voices*; *Mercy*; *Blessing the Boats: New and Selected Poems 1988–2000* (which won the National Book Award); *The Terrible Stories* (which was nominated for the National Book Award); *The Book of Light*; *Quilting: Poems 1987–1990*; and *Next: New Poems*. Her collection *Good Woman: Poems and a Memoir 1969–1980* was nominated for a Pulitzer Prize; *Two-Headed Woman*, also a Pulitzer Prize nominee, received the University of Massachusetts Press's Juniper Prize. She also wrote more than sixteen books for children. Other honors include an Emmy Award from the American Academy of Television Arts and Sciences; a Lannan Literary Award; two fellowships from the National Endowment for the Arts; the Shelley Memorial Award; the YM-YWHA Poetry Center Discovery Award; and the 2007 Ruth Lilly Prize. In 1999 she was elected a chancellor of the Academy of American Poets. She has served as Poet Laureate for the State of Maryland and Distinguished Professor of Humanities at St. Mary's College of Maryland.

R. D. Coleman has lived in New York City his entire life. He has worked as a union organizer, with street gangs on the Lower East Side, as a worker in and director of homeless shelters, and as an assistant commissioner in the NYC Department of Homeless Services. His collection of poems, *Beach Tracks*, was released by New York Quarterly Books in 2010.

Durward Collins Jr. (1939–87) was born in Houston and earned degrees from the University of Michigan and City College in New York. He held positions with the New York City Board of Education, Harlem Center for the Child, York College of New York, and Bronx Community College. Collins was also a professional model and actor. He resided in Upper Grandview, New York, with his wife, Veronica Jones Collins.

Margaret Danner (1915–84) was born in Pryorsburg, Kentucky, and grew up in Chicago. Her collections of poems include *Impressions of African Art Forms*; *To Flower*; *Iron Lace*; *Not Light, Nor Bright, Nor*; *Poem Counterpoem*, with Dudley Randall; and *The Down of a Thistle: Selected Poems, Prose Poems, and Songs*.

Diane di Prima (1934–) was born in Brooklyn and became an influential member of the beat movement. She co-founded the New York Poets Theatre, founded the Poets Press, and edited a literary magazine, *The Floating Bear,* with Amiri Baraka. She has written more than forty books of poetry and prose, including *Revolutionary Letters.* Her work has appeared in over four hundred literary magazines, newspapers, and anthologies. She was selected as poet laureate of San Francisco in 2009.

Ebon Dooley (1942–2006) was born Leo Thomas Hale in Milan, Tennessee, and graduated from Columbia Law School. His collection, *Revolution: A Poem,* was published by Third World Press in 1968. He was a renowned community activist, bookstore manager, and public radio host in Atlanta for WRFG-FM (Radio Free Georgia, 89.3) for more than thirty years. He served as president of the board of directors, broadcast director, and affiliate representative for the station on the Pacifica Radio Board.

Harry Edwards (1942–) was born in St. Louis and earned a B.A. degree from San Jose State University, and M.A. and Ph.D. degrees from Cornell University. Edwards was on the sociology faculty at the University of California, Berkeley from 1970 to 2001. He is the architect of the Olympic Project for Human Rights, which led to the Black Power Salute protest by African American athletes at the 1968 Summer Olympics in Mexico City. His works include *The Sociology of Sport*; *The Struggle that Must Be*; and *The Revolt of the Black Athlete.* He is a consultant to the San Francisco Forty-Niners and Golden State Warriors.

James Emanuel (1921–) was born in Alliance, Nebraska. He earned a B.A. from Howard University, an M.A. from Northwestern University, and a Ph.D. from Columbia University. Among his books of poetry are *Jazz from the Haiku King*; *De la rage au Coeur* (translated by Jean Migrenne and Amiot Lenganey); *Whole Grain: Collected Poems, 1958–1989*; *The Quagmire Effect*; *Deadly James and Other Poems*; *The Broken Bowl: New and Uncollected Poems*; *Black Man Abroad: The Toulouse Poems*; and *At Bay*. He is also the author of *Langston Hughes* and the editor, with Theodore L. Gross, of *Dark Symphony: Negro Literature in America.* He lives in Paris.

Lawrence Ferlinghetti (1919–) was born in Yonkers, New York, and spent his early childhood in France. He received a B.A. from the University of North Carolina, an M.A. from Columbia University, and a Ph.D. from the Sorbonne. In 1953 Ferlinghetti and Peter Martin began to publish *City Lights* magazine. They also opened the City Lights Books Shop in San Francisco to help support the magazine. In 1955 they launched City Lights Publishing, a book-publishing venture. City Lights became known as the heart of the beat movement. Ferlinghetti is the author of more than thirty books of poetry, including *Americus, Book I*; *San Francisco Poems*; *How to Paint Sunlight*; *A Far Rockaway of the Heart*; *These Are My Rivers: New & Selected Poems, 1955–1993*; *Over All the Obscene Boundaries: European Poems & Transitions*; *Who Are We Now?*; *The Secret Meaning of Things*; and *A Coney Island of the Mind.* He has translated the work of a number of poets, including Nicanor Parra, Jacques Prevert, and Pier Paolo Pasolini. Ferlinghetti is also the author of more than eight plays and of the novels *Love in the Days of Rage* and *Her*. San Francisco renamed a street in his honor in 1994 and made him its first poet laureate in 1998. In 2000, he received the lifetime achievement award from the National Book Critics Circle.

Richard Frost (1929–) was born in Redwood City, California, and earned degrees from San Jose State University. His collections include *The Circus Villains; Getting Drunk with the Birds; Jazz for Kirby; The Family Way*; and *Neighbor Blood*. He is a jazz drummer and Emeritus Professor of English at the State University College, Oneonta, New York.

Dorothy Gilbert's poetry has appeared in *The New Yorker; The Nation; The Iowa Review; Southern Lights: PEN South Anthology*; and in the online journal *Tattoo Highway*. She translates poetry from medieval French and English, and her verse translations of two *lais* of Marie de France are included in the 2007 edition of *The Norton Anthology of Literature by Women*. She is preparing a Norton Critical Edition, with her English rhymed version, of Marie's oeuvre. Gilbert has worked for PEN American Center since 1990 and teaches in a special program for freshmen at the University of California, Berkeley.

Zack Gilbert (1925–95) was born Lerman Gilbert in McMullin, Missouri. He published his first poem in the *Chicago Defender* while in grade school and subsequently published in *Negro Digest* and *Black World*. He published two collections of poems, *My Own Hallelujahs* and *Up North Big City Street*.

Allen Ginsberg (1926–97) was born in Newark, New Jersey, and attended Columbia University. He began close friendships with William S. Burroughs, Neal Cassady, and Jack Kerouac, all of whom later became leading figures of the beat movement. In 1954 Ginsberg moved to San Francisco, and two years later City Lights published his *Howl and Other Poems*, which was banned for obscenity. The work overcame censorship trials, however, and became one of the most widely read poems of the century, translated into over twenty-two languages. Ginsberg went on publish numerous collections of poetry, including *Kaddish and Other Poems; Planet News*; and *The Fall of America: Poems of These States* (which won the National Book Award). In 1993 Ginsberg received the Chevalier des Arts et des Lettres (Order of Arts and Letters) from the French Minister of Culture. He co-founded and directed the Jack Kerouac School of Disembodied Poetics at the Naropa Institute in Colorado. In his later years Ginsberg became a Distinguished Professor at Brooklyn College.

Yolanda Cornelia "Nikki" Giovanni (1943–) was born in Knoxville, Tennessee, and raised in Cincinnati, Ohio. In 1960 she entered Fisk University in Nashville, Tennessee, where she worked with the school's Writer's Workshop and edited the literary magazine. After receiving her B.A. degree in 1967 she organized the Black Arts Festival in Cincinnati before attending graduate school at the University of Pennsylvania and Columbia University. In her first two collections, *Black Feeling, Black Talk* and *Black Judgement*, Giovanni reflects on African American identity. She has published *Bicycles: Love Poems; Acolytes; The Collected Poetry of Nikki Giovanni: 1968–1998; Quilting the Black-Eyed Pea: Poems and Not-Quite Poems; Blues For All the Changes: New*

Poems; *Love Poems*; and *Selected Poems of Nikki Giovanni*. A survivor of lung cancer, Giovanni has also contributed an introduction to the anthology *Breaking the Silence: Inspirational Stories of Black Cancer Survivors*. Her honors include three NAACP Image Awards for Literature in 1998; the Langston Hughes award for Distinguished Contributions to Arts and Letters in 1996; and over twenty honorary degrees from national colleges and universities. Giovanni was the first recipient of the Rosa Parks Woman of Courage Award, and national magazines have named her Woman of the Year. She has served as poetry judge for the National Book Awards and was a finalist for a Grammy Award in the category of Spoken Word. She is currently professor of English and Gloria D. Smith Professor of Black Studies at Virginia Tech, where she has taught since 1987.

Donald L. Graham (1944–71) was born in Gary, Indiana, and graduated from Fisk University. He taught at Fisk and served as director of the Fisk Writers Workshop. His poems appeared in *Dynamite Voices I: Black Poets of the '60s*; *Journal of Black Poetry*; *Black Fire*; and *Kaleidoscope*. His published books include *Black Song*; *Soul Motion*; and *Soul Motion II*.

Barbara Guest (1920–2006) was born in Wilmington, North Carolina. She attended the University of California, Los Angeles, and the University of California, Berkeley, graduating in 1943. Guest has published numerous collections of poetry, among them *The Red Gaze*; *Miniatures and Other Poems*; *Symbiosis*; *Defensive Rapture*; *Fair Realism*; *Musicality*; *The Nude*; *Quilts*; and *Biography*. Her honors include the Robert Frost Medal for Distinguished Lifetime Achievement from the Poetry Society of America; the Longwood Award; a San Francisco State award for poetry; the Lawrence Lipton Award for Literature; the Columbia Book Award; and a grant from the National Endowment for the Arts.

Nicolás Guillén (1902–89) was born in Camagüey, Cuba, and became the national poet of his country. He was also a journalist, typographer, and political activist, and he strove to infuse his work with influences from his African and Spanish heritage. His major collections include *Songoro Cosongo*; *La Paloma De Vuelo Popular*; *Yoruba from Cuba: Selected Poems*; *El Gran Zoo*; and *Las Grandes Elegias Y Otros Poemas*.

Michael S. Harper (1938–) was born in Brooklyn and earned a B.A. and an M.A. from California State University, and an M.F.A. from the University of Iowa. He has published more than ten books of poetry, including *Selected Poems*; *Songlines in Michaeltree: New and Collected Poems*; *Honorable Amendments*; and *Healing Song for the Inner Ear*. His other collections include: *Images of Kin* (which won the Melville-Cane Award from the Poetry Society of America and was nominated for the National Book Award); *Nightmare Begins Responsibility*; *History is Your Heartbeat* (which won the Black Academy of Arts and Letters Award for poetry); and *Dear John, Dear Coltrane* (which was nominated for the National Book Award). Harper edited the *Collected Poems of Sterling A. Brown*. He is co-editor with Anthony Walton of *The Vintage Book of African American Poetry* and *Every Shut Eye Ain't Asleep: An Anthology of Poetry by African Americans Since 1945*, and with Robert B. Stepto of *Chant of Saints:*

A Gathering of Afro-American Literature, Art, and Scholarship. He was the first Poet Laureate of Rhode Island and has received many other honors, including a fellowship from the Guggenheim Foundation and a National Endowment for the Arts Creative Writing Award. Harper is University Professor and professor of English at Brown University, where he has taught since 1970. He lives in Barrington, Rhode Island.

Bruce Hartford is webmaster for the Civil Rights Movement Veterans website (http://crmvet.org). During the 1960s he was a civil rights worker in Alabama and Mississippi for the SCLC before becoming a student activist with Students for a Democratic Society at San Francisco State College and a freelance journalist covering military affairs during the Vietnam War. For the past thirty years, he has been a technical writer for Silicon Valley software firms. He was a founding member of, and is a longtime national officer of, the National Writers Union.

Robert Hayden (1913–80) was raised in Detroit and attended Wayne State University. Hayden published his first book of poems, *Heart-Shape in the Dust*, in 1940. He enrolled in a graduate English Literature program at the University of Michigan, where he studied with W. H. Auden. Hayden's poetry gained international recognition in the 1960s; in 1966 he was awarded the grand prize for poetry at the First World Festival of Negro Arts in Dakar, Senegal, for *Ballad of Remembrance*. In 1976 he became the first black American to be appointed as Consultant in Poetry to the Library of Congress (later called the Poet Laureate).

David Henderson (1942–) was born in Harlem and raised there and in the Bronx. He was a founding member of the Umbra Poets, an influential collective of poets and writers who were central to the black arts movement. His books include *De Mayor of Harlem*; *'Scuse Me While I Kiss the Sky*; *Jimi Hendrix: Voodoo Child*; and *Neo-California*. He has been widely published in anthologies and magazines. He has read from his poetry for the permanent archives of the Library of Congress. Henderson lives in downtown New York City.

Anselm Hollo (1934–) is the author of over thirty books, most recently the essay collection *Caws and Causeries* and *Notes on the Possibilities and Attractions of Existence: New and Selected Poems 1965–2000* (which received the San Francisco Poetry Center's Book Award for 2001). His work has been widely anthologized and translated into several languages. His translation of *Pentii Saarikoski's Trilogy* received the 2004 Harold Morton Landon Translation Award from the Academy of American Poets. He is a recipient of a National Endowment for the Arts Fellowship in Poetry; two grants from The Fund for Poetry; and the government of Finland's Distinguished Foreign Translator's Award. A native of Helsinki, he has lived in the United States since 1967, teaching poetics and translation at colleges and universities. He is a professor of writing and poetics at Naropa University in Boulder, Colorado, where he lives with his wife, the visual artist Jane Dalrymple-Hollo.

Barbara Howes (1919–46) grew up in a suburb of Boston and graduated from Bennington College in Vermont. She served as editor of *Chimera: A Literary Magazine* for three years and later edited three short story anthologies: *From the Green An-*

tilles: Writings of the Caribbean; The Eye of the Heart: Short Stories from Latin America; and *The Sea-Green Horse.* She published eight collections of poetry, including *The Undersea Farmer; Looking Up at Leaves;* and *Moving.*

Ericka Huggins (1951–) became a leader in the Los Angeles chapter of the Black Panther Party with her husband John Huggins in 1969. In 1972 she became writer and editor of the Black Panther Intercommunal News Service, and in 1974 she published *Poems and Insights* with Huey P. Newton. Huggins is a professor of women's studies at California State University, East Bay. She lives in Oakland.

Langston Hughes (1902–67) was born in Joplin, Missouri. In November 1924 he moved to Washington, D.C. Hughes's first book of poetry, *The Weary Blues,* was published by Alfred A. Knopf in 1926. He finished his college education at Lincoln University in Pennsylvania three years later. In 1930 his first novel, *Not Without Laughter,* won the Harmon gold medal for literature. In addition to a large body of poetry, Hughes wrote eleven plays and countless works of prose, including the well-known "Simple" books: *Simple Speaks His Mind; Simple Stakes a Claim; Simple Takes a Wife;* and *Simple's Uncle Sam.* He edited the anthologies *The Poetry of the Negro* and *The Book of Negro Folklore,* wrote an acclaimed autobiography (*The Big Sea*), and wrote the play *Mule Bone* with Zora Neale Hurston.

David Ignatow (1914–97) was born in Brooklyn. He published numerous books of poetry, including *Living Is What I Wanted: Last Poems; At My Ease: Uncollected Poems of the Fifties and Sixties; I Have a Name; Against the Evidence: Selected Poems, 1934–1994; Despite the Plainness of the Day: Love Poems; Shadowing the Ground; New and Collected Poems, 1970–1985; Leaving the Door Open, Poems: 1934–1969; Rescue the Dead; Earth Hard: Selected Poems;* and *Figures of the Human.* Ignatow was an editor of *American Poetry Review, Analytic, Beloit Poetry Journal,* and *Chelsea Magazine;* the poetry editor of *The Nation;* and a professor at seven colleges and universities. He was the president of the Poetry Society of America from 1980 to 1984 and the poet-in-residence at the Walt Whitman Birthplace Association in 1987. His many honors include a Bollingen Prize, two Guggenheim fellowships, the John Steinbeck Award, and a National Institute of Arts and Letters award. He received the Shelley Memorial Award, the Frost Medal, and the William Carlos Williams Award of the Poetry Society of America.

Will Inman (1923–2009) was born in Wilmington, North Carolina, and graduated from Duke University in 1943. For many years he was an activist in labor unions and other groups. In 1973 Inman moved to Tucson, Arizona, where he co-founded the Tucson Poetry Festival in 1981. His books of poetry include *What Friend in the Labyrinth: Meditation in Thirty-Six Parts; you whose eyes open naked into me; Surfing the Dark Sound; Sacred Chaff; Center Walking; Shadow Experiences: Poems and Potentials; A Trek of Waking; A Way Through for the Damned; Selected Poems; Voice of the Beech Oracle: A Shaman Song; The Wakers in the Tongue;* and *108 Verges Unto Now.*

Lance Jeffers (1919–85) was born in Freemont, Nebraska, and earned degrees from Columbia University. He taught at several colleges and universities, including California State College at Long Beach and North Carolina State University. His poems appeared in *The Best Short Stories of 1948; Burning Spear; A Galaxy of Black Writing; New Black Voices; Black Fire; Phylon;* and the *Tamarack Review*. His books of poetry include *My Blackness is the Beauty of This Land; When I Know the Power of My Black Hand; O Africa; Where I Baked My Bread;* and *Grandsire*.

June Jordan (1936–2002) was born in New York City in 1936. Her books of poetry include *Kissing God Goodbye: Poems, 1991–1997; Haruko/Love Poems; Naming Our Destiny: New and Selected Poems; Living Room; Passion;* and *Things That I Do in the Dark*. She is also the author of children's books; plays; a novel; a guide to writing, teaching, and publishing poetry *(Poetry for the People: A Blueprint for the Revolution)*; and a memoir (*Soldier: A Poet's Childhood*). Her collections of political essays include *Affirmative Acts: Political Essays* and *Technical Difficulties*. Jordan received a Rockefeller Foundation grant, the National Association of Black Journalists Award, and fellowships from the Massachusetts Council on the Arts, the National Endowment for the Arts, and the New York Foundation for the Arts. She taught at the University of California, Berkeley, where she founded Poetry for the People.

Donald Justice (1925–2004) was born in Miami in 1925. A graduate of the University of Miami, he attended the University of North Carolina, Stanford University, and the University of Iowa. His books include *New and Selected Poems; A Donald Justice Reader; The Sunset Maker; Selected Poems* (for which he won a Pulitzer Prize); *Departures; Night Light;* and *The Summer Anniversaries* (which received the Academy's Lamont Poetry Selection). He has held teaching positions at Syracuse University; the University of California, Irvine; Princeton University; the University of Virginia; and the University of Iowa. From 1982 until his retirement in 1992 he taught at the University of Florida, Gainesville. He won the Bollingen Prize in Poetry in 1991 and received grants in poetry from the Guggenheim Foundation, the Rockefeller Foundation, and the National Endowment for the Arts. He served as a chancellor of the Academy of American Poets from 1997 to 2003.

X. J. (Joseph Charles) Kennedy (1929–) was born in Dover, New Jersey. After studying at Seton Hall, Columbia University, and the University of Michigan, he served four years in the U.S. Navy's Atlantic Fleet as a journalist, and then attended the Sorbonne in Paris for one year in 1955. In the early 1970s Kennedy published *Counter/Measures*, a magazine devoted to the use of traditional form in poetry. Kennedy's first collection of poetry, *Nude Descending a Staircase*, won the Lamont Poetry Selection. His other awards include a Guggenheim fellowship, a National Endowment for the Arts grant, the Bess Hokin Prize from *Poetry* magazine, and a *Los Angeles Times* Book prize. Kennedy has taught at numerous colleges and universities. He is a former poetry editor of *The Paris Review*, and his poems have appeared in the *New Yorker, Poetry*, and *The Hudson Review*. In addition to his collection *Dark Horses: New Poems* (1992), he has published numerous works for children. Kennedy lives in Bedford, Massachusetts, with his wife and their five children.

Galway Kinnell (1927–) was born in Providence, Rhode Island, and attended Princeton University and the University of Rochester. His first book of poems, *What a King-*

dom It Was, was published in 1960, followed by *Flower Herding on Mount Monadnock*. Kinnell joined CORE as a fieldworker, spending much of the 1960s involved in the civil rights movement, and he was arrested while participating in a workplace integration in Louisiana. He captured much of his civil rights activity in his collection *Body Rags*. Kinnell has published several other books of poetry, including *Strong Is Your Hold*; *A New Selected Poems* (a finalist for the National Book Award); *Imperfect Thirst*; *When One Has Lived a Long Time Alone*; *Selected Poems* (for which he received both a Pulitzer Prize and the National Book Award); and *Mortal Acts, Mortal Words*. Kinnell's other honors include the Wallace Stevens Award; a MacArthur Fellowship; a Rockefeller Grant; the 1974 Shelley Prize of the Poetry Society of America; and the 1975 Medal of Merit from National Institute of Arts and Letters. He has served as a poet-in-residence at numerous colleges and universities. Kinnell divides his time between Vermont and New York City, where he was the Erich Maria Remarque Professor of Creative Writing at New York University.

Carolyn Kizer (1925–) was born in Spokane, Washington. She is the author of eight books of poetry: *Cool, Calm, and Collected: Poems 1960–2000*; *Harping On: Poems 1985–1995*; *The Nearness of You: Poems for Men*; *Yin* (which won a Pulitzer Prize); *Mermaids in the Basement: Poems for Women*; *Midnight Was My Cry: New and Selected Poems*; *Knock Upon Silence*; and *The Ungrateful Garden*. She has also written *Picking and Choosing: Prose on Prose*; *Proses: Essays on Poets and Poetry*; and *Carrying Over: Translations from Chinese, Urdu, Macedonian, Hebrew, and French-African*. She is the editor of *100 Great Poems by Women* and *The Essential Clare*. In 1959 she founded *Poetry Northwest* and served as its editor until 1965. From 1966 to 1970, she served as the first director of the Literature Program at the National Endowment for the Arts. Kizer has received an American Academy of Arts and Letters award, the Frost Medal, the John Masefield Memorial Award, and the Theodore Roethke Memorial Poetry Award. She is a former chancellor of the Academy of American Poets and lives in Sonoma, California, and Paris.

Etheridge Knight (1931–91) was born in Corinth, Mississippi. In 1960 he was arrested for robbery and sentenced to eight years in the Indiana State Prison, during which he began writing poetry and corresponded with and received visits from such established African American literary figures as Dudley Randall and Gwendolyn Brooks. Randall's Broadside Press published *Poems from Prison*, Knight's first book, a year before he was released from prison. In 1970 Knight edited a collection titled *Black Voices from Prison*. Knight's books and oral performances drew both popular and critical acclaim, and he received honors from such institutions as the Guggenheim Foundation, the National Endowment for the Arts, and the Poetry Society of America. In 1990 he earned a bachelor's degree in American poetry and criminal justice from Martin Center University in Indianapolis.

Stanley Koehler (1915–2010) was born in West Orange, New Jersey, graduated from Princeton University as class valedictorian, and later received advanced degrees from Harvard and Princeton. After serving in the U.S. Navy during the Second World War, he taught at Oklahoma State College, Kansas University, Yale University, and the

University of Massachusetts, Amherst, where he was a founding member of the *Massachusetts Review*. He published several works, including *The Fact of Fall: Poems* and *Countries of the Mind: The Poetry of William Carlos Williams.*

Aaron Kramer (1921–97) was born in Brooklyn and earned degrees from Brooklyn College and New York University. He taught at Dowling College in Oakdale, New York, for nearly forty years and was a founding co-editor of *West Hills Review: A Whitman Journal.* He published more than twenty collections of poetry, including *'Til the Grass is Ripe for Dancing* and *Border Incident.* He was a leading resistance poet during the McCarthy era with such texts for music as *Denmark Vesey* and such books as *Roll the Forbidden Drums!*. In 1958 he collaborated with a dozen artists on *The Tune of the Calliope: Poems and Drawings of New York.* His scholarly works include *The Prophetic Tradition in American Poetry; Melville's Poetry: Toward the Enlarged Heart*; and *Neglected Aspects of American Poetry.* He edited *On Freedom's Side: An Anthology of American Poems of Protest* and translated several books, including *A Century of Yiddish Poetry* and *The Last Lullaby: Poems of the Holocaust.*

Julius Lester (1939–) was born in St. Louis and grew up in Kansas City, Kansas, and Nashville, Tennessee. After graduating from Fisk University, he moved to New York City, where he hosted a talk radio show on WBAI FM, and hosted a television talk show on WNET. He has published more than forty books, including *The Folksinger's Guide to the 12-String Guitar as Played by Leadbelly* (co-authored with Pete Seeger); *Revolutionary Notes; Ackamarackus: Julius Lester's Sumptuously Silly Fantastically Funny Fables*; and *The Autobiography of God.* He has published hundreds of essays and reviews in numerous journals, magazines, and newspapers. Part of the permanent collection at Howard University, his collection of photographs from the civil rights movement has been exhibited at the Smithsonian Institution.

Denise Levertov (1923–97) was born in Ilford, Essex, England, and became a naturalized U.S. citizen in 1956. Her first American collections, *Here and Now* and *With Eyes at the Back of our Heads,* established her as a significant voice in American letters. She published over twenty additional poetry books, including *The Sorrow Dance; Freeing the Dust* (which won the Lenore Marshall Poetry Prize); *Poems 1968–1972; Breathing the Water; A Door in the Hive; Evening Train*; and *The Sands of the Well.* She also wrote four books of prose, including *Tesserae,* and translated three books of poetry, among them Jean Joubert's *Black Iris.*

Philip Levine (1928–), the poet laureate of the United States, was born in Detroit, Michigan. He is the author of numerous books of poetry, including *News of the World, Breath; The Mercy; The Simple Truth* (which won a Pulitzer Prize); *What Work Is* (which won the National Book Award); *New Selected Poems; Ashes: Poems New and Old* (which received the National Book Critics Circle Award and the first American Book Award for Poetry); *7 Years From Somewhere* (which won the National Book Critics Circle Award); and *The Names of the Lost* (which won the Lenore Marshall Poetry Prize). Levine has also published a collection of essays, *The Bread of Time: Toward an Autobiography*; edited *The Essential Keats*; and co-edited and translated *Off the Map: Selected Poems of Gloria Fuertes* (with Ada Long) and *Tarumba: The Selected Poems of*

Jaime Sabines (with Ernesto Trejo). Levine has received the Ruth Lilly Poetry Prize; the Harriet Monroe Memorial Prize from *Poetry*; the Frank O'Hara Prize; and two Guggenheim Foundation fellowships. He served as the chair of the Literature Panel of the National Endowment for the Arts and was elected a chancellor of the Academy of American Poets in 2000. He lives in New York City and Fresno, California, and teaches at New York University.

Audre Lorde (1934–92) was born in New York City and received a B.A. degree from Hunter College and an M.L.S. degree from Columbia University. Her first book of poems, *The First Cities* (1968) was followed by *Cables to Rage*; *From a Land Where Other People Live* (which was nominated for a National Book Award); *New York Head Shot and Museum*; *Coal*; and *The Black Unicorn* among others. Her first prose collection, *The Cancer Journals*, won the Gay Caucus Book of the Year award for 1981. Her other prose collections include *Zami: A New Spelling of My Name*; *Sister Outsider: Essays and Speeches*; and *A Burst of Light* (which won a National Book Award).

Robert Lowell (1917–77) was born in Boston and attended Harvard before transferring to Kenyon College, where he received an undergraduate degree. His second collection of poetry, *Lord Weary's Castle*, won the Pulitzer Prize in 1947 and established Lowell as a major American poet. He served as U.S. Poet Laureate from 1947 to 1948; won the National Book Award in 1960 for *Life Studies*; was elected a chancellor of the Academy of American Poets in 1962; won a second Pulitzer Prize in 1974 for *The Dolphin*; and received a National Book Critics Circle Award in 1977 for *Day by Day*. Other of his published works include *The Mills of the Kavanaughs*; *Imitations*; *For the Union Dead*; *Selected Poems*; *Notebooks*; and *History*.

Phillip Abbott Luce

Charles Lynch (1943–) grew up in Baltimore and received degrees from Kenyon College and City College of New York. His work has appeared in many literary magazines and in several anthologies, including *The Poetry of Black America*; *Celebrations*; *Leaving the Bough*; *Sweet Nothings: An Anthology of Rock and Roll in American Poetry*; and three Cave Canem anthologies (2004, 2006, and 2007). He is an assistant professor of English at New Jersey City University and lives in Brooklyn with his wife, Gail.

Naomi Long Madgett (1925–) was born in Norfolk, Virginia, and grew up in East Orange, New Jersey. She has earned degrees at Virginia State University, Wayne State University, and the Institute for Advanced Studies at Greenwich University. She is the founder, publisher, and editor of Lotus Press. Among her books of poetry are *Remembrances of Spring: Collected Early Poems*; *Octavia: Guthrie and Beyond*; and *Connected Islands: New and Selected Poems*. Madgett lives in Detroit, where she serves as the poet laureate of the city.

Haki R. Madhubuti (Don L. Lee) (1942–), a poet, essayist, and editor, was born in Little Rock, Arkansas and attended the University of Illinois and the University of Iowa, from which he received an M.F.A. He is the author of more than twenty books of poetry, including *Heart Love: Wedding and Love Poems*; *GroundWork: New and Selected Poems of Don L. Lee*; *Killing Memory*; *Seeking Ancestors*; *Earthquakes and Sun-*

rise Missions: Poetry and Essays of Black Renewal, 1973–1983; Book of Life; and *Directionscore: Selected and New Poems.* His prose works include *Claiming Earth: Race, Rage, Rape, Redemption*; *Black Men: Obsolete, Single, Dangerous?*; *Enemies: The Clash of Races*; and *Dynamite Voices I: Black Poets of the 1960s.* Madhubuti is the founder and editor of Third World Press and *Black Books Bulletin,* and director the Institute of Positive Education. Among his honors and awards are an American Book Award and fellowships from the National Endowment for the Arts and the National Endowment for the Humanities.

Marvin X (Marvin E. Jackmon) (1944–) was born in Fowler, California, and attended Merritt College along with Huey P. Newton and Bobby Seale. He received B.A. and M.A. degrees in English from San Francisco State University. He is well known as a poet, playwright, and essayist of the black arts movement, and his works include *Flowers for the Trashman*; *The Black Bird*; *The Trial, Resurrection of the Dead*; and *In the Name of Love.*

Eve Merriam (1916–92) was born in Philadelphia and earned a degree from the University of Pennsylvania. Her first book, *Family Circle,* was selected for the Yale Series of Younger Poets. She published eight additional collections of poems for adult audiences, including *Montgomery, Alabama, Money, Mississippi, and Other Places,* as well as biographies, essays, and plays. Her prolific works for children include *There is No Rhyme for Silver*; *It Doesn't Always Have to Rhyme*; *The Inner City Mother Goose*; *Catch a Little Rhyme*; *Finding a Poem*; *Out Loud*; and *Rainbow Writing.*

Robert Mezey (1935–) was born in Philadelphia and educated at Kenyon College, the University of Iowa, and Stanford University. His books of poetry include *The Lovemaker*; *White Blossoms*; *A Book of Dying*; *The Mercy of Sorrow*; *The Door Standing Open: New and Selected Poems*; *Couplets*; *Small Song*; *Selected Translations*; *Evening Wind*; *Natural Selection*; and *Collected Poems 1952–1999.* He has received the Robert Frost Prize and the Lamont Poetry Prize among other literary awards.

Marjorie Mir (1934–) has edited poetry for *Monhegan Commons* for more than ten years, and her own books of poetry include *The Planet First Observed and Other Poems*; *Companions: Poems New and Selected*; and *Poet's Cove.* In 2000 she was awarded first prize in the *Atlanta Review*'s international competition. She lives in Bronxville, New York, where she is a retired librarian and a member of Poetry Caravan, a group of Westchester writers who share poetry with the residents of nursing homes and assisted living facilities.

Pauli Murray (1910–85) was born in Baltimore and grew up in Durham, North Carolina. She graduated from Hunter College in New York and applied to law school at the University of North Carolina but was denied admission on the basis of race. She graduated from Howard University Law School as valedictorian and later became the first African American to earn a Ph.D. from Yale and the first African American woman in America to be ordained as an Episcopal priest. Among her publications are *Dark Testament and Other Poems*; *Song in a Weary Throat: An American Pilgrimage*; and *Proud Shoes: The Story of an American Family.*

Larry Neal (1937–81) was born in Atlanta, grew up in Philadelphia, and earned degrees from Lincoln University and the University of Pennsylvania. He became a central figure in the black arts movement and with Amiri Baraka edited *Black Fire: An Anthology of Afro-American Writing,* a defining book of the movement. His writings appeared in several journals, including *Liberator, Negro Digest, Black Theatre, Partisan Review,* and *Drama Critique.* He published two collections of poems: *Black Boogaloo: Notes on Black Liberation* and *Hoodo Hollerin Bebop Ghosts.*

Huey P. Newton (1942–89) was born in Monroe, Louisiana, and reared in Oakland, California, where he met Bobby Seale at Merritt College and formed the Black Panther Party for Self-Defense, a group designed to protect the community from police brutality. Newton earned a Ph. D. in social philosophy from the University of California, Santa Cruz. He published *Revolutionary Suicide* and *Poems and Insights* (with Ericka Huggins) among other writings.

Melvin Newton

Thich Nhat Hanh (1926–) was born in central Vietnam and became a monk at sixteen. His influence was instrumental in Dr. King's decision to oppose the Vietnam War in 1967. He has published more than eighty books of poetry, prose, and prayers, including *Call Me by My True Names*; *Peace Is Every Step*; *Being Peace*; *Touching Peace*; *Living Buddha Living Christ*; *Teachings on Love*; *The Path of Emancipation*; and *Anger.* He currently lives in Plum Village, a Buddhist community in exile in France.

Ojenke (Alvin Saxon) (1947–) grew up in Watts and became a member of the Watts Writers Workshop in 1966 and an influential reader and performer. His poetry has appeared in the *Antioch Review*; *Negro Digest*; *From the Ashes: Voices of Watts*; *Watts Poets and Writers*; and *Giant Talk: An Anthology of Third World Writing.*

George Oppen (1908–84) was born in New Rochelle, New York, and moved to San Francisco with his family before reaching his teenage years. His first book of poetry, *Discrete Series,* was published in 1934, and his poems also appeared in literary journals such as *Active Anthology, Poetry,* and *Hound and Horn.* His third collection, *Of Being Numerous,* was awarded the Pulitzer Prize for poetry in 1969. His other collections include *The Materials*; *This in Which*; and *Myth of the Blaze,* among others.

Gregory Orr (1947–) was born in Albany and received degrees from Antioch College and Columbia University. He is the author of several collections of poetry, including *How Beautiful the Beloved*; *Concerning the Book that is the Body of the Beloved*; *The Caged Owl: New and Selected Poems*; *Orpheus and Eurydice*; *Burning the Empty Nests*; *City of Salt* (which was a finalist for the *L.A. Times* Poetry Prize); and *Gathering the Bones Together.* He is also the author of a memoir, *The Blessing* (2002), which was chosen by *Publisher's Weekly* as one of the fifty best nonfiction books that year, and three books of essays, including *Poetry as Survival* and *Stanley Kunitz: An Introduction to the Poetry.* He has received a Guggenheim fellowship and two poetry fellowships from the National Endowment for the Arts. In 2003 he was presented the Award in Literature by the American Academy of Arts and Letters, and he was a Rockefeller

Fellow at the Institute for the Study of Culture and Violence. He teaches at the University of Virginia, where he founded the M.F.A Program in Writing in 1975, and served from 1978 to 2003 as the poetry editor of the *Virginia Quarterly Review*.

Raymond Patterson (1929–2001) was born in Harlem and graduated from Lincoln University in Pennsylvania and New York University. His poetry appeared in *Transatlantic Review, Ohio Review,* and *Beloit Poetry Journal,* and in the anthologies *The Poetry of the Negro*; *New Black Voices*; *The Norton Introduction to Literature*; and *Best American Poetry of 1996*. His poetry collections include *26 Ways of Looking at a Black Man* and *Elemental Blues*.

Born in Massachusetts, **Oliver Pitcher** (1924–) is a poet, playwright, and surrealist painter. His poems have appeared in such journals as *Totem, The Tiger's Eye,* and *Umbra* and in a collection, *Dust of Silence*.

The influential Canadian poet **Al Purdy** (1918–2000) was born in Wooler, Ontario. He published more than thirty books of poetry and won numerous awards, including the Canadian Authors Association Award, two Governor General's Awards (for *The Cariboo Horses* in 1965 and *The Collected Poems of Al Purdy, 1956–1986* in 1986), and the Voice of the Land Award, a special award created by the League of Canadian Poets specifically to honor Purdy's unique contribution to Canada. He was appointed to the Order of Canada in 1982 and to the Order of Ontario in 1987.

Craig Randolph Pyes is a correspondent for the Center for Investigative Reporting (CIR) specializing in international investigations. He shared a 2002 Pulitzer Prize for explanatory reporting at the *New York Times* for stories on the threat of al Qaeda prior to 9/11 and was a member of the small *New York Times* team that won the 1998 Pulitzer Prize for international reporting for articles about the corrosive effects of drug corruption in Mexico. He has worked as an off-air investigative producer on projects for *Sixty Minutes, Dateline,* and *Primetime Live*. He was a staff investigative reporter for the *Albuquerque Journal* before becoming the co-director of CIR's Human Rights Project.

Dudley Randall (1914–2000) was born in Washington, D.C., but moved to Detroit at an early age. After serving in the Second World War he earned a B.A. degree from Wayne State University in Detroit, and an M.A. degree from the University of Michigan. A pioneering figure in Detroit's literary community, Randall founded Broadside Press, one of the most influential black presses in the country. He published several books of poetry, including *Poem Counterpoem* and *After the Killing*. He also edited numerous works, including *For Malcolm: Poems on the Life and Death of Malcolm X* and *Black Poets*.

Adrienne Rich's (1929–) most recent books of poetry are *Tonight No Poetry Will Serve* and *Telephone Ringing in the Labyrinth*. She edited Muriel Rukeyser's *Selected Poems* for the Library of America. Her *A Human Eye: Essays on Art in Society,* appeared in 2009. She was the 2006 recipient of the National Book Foundation's Medal for Distinguished Contribution to American Letters. Rich lives in California.

Victor Manuel Rivera-Toledo (1907–84) was born in Quetzaltenango, Guatemala. He worked for the Guatemala government for more than forty years in the Ministry of the Interior and the Ministry of Foreign Relations, finishing his career in 1974 as consul in New York. He was awarded his country's highest honor, La Orden del Quetzal, for his years of service and valuable contributions. He was also an accomplished writer, publishing poems and humorous articles in Guatemalan newspapers and magazines. His poem "Requiem for the Fallen" appeared posthumously in *The Second Lost Art* in 1996. Also published posthumously were *Lira Ausente* (2001) and *La Filosofia de la Risa* (2002) by his son, Luis Eduardo Rivera-Solis.

Conrad Kent Rivers (1933–68) was born in Atlantic City, New Jersey, and earned degrees from Wilberforce University, Chicago Teachers College, and Indiana University. His writings appeared in *Kenyon Review, Negro Digest, American Negro Poetry,* and *For Malcolm.* His collections of poems included *Perchance to Dream; Othello; These Black Bodies and This Sunburnt Face; Dusk at Selma;* and *The Still Voice of Harlem.*

Muriel Rukeyser (1913–80) was born in New York City and attended Vassar College and Columbia University. Her first collection of poetry, *Theory of Flight,* was selected by Stephen Vincent Benét for the Yale Younger Poets series in 1935. Her subsequent collections include *A Turning Wind; Beast in View; The Green Wave; Elegies; Body of Waking; The Speed of Darkness; Breaking Open; The Gates;* and *Collected Poems.* She also published fiction, drama, screenplays, translations, and biographies of Willard Gibbs, Wendell Willkie, and Thomas Hariot.

Sonia Sanchez (1934–) was born in Birmingham, Alabama, and earned a B.A. in political science from Hunter College. She is the author of more than a dozen books of poetry, including *Shake Loose My Skin: New and Selected Poems; Like the Singing Coming Off the Drums: Love Poems; Does Your House Have Lions?* (which was nominated for both the NAACP Image and National Book Critics Circle awards); *Wounded in the House of a Friend; Under a Soprano Sky; Homegirls and Handgrenades* (which won an American Book Award from the Before Columbus Foundation); *I've Been a Woman: New and Selected Poems; A Blues Book for Blue Black Magical Women; Love Poems; Liberation Poem; We a BaddDDD People;* and *Homecoming.* She has received the Community Service Award from the National Black Caucus of State Legislators; the Lucretia Mott Award; the Outstanding Arts Award from the Pennsylvania Coalition of 100 Black Women; the Peace and Freedom Award from Women International League for Peace and Freedom; the Pennsylvania Governor's Award for Excellence in the Humanities; a National Endowment for the Arts award; and a Pew Fellowship in the Arts. She lives in Philadelphia.

Edward Sanders (1939–) was born in Kansas City, Missouri, and graduated from New York University. He co-founded the rock band The Fugs, opened the Peace Eye Bookstore in New York's Lower East Side, and appeared on the cover of *Life* magazine (17 February 1967). He is a classics scholar, pioneer in investigative poetics, inventor of musical instruments, publisher of *The Woodstock Journal,* and author of many books, including the Charles Manson exposé *The Family* and the multi-volume project, *America: A History in Verse*. Sanders has received a number of awards and fellowships, including a Guggenheim Fellowship in poetry and a National Endowment for the Arts Fellowship in poetry. His *Thirsting for Peace in a Raging Century, Selected Poems 1961–1985* won an American Book Award in 1988. He lives in Woodstock, New York.

Armand Schwerner (1927–99) was born in Antwerp and immigrated to the United States in the mid-1930s. He earned B.A. and M.A. degrees from Columbia University. His first book of poetry, *The Lightfall*, was published in 1963, and soon after he began his serial epic poem, "The Tablets," which consists of translations on clay tablets from an extinct culture in the Near East. Twenty-seven complete tablets were published shortly after Schwerner's death. His other books include *If Personal*; *Seaweed*; the *Bacche Sonnets*; *This Practice*; *The Work*; *The Joy and the Triumph of the Will*; *Sounds of the River Naranjana*; and *Selected Shorter Poems*.

Edith Segal (1902–97) was born in New York City and developed as a dancer, teacher, and writer. In the 1950s she supported many friends who were persecuted for their political beliefs. She herself was asked to appear before New York commission hearings on communist influence in summer camps. During this time she also began to publish her poetry. Segal eventually published more than ten books, including *Poems and Songs for Ethel and Julius Rosenberg*; *Poems and Songs for Dreamers Who Dare*; and *Take My Hand: Poems and Songs for Lovers and Rebels*.

Léopold Sédar Senghor (1906–2001) was born in Joal, Senegal, and educated in Senegal and France. He was president of the Republic of Senegal from 1960 to 1981, and in 1983 became the first African elected to the French Academy. He was considered by many to be Africa's most famous poet. A co-founder of the Négritude cultural movement, he is recognized as one of the most significant figures in African literature. In 1978 he was awarded the Prix mondial Cino Del Duca, an international literary award established in 1969 in France. His *Collected Poems* was released in the U.S. in 1998 by the University of Virginia Press.

Marvin Solomon

A. B. Spellman (1935–) was born in Elizabeth City, North Carolina, and graduated from Howard University. His first collection of poems, *The Beautiful Days*, was published in 1964. Two years later he published a book on African American music, *Four Lives in the Bebop Business*. He taught African American studies at Harvard University from 1972 to 1975 and held a variety of positions with the National Endowment for the Arts from 1975 to 2005.

Lorenzo Thomas (1944–2005) was born in the Republic of Panama and grew up in New York City. He graduated from Queens College in New York and later joined the faculty of the University of Houston. His poetry collections included *Chances Are Few*; *The Bathers*; and *Dancing on Main Street*. He was posthumously awarded the American Book Award in 2008 for *Don't Deny My Name: Words and Music and the Black Intellectual Tradition* (edited by Aldon Lynn Nielsen).

Born in St. Louis, **Quincy Troupe** (1939–) is the author of eight volumes of poetry, three children's books, and six nonfiction works. In 2010 he received the American Book Award for Lifetime Literary Achievement. Among his bestselling works are *Miles: The Autobiography of Miles Davis* and his memoir, *Miles and Me*. His other books include *The Pursuit of Happyness*, an autobiography he wrote with Chris Gardner that was a *New York Times* bestseller for over forty weeks and became a major motion picture, and *The Architecture of Language*, a book of poems that won the 2007 Paterson Award for Sustained Literary Achievement. *Transcircularities: New and Selected Poems* won the 2003 Milt Kessler Poetry Award and was selected by *Publishers Weekly* as one of the ten best books of poetry in 2002. He is editor of *Black Renaissance Noire*, a literary journal of the Institute of Africana Studies at New York University.

Lewis Turco (1934–)was born in Buffalo and earned a B.A. degree from the University of Connecticut and an M.A. degree from the University of Iowa. He is the author of over fifty books, including *The Book of Forms: A Handbook of Poetics; The Museum of Ordinary People and Other Stories; Satan's Scourge, A Narrative of the Age of Witchcraft;* and *La Famiglia / The Family, Memoirs.*

Jean Valentine (1934–) was born in Chicago, earned a B.A. degree from Radcliffe College, and has taught at Sarah Lawrence College, the Graduate Writing Program of New York University, Columbia University, and the 92nd Street Y in Manhattan. Her first book, *Dream Barker*, was chosen for the Yale Series of Younger Poets in 1965. Her recent collections include *Break the Glass; Door in the Mountain: New and Collected Poems* (which won the National Book Award); *The Cradle of the Real Life; Growing Darkness, Growing Light; The River at Wolf;* and *Home Deep Blue: New and Selected Poems*. She is the editor of *The Lighthouse Keeper: Essays on the Poetry of Eleanor Ross Taylor*. Valentine was the State Poet of New York from 2008 to 2010. She received the 2009 Wallace Stevens Award from the Academy of American Poets, and has received a Guggenheim Fellowship and awards from the NEA, the Bunting Institute, the Rockefeller Foundation, the New York Council for the Arts, and the New York Foundation for the Arts, as well as the Maurice English Prize, the Teasdale Poetry Prize, and the Poetry Society of America's Shelley Memorial Prize in 2000.

Maria Varela (1940–) grew up in several eastern and midwestern cities and attended Alverno College, a Catholic women's college in Milwaukee, where she was president of the student body. In her teens she became active in Young Christian Students (YCS), and she worked on the staff of the progressive Catholic social justice organization after graduation. In 1962 she joined the staff of SNCC. She has since worked in many land-based struggles and organizations with Hispanic people of the rural southwest. Varela promotes sustainable development in poor rural communities, including agriculture, human and environmental health, cultural survival, and environmental conservation and restoration. She was rewarded for her efforts in 1991 with a MacArthur Fellowship. She lives in Albuquerque.

Derek Walcott (1930–) was born in Castries, Saint Lucia, and graduated from the University of the West Indies. He has published numerous collections of poetry, including *White Egrets*; *Selected Poems*; *The Prodigal*; *Tiepolo's Hound*; and *Omeros*. He has also written several plays produced throughout the United States, including *The Odyssey: A Stage Version*; *The Isle is Full of Noises*; *Remembrance and Pantomime*; *The Joker of Seville*; *O Babylon!*; and *Dream on Monkey Mountain and Other Plays,* which won the Obie Award for distinguished foreign play of 1971. He has also received the 1992 Nobel Prize in Literature, a MacArthur Fellowship, a Royal Society of Literature Award, and, in 1988, the Queen's Medal for Poetry. He is an honorary member of the American Academy and Institute of Arts and Letters.

Alice Walker (1944–) was born in Eatonton, Georgia, attended Spelman College, and received a B.A. degree from Sarah Lawrence College. Her books of poetry include *A Poem Traveled Down My Arm: Poems And Drawings*; *Absolute Trust in the Goodness of the Earth*; *Her Blue Body Everything We Know: Earthling Poems, 1965–1990*; *Horses Make the Landscape More Beautiful*; *Goodnight, Willie Lee, I'll See You in the Morning*; *Revolutionary Petunias and Other Poems*; and *Once: Poems*. Among her novels and short story collections are *Now is the Time to Open Your Heart*; *The Way Forward Is with a Broken Heart*; *By the Light of My Father's Smile*; *Possessing the Secret of Joy*; *The Temple of My Familiar*; *To Hell with Dying*; *The Color Purple* (which won a Pulitzer Prize and an American Book Award); and *You Can't Keep a Good Woman Down*. Walker has won numerous awards and honors, including the Lillian Smith Award from the National Endowment for the Arts; the Rosenthal Award from the National Institute of Arts and Letters; fellowships from the Radcliffe Institute; a Merrill Fellowship; and a Guggenheim Fellowship. She lives in Mendocino, California.

Margaret Walker (1915–98) was born in Birmingham, Alabama, and earned degrees from Northwestern University and the University of Iowa. She is best known for her poem "For My People," published in 1942, and her bestselling novel, *Jubilee* (1966), based on her family's experiences during slavery and immediately after the Civil War. Her collection of poems, *Prophets for a New Day,* is heavily influenced by the civil rights movement and its leaders.

Yevgeny Yevtushenko (1933–) was born in Siberia and moved to Moscow after the Second World War. He has produced a large body of work since the 1950s, including poetry, fiction, essays, and screenplays, and is considered one of Russia's most gifted writers. His numerous books of poetry include *The City of the Yes and the City of the No and Other Poems*; *Flowers and Bullets*; *Freedom to Kill*; *Stolen Apples*; and *From Desire to Desire*.

ACKNOWLEDGMENT OF COPYRIGHT

A. R. Ammons. "Belief." Courtesy of the author and Writers Representatives, LLC.

Maya Angelou. "Riot: 60's" from *Just Give Me a Cool Drink of Water 'fore I Die* by Maya Angelou, copyright © 1971 by Maya Angelou. Used by permission of Random House, Inc., and Little, Brown Group Limited.

W. H. Auden. "Elegy for JFK," copyright © 1976 by Edward Mendelson, William Meredith, and Monroe K. Spears, Executors of the Estate of W. H. Auden, from *Collected Poems of W. H. Auden* by W. H. Auden. Used by permission of Random House, Inc., and the Wylie Agency.

Keith E. Baird. "Poplarville II" and "Attica — U.S.A." Courtesy of the author.

Amiri Baraka. "A Poem for Black Hearts," "Black Art," and "Poem for HalfWhite College Students" are reprinted by permission of SLL/Sterling Lord Literistic, Inc. Copyright by Amiri Baraka.

Gerald W. Barrax. "For Malcolm: After Mecca." Courtesy of Gerald W. Barrax.

Bruce Bartford. "Grenada March #107" and "Mississippi Voter Rally." Courtesy of the author. See also the Civil Rights Movement Veterans website, www.crmvet.org.

John Beecher. "The Better Sort of People," "Free World Notes," "Georgia Scene: 1964," "A Commemorative Ode," and "Escort for a President" are reprinted with permission of New South Books from *One More River to Cross: The Selected Poetry of John Beecher* (2002), edited by Steven Ford Brown. For more information: www.newsouthbooks.com.

Jim "Arkansas" Benston. "Ode to Jimmy Lee." Courtesy of Strider "Arkansas" Benston.

John Berryman. "Formal Elegy" from *Collected Poems: 1937–1971* by John Berryman. Copyright © 1989 by Kate Donahue Berryman. Reprinted by permission of Farrar, Straus and Giroux, LLC, and Faber and Faber Ltd.

Robert Bly. "War and Silence" is reprinted by permission of the author.

June Brindel. "The Road to Selma," © 1965 June Rachuy Brindel. Originally published in *The Chicago Defender* 1965.

Louis Daniel Brodsky. "Selma, Alabama, 3/6/65." Courtesy of the author.

Gwendolyn Brooks. "A Bronzeville Mother Loiters in Mississippi. Meanwhile, a Mississippi Mother Burns Bacon," "The Last Quatrain of the Ballad of Emmett Till," "The *Chicago Defender* Sends a Man to Little Rock," "Medgar Evers (for Charles Evers)," "Malcolm X (for Dudley Randall)," "Martin Luther King, Jr.," and "Riot" are reprinted by consent of Brooks Permissions. "The Assassination of John F. Kennedy" from *Of Poetry and Power: Poems Occasioned by the Presidency and by the Death of John F. Kennedy*, edited by Erwin A. Glikes. Reprinted by permission of Basic Books, a member of Perseus Books Group.

Charles Bukowski. "finish" from *The Days Run Away Like Wild Horses over the Hills* by Charles Bukowski. Copyright © 1969 by Charles Bukowski. Reprinted by permission of Harper Collins Publishers.

Karl Carter. "Heroes" and "Judas." Courtesy of the author.

Aimé Césaire. "On the State of the Union." Translated from the French by Clayton Eshleman and Annette Smith.

Kathleen Cleaver. "The Black Mass Needs but One Crucifixion." Courtesy of the author.

Lucille Clifton. "apology," "malcolm," and "the meeting after the savior gone" from *Good Woman: Poems and a Memoir 1969–1980*. Copyright © 1987 by Lucille Clifton. Reprinted with the permission of BOA Editions, Ltd., www.boaeditions.org.

R. D. Coleman. "American (In Memory of Medgar Evers)." Courtesy of the author.

Durward Collins Jr. "Temperate Belt: Reflections on the Mother of Emmett Till." Courtesy of Veronica Jones.

Margaret Danner. "Passive Resistance" is used by permission of Broadside Press.

Diane di Prima. "Revolutionary Letters" copyright 1971, 1980 by Diane di Prima. Used by permission of the author.

Ebon Dooley. "A Poem to My Brothers Killed in Combat or Something about a Conversation with My Father after Rev. King Was Killed." Courtesy of the author.

Harry Edwards. "How to Change the U.S.A." Courtesy of the author.

James A. Emanuel. "Emmett Till" from *The Force and the Reckoning* © 2001 by James A. Emanuel, published by Lotus Press, Detroit, is reprinted by permission of the author. "Freedom Rider: Washout" from *Whole Grain: Collected Poems, 1958–1989* © 1991 by James A. Emanuel, published by Lotus Press, is reprinted by permission of the author.

Lawrence Ferlinghetti. "Assassination Raga," from *These Are My Rivers*, copyright © 1969 by Lawrence Ferlinghetti. Reprinted by permission of New Directions Publishing Corp.

Richard Frost. "On Not Writing an Elegy." Courtesy of the author.

Dorothy Gilbert. "At the Brooklyn Docks, November 23, 1963." Courtesy of the author.

Allen Ginsberg. "May King's Prophecy." Copyright © 1970 The Allen Ginsberg Estate, reprinted by permission of The Wylie Agency LLC.

Nikki Giovanni. "Black Power," "Reflections on April 4, 1968," "Adulthood," "Nikki-Rosa" from *Black Feeling, Black Talk, Black Judgement* by Nikki Giovanni. Copyright © 1968, 1970 by Nikki Giovanni. Reprinted by permission of Harper Collins Publishers.

Barbara Guest. "Verba in Memoriam." Courtesy of Hadley Guest.

Nicolás Guillén. "Elegy for Emmett Till," "Little Rock," and "What Color?" are reprinted from *Man-Making Words: Selected Poems of Nicholás Guillén*. Copyright © 1972 by Roberto Márquez and published by the University of Massachusetts Press.

Michael S. Harper. "American History," "Here Where Coltrane Is," "A Mother Speaks: The Algiers Motel Incident, Detroit," "Newsletter from My Mother: 8:30 a.m., December 8, 1969." © Michael S. Harper, 1970.

Robert Hayden. "El Hajj Malik El-Shabazz" and "Words in the Mourning Time." Copyright © 1970 by Robert Hayden, from *Collected Poems of Robert Hayden* by Robert Hayden, edited by Frederick Glaysher. Copyright © 1985 by Emma Hayden. Used by permission of Liveright Publishing Corporation. "School Integration Riot." Courtesy of Maia Patilla.

David Henderson. "Keep on Pushing" is used by permission of the author.

Anselm Hollo. "Until Death Do Us Part." Courtesy of the author.

Barbara Howes. "A Night Picture of Pownal" from *Looking Up at Leaves*, by Barbara Howes, published by Alfred A. Knopf, Inc. Copyright © 1966 by Barbara Howes, reprinted by permission.

Ericka Huggins. "[let the fault be with the man]." Courtesy of the author.

Langston Hughes. "Birmingham Sunday" and "Mississippi—1955" from *The Collected Poems of Langston Hughes* by Langston Hughes, edited by Arnold Rampersad with David Roessel, Associate Editor, copyright © 1994 by the Estate of Langston Hughes. Used by permission of Alfred A. Knopf, a division of Random House, Inc., and by permission of Harold Ober Associates Incorporated.

David Ignatow. "For Medgar Evers" from *Against the Evidence: Selected Poems, 1934–1994* © 1994 by David Ignatow. Reprinted with permission of Wesleyan University Press. "Before the Sabbath." Courtesy of the Estate of David Ignatow. From *Of Poetry and Power: Poems Occasioned by the Presidency and by the Death of John F. Kennedy* (Basic Books, 1964).

Will Inman. "Jacqueline." Courtesy of Roberta L. Howard.

Lance Jeffers. "My Blackness Is the Beauty of This Land" is used by permission of Broadside Press.

June Jordan. "Poem against the State (of Things): 1975." Copyright 2005 June Jordan Literary Estate trust. Reprinted by permission. www.junejordan.com.

Donald Justice. "The Assassination" from *Collected Poems of Donald Justice* by Donald Justice, copyright © 2004 by Donald Justice. Used by permission of Alfred A. Knopf, a division of Random House, Inc.

X. J. Kennedy. "Down in Dallas" is reprinted by permission of the author. From *Of Poetry and Power: Poems Occasioned by the Presidency and by the Death of John F. Kennedy* (Basic Books, 1964).

Galway Kinnell. "The Last River" from *Body Rags* by Galway Kinnell. Copyright © 1967, renewed 1995 by Galway Kinnell. Reprinted with permission of Houghton Mifflin Harcourt Publishing Company. All rights reserved.

Carolyn Kizer. "Race Relations" from *Yin*. Copyright © 1984 by Carolyn Kizer. Reprinted with permission of BOA Editions, Ltd., www.BOAEditions.org. "Poem, Small and Delible" and "Season of Lovers and Assassins" from *Calm, Cool, and Collected: Poems 1960–2000*. Copyright © 2001 by Carolyn Kizer. Reprinted with the permission of Copper Canyon Press, www.coppercanyonpress.org.

Etheridge Knight. "Portrait of Malcolm X (for Charles Baxter)" is used by permission of Broadside Press.

Stanley Koehler. "In Arlington Cemetery." Courtesy of the author. From *Of Poetry and Power: Poems Occasioned by the Presidency and by the Death of John F. Kennedy* (Basic Books, 1964).

Aaron Kramer. "Blues for Medgar Evers." Courtesy of Laura Kramer. Aaron Kramer's papers are archived at the University of Michigan. For a collection of his work, readers can consult *Wicked Times*, University of Illinois Press, 2004.

Julius Lester. "On the Birth of My Son, Malcolm Coltrane" and "Revolutionary Mandate 1" are reprinted by permission of the author.

Denise Levertov. "The Gulf" and "The Day the Audience Walked Out on Me, and Why," from *Poems 1968–1972*, copyright © 1970 by Denise Levertov. "A Note to Olga," from *Poems 1960–1967*, copyright © 1966 by Denise Levertov. Reprinted by permission of New Directions Publishing Corp.

Philip Levine. "Coming Home" from *New Selected Poems* by Philip Levine. Copyright © 1991 by Philip Levine. Used by permission of Alfred A. Knopf, a division of Random House, Inc.

Audre Lorde. "Rites of Passage." Copyright © 1976 by Audre Lorde. "Suffer the Children." Copyright © 1968 by Audre Lorde, from *The Collected Poems of Audre Lorde* by Audre Lorde. Used by permission of W. W. Norton and Company, Inc., and the Charlotte Sheedy Literary Agency.

Robert Lowell. "For the Union Dead," "For Robert Kennedy," and "Two Walls" from *Collected Poems* by Robert Lowell. Copyright © 2003 by Harriet Lowell and Sheridan Lowell. Reprinted by permission of Farrar, Straus and Giroux, LLC.

Charles Lynch. "If We Cannot Live as People." Courtesy of the author.

Naomi Long Madgett. "Alabama Centennial" and "Midway" from *Star by Star* by Naomi Long Madgett. Reprinted in *Connected Islands: New and Selected Poems* by Naomi Long Madgett (Detroit: Lotus Press, Inc., 2004).

Haki Madhubuti. "One Sided Shoot-out" from *Groundwork: New and Selected Poems*. Copyright 1996, by Haki R. Madhubuti. "Assassination," from *Don't Cry, Scream*. Copyright 1969, by Haki R. Madhubuti. Reprinted by permission of Third World Press, Inc., Chicago.

Marvin X. "That Old Time Religion." Courtesy of the author.

Eve Merriam. "Money, Mississippi" is used by permission of Marian Reiner.

Robert Mezey. "April Fourth" is used by permission of the author.

Marjorie Mir. "Four Days in November." Courtesy of the author. From *Of Poetry and Power: Poems Occasioned by the Presidency and by the Death of John F. Kennedy* (Basic Books, 1964). "Mississippi, 1964." Courtesy of the author.

Pauli Murray. "For Mack C. Parker" and "Collect for Poplarville." © 1970 by the Estate of Pauli Murray. Reprinted by permission of the Charlotte Sheedy Literary Agency.

Larry Neal. "Malcolm X—An Autobiography," from the book *Visions of a Liberated Future* by Larry Neal. Copyright © 1989 by Evelyn Neal. Appears by permission of the publisher, Thunder's Mouth Press, a division of Avalon Publishing Group. "Kuntu." Courtesy of Evelyn Neal.

Huey P. Newton. "Revolutionary Suicide." Courtesy of the Huey P. Newton Foundation.

Thich Nhat Hanh. "The Sun of the Future" is reprinted from *Call Me by My True Names* (1999) by Thich Nhat Hanh with permission of Parallax Press, Berkeley, California, www.parallax.org.

Ojenke. "Watts." Courtesy of the author.

George Oppen. "The Book of Job and a Draft of a Poem to Praise the Paths of the Living." By George Oppen, from *New Collected Poems,* copyright © 1975 by George Oppen. Reprinted by permission of New Directions Publishing Corp. and Carcanet Press Limit.

Gregory Orr. "The Demonstration" and "On a Highway East of Selma, Alabama" from *The Caged Owl: New and Selected Poems.* Copyright © 2002 by Gregory Orr. Reprinted with the permission of Copper Canyon Press, www.coppercanyonpress.org.

Raymond Patterson. "Birmingham 1963," "Schwerner, Chaney, Goodman," and "At That Moment" are used by permission of the Estate of Raymond R. Patterson.

Al Purdy. "For Robert Kennedy." Courtesy of Harbour Publishing.

Craig Randolph Pyes. "The Panther / After Rilke." Courtesy of the author.

Dudley Randall. "Ballad of Birmingham" is used by permission of Broadside Press.

Adrienne Rich. From "Ghazals: Homage to Ghalib." Copyright © 1993 by Adrienne Rich. Copyright © 1969 by W. W. Norton and Company, Inc., from *Collected Early Poems: 1950–1970* by Adrienne Rich. Used by permission of the author and W. W. Norton and Company, Inc.

Victor Manuel Rivera-Toledo. "Black Thursday." Courtesy of Luis Rivera.

Muriel Rukeyser. "Martin Luther King, Malcolm X" is reprinted by permission of International Creative Management, Inc. Copyright © 2005.

Sonia Sanchez. "malcolm," from *Shake Loose My Skin: New and Selected Poems* by Sonia Sanchez. Copyright © 1999 by Sonia Sanchez. Reprinted by permission of Beacon Press, Boston.

Edward Sanders. "A Flower from Robert Kennedy's Grave" from *Thirsting for Peace in a Raging Century: Selected Poems 1961–1985.* Copyright © 1987 by Edward Sanders. Reprinted with the permission of Coffee House Press, www.coffeehousepress.com.

Armand Schwerner. "Speech for LeRoi" is used by permission of the estate of Armand Schwerner.

Edith Segal. "Ballad for Four Children and a President." Courtesy of Shari Segel Goldberg.

Léopold Sédar Senghor. "Elegy for Martin Luther King," from *The Collected Poetry,* translated by Melvin Dixon. © 1991 by the Rector and Visitors of the University of Virginia Press. Reprinted with permission of University of Virginia Press.

Marvin Solomon. "Sonnet for John-John," from *Of Poetry and Power: Poems Occasioned by the Presidency and by the Death of John F. Kennedy* (Basic Books, 1964).

A. B. Spellman. "When Black People Are" and "In Orangeburg My Brothers Did." Courtesy of the author.

Lorenzo Thomas. "Not That Hurried Grief, for John F. Kennedy" from *Of Poetry and Power: Poems Occasioned by the Presidency and by the Death of John F. Kennedy,* edited by Erwin A. Glikes. Reprinted by permission of Basic Books, a member of Perseus Books Group.

Qunicy Troupe. "For Malcolm Who Walks in the Eyes of Our Children" and "White Weekend (April 5–8, 1968)" from *Transcircularities: New and Selected Poems,* published by Coffee House Press, 2002. © Copyright by Quincy Troupe.

Lewis Turco. "November 22, 1963" appeared originally in *Poetry* in 1964. Copyright 1968, 1986, 2006 by Lewis Turco.

Jean Valentine. "September 1963" from *Door in the Mountain: New and Collected Poems.* © 2004 by Jean Valentine and reprinted by permission of Wesleyan University Press.

Maria Varela. "Crumpled Notes (found in a raincoat) on Selma." Courtesy of the author.

Derek Walcott. "Elegy" and "The Gulf" from *Collected Poems 1948–1984* by Derek Walcott. Copyright © 1986 by Derek Walcott. Reprinted by permission of Farrar, Straus and Giroux, LLC, and Faber and Faber Ltd.

Alice Walker. "Be Nobody's Darling" from *Revolutionary Petunias and Other Poems.* Copyright 1972 by Alice Walker. Reprinted with permission by Harcourt, Inc., and by The Wendy Weil Agency, Inc.

Margaret Walker. "Micah (In Memory of Medgar Evers of Mississippi)," "For Andy Goodman, Michael Schwerner, and James Chaney," "For Malcolm X," "Amos, 1963," and "Amos (Postscript, 1968)." From Margaret Walker, *This Is My Century: New and Collected Poems.* © 1989 by Margaret Walker Alexander. Published by The University of Georgia Press. Used by permission of The University of Georgia Press.

Yevgeny Yevtushenko. "Freedom to Kill," from *Stolen Apples* by Yevgeny Yevtushenko. Copyright © 1971 by Doubleday, a division of Random House, Inc. Used by permission of Doubleday, a division of Random House, Inc.

Every reasonable effort has been made to obtain permission. We invite copyright holders to inform us of any oversights.

INDEX

JEFFREY LAMAR COLEMAN is an associate professor of English at St. Mary's College of Maryland. He is the author of *Spirits Distilled* (2006).

Library of Congress Cataloging-in-Publication Data
Words of protest, words of freedom : poetry of the American civil rights movement and era / Jeffrey Lamar Coleman, ed.
p. cm.
Includes bibliographical references and index.
ISBN 978-0-8223-5092-7 (cloth : alk. paper)
ISBN 978-0-8223-5103-0 (pbk. : alk. paper)
1. Civil rights movements—United States—History—20th century—Poetry. 2. Civil rights movements—Poetry.
3. American poetry—20th century. I. Coleman, Jeffrey Lamar.
PS595.R32W549 2012
811'.540803587392—dc23 2011030939